Praise for
The Digital Revolution

"By 2020, 75 percent of businesses will be fully digital, yet only a few have a real digital strategy. *The Digital Revolution* provides powerful insights and practical examples of how to develop a digital roadmap. Countries, cities, and companies must disrupt themselves or be disrupted in this new digital world."

—John Chambers, Executive Chairman, Cisco Systems

"The online digital revolution is affecting all parts of our world. This timely book is filled with interesting scenarios of disruption and discusses a variety of challenges arising in the new information age. Reading it will help you understand how this revolution will affect your job, your company, and your future."

—John Hennessy, President, Stanford University
Board Member, Google and Cisco

"*The Digital Revolution* is a thoughtful and creative addition to the conversation on one of *the* major forces shaping our world—digital disruption. Inder Sidhu explores both the challenges and opportunities arising from new technologies. He offers valuable insight into the ways in which organizations will need to adapt and change—from becoming radically transparent, to engaging connected consumers, to increasing asset utilization, to redesigning the organization, to innovating at speed."

—Dominic Barton, Global Managing Director, McKinsey & Company

"Inder Sidhu has his finger on the pulse of 'The Internet of Everything'—not only today's cutting edge from Tesla to Uber, but also where the digital revolution will take us. He has convinced me that the best is yet to come, indeed that we are only at the beginning of the transformative impact of digitization."

—Geoffrey Garrett, Dean, The Wharton School

The Digital Revolution

How Connected Digital Innovations Are Transforming Your Industry, Company, and Career

Inder Sidhu
with T.C. Doyle

Publisher: Paul Boger
Editor-in-Chief: Amy Neidlinger
Editorial Assistant: Olivia Basegio
Cover Designer: Alan Clements
Managing Editor: Kristy Hart
Senior Project Editor: Betsy Gratner
Copy Editor: Box Twelve Communications
Proofreader: Debbie Williams
Indexer: WordWise Publishing Services
Senior Compositor: Gloria Schurick
Manufacturing Buyer: Dan Uhrig

© 2016 by Inder Sidhu
Published by Pearson Education, Inc.
Old Tappan, New Jersey 07675

For information about buying this title in bulk quantities, or for special sales opportunities (which may include electronic versions; custom cover designs; and content particular to your business, training goals, marketing focus, or branding interests), please contact our corporate sales department at corpsales@pearsoned.com or (800) 382-3419.

For government sales inquiries, please contact governmentsales@pearsoned.com.

For questions about sales outside the U.S., please contact international@pearsoned.com.

Company and product names mentioned herein are the trademarks or registered trademarks of their respective owners.

First Printing December 2015

ISBN-10: 0-13-429131-X
ISBN-13: 978-0-13-429131-4

Pearson Education LTD.
Pearson Education Australia PTY, Limited
Pearson Education Singapore, Pte. Ltd.
Pearson Education Asia, Ltd.
Pearson Education Canada, Ltd.
Pearson Educación de Mexico, S.A. de C.V.
Pearson Education—Japan
Pearson Education Malaysia, Pte. Ltd.

Library of Congress Control Number: 2015916019

__To my wife, Deepna__
You make everything possible.

and

__To Sonia, Sabrina, and Neal__
The digital revolutionaries.

Contents

Acknowledgments

For their guidance, support, and sponsorship, I am grateful to John Chambers, Rob Lloyd, Wim Elfrink, and Chuck Robbins.

Writing this book required me to draw upon the best and the brightest practitioners who are leading the digital revolution from the front lines today. For the countless hours they spent in discussions with me, I am deeply indebted to

- John Hennessy, President of Stanford University and Board Member of Google & Cisco

- Rick Levin, President Emeritus of Yale University and CEO of Coursera

- Geoffrey Garrett, Dean of the Wharton School, University of Pennsylvania

- Daphne Koller, Co-founder and President of Coursera

- Salman Khan, Founder and CEO of Khan Academy

- Bernard Tyson, CEO of Kaiser Permanente

- Dr. Charles Sorenson, CEO of Intermountain Healthcare

- Dr. Martin Harris, Chief Information Officer of Cleveland Clinic

- Vance Moore, Head of Operations at Mercy

- Greg Poulsen, Chief Strategy Officer of Intermountain Healthcare

- Suja Chandrasekaran, Chief Technology Officer and Chief Data Officer of Walmart Stores

- Malachy Moynihan, Vice President of Digital Products at Amazon (Lab 126)

- Rachael Antalek, Vice President of Concept Innovation at Starbucks

- Prof. Carlo Ratti, Director of Senseable City Laboratory at MIT
- Dr. Anil Menon, President of Smart Connected Communities at Cisco
- David Hoffman, Global Privacy Officer of Intel
- Michelle Dennedy, Chief Privacy Officer of Cisco
- Prof. Alex "Sandy" Pentland of Massachusetts Institute of Technology (MIT), Co-creator of the MIT Media Lab, and Chair of the World Economic Forum's Data Driven Development Council
- Mark Chandler, Chief Legal Officer of Cisco
- Amit Yoran, President of RSA
- Chris Young, President of Intel Security
- John Stewart, Chief Security Officer of Cisco
- Michael Siegel, Principal Research Scientist and Associate Director of MIT's Interdisciplinary Consortium for Improving Critical Infrastructure Cybersecurity, known as MIT-(IC)^3
- Michael Timmeny, Senior VP of Government and Community Relations at Cisco
- Travis LeBlanc, Bureau Chief of the Enforcement Division at the Federal Communications Commission (FCC)
- Dr. Robert Pepper, Vice President of Public Policy at Cisco
- Kelly Kramer, Chief Financial Officer of Cisco
- Saori Casey, Vice President and Head of Corporate Finance at Apple
- Doug Davis, General Manager of the Internet of Things Group at Intel
- Prof. Peter Fader of the Wharton School at the University of Pennsylvania and Co-director of the Wharton Customer Analytics Initiative

- Ed Jimenez, Director of the Customer Experience Practice at Cisco

- Carlos Dominguez, President of Sprinklr, a social media management leader

- Lori Goler, Head of Human Resources at Facebook

- Prasad Setty, Vice President of HR and Head of People Analytics at Google

- Fran Katsoudas, Chief Human Resources Officer of Cisco

For helping shape every chapter in this book through their insightful discussions, I am deeply grateful to Vijeev Verma and Mukundh Thirumalai—great guys, amazing friends, awesome thinkers.

For helping me every working day for the last fifteen years—always with a pleasant disposition, and positive, can-do attitude—I owe a deep debt of eternal gratitude to my assistant, Heather Scharnow.

I also owe a debt of gratitude to my Cisco colleagues who shared ideas and provided ongoing encouragement along the journey, including Nick Adamo, Kelly Ahuja, Graham Allen, Mala Anand, Wendy Bahr, Joel Barbier, Jeanne Beliveau-Dunn, Ravi Bhavanasi, Roger Biscay, Kevin Bloch, Ken Boal, Phyllis Bond, Jordi Botifoll, Bruce Botto, Joseph Bradley, John Brigden, Nancy Cam-Winget, Sean Caragata, Barbara Casey, Owen Chan, Ravi Chandrasekaran, Blair Christie, Howard Charney, Enrico Conedera, Chris Dedicoat, Guillermo Diaz, Paula Dowdy, Debbie Dunnam, Nick Earle, John Earnhardt, Par Edin, Pat Finn, Larisa Fong, Lance Ford, John Garrity, Alison Gleeson, Michael Ganser, Michael Glickman, David Goeckeler, Chris Gow, Debbie Gross, Jim Grubb, Ward Hamilton, Faisal Hanafi, Rick Heller, Caspar Herzberg, Sandy Hogan, Rebecca Jacoby, Prem Jain, Soni Jiandani, Brian Jin, John Kern, Munish Khetrapal, Shaun Kirby, Bruce Klein, Leon Kofman, Oliver Kohler, Maciej Kranz, Vijay Krish, Jill Larsen, Inbar Lasser-Raab, Rhonda Le, Su Le, Gerard Lithgow, Anand Malani, Dinesh Malkani, John Manville, Kim Marcelis, Lorena Marciano, Brian Marlier, Steve Martino, Alan McGinty, Joe McMorrow, Doug McNitt, Martin McPhee, Angel Mendez, Anil Menon, Duncan Mitchell, Gary Moore, Neils Munster-Hansen, Plamen Nedeltchev, Andy Noronha, John O'Connor, Edzard Overbeek,

Edwin Paalvast, Marty Palka, Frank Palumbo, Pankaj Patel, Smita Patel, Mark Patterson, Robert Pepper, Edison Peres, Lance Perry, Shannon Pina, Joe Pinto, Randy Pond, Don Proctor, Marivell Quinonez, Ron Ricci, Hilton Romanski, Vickie Rose, Nilima Sant, Felicia Schulter, Woody Sessoms, Parvesh Sethi, Faiyaz Shahpurwala, Tony Shakib, Stephen Sinclair, Pavan Singh, Jim Smith, Matthew Smith, Kris Snow, Rob Soderbery, Marc Surplus, Manjula Talreja, Irving Tan, Greg Thomas, Bastiaan Toeset, Denny Trevett, Rowan Trollope, Pastora Valero, Karen Walker, Mike Walker, Jim Walsh, Padmasree Warrior, Eric Wenger, Chris White, Paul Wingate, KC Wu, John Wunder and Tae Yoo.

I also want to thank the team at Pearson including Paul Boger, Amy Neidlinger, Olivia Basegio, Alan Clements, Kristy Hart, Gloria Schurick, Dan Uhrig, Debbie Williams, and Betsy Gratner for all their efforts in making this book a reality.

No one has had a greater impact on the ideas in this book than my coauthor, T.C. Doyle. Our partnership started several years ago, when we collaborated on our first book, and I firmly believe that if it were not for him, this book would not exist. From writing to researching to arguing to shaping the content, T.C.'s contributions have been invaluable.

For the endless support and unconditional love that make everything in my life possible, I am lucky to have my wonderful wife, Deepna. She also provided many insightful suggestions on the manuscript and researched many topics. She is the best thing that ever happened to me. And our three wonderful children—Sonia, Sabrina, and Neal—their enthusiastic and unwavering belief in me (except for my fashion sense) gives meaning to my every effort. Seeing them every day reminds me of all that is good in the world. While I wrote about the digital revolution, they lived it.

Introduction

There's Something Happening Here

As a veteran of Silicon Valley for more than two decades, I like to believe that I have developed a sense of when "the next big thing" is about to hit.

All throughout 2013 and 2014 I felt something was imminent. Yet when I looked around, there were only hints and suggestions of what was to come.

In the news, of course, were stories about the next iPhone (duh), virtual reality headsets, cloud computing, big data, and more. Some in the industry said any *one* of these technologies would usher in the next wave of computing—be it the third, fourth, or fifth wave, depending on how you were counting.

When I looked at the market, however, I didn't see anything as revolutionary on the near horizon as an iPhone, Facebook, or Amazon. What I did see was report after report discussing the impact that one Bay Area company was having on transportation: Uber.

Uber, of course, is the company behind the namesake consumer app that connects passengers who need to get somewhere fast with drivers at the ready. While the concept sounds pedestrian, the execution is not.

Rather than hire a legion of drivers or buy a fleet of cars, Uber entered the transportation market in a much more nimble fashion. It developed an ingenious app that made use of innovations and investments made by others to connect drivers and passengers. (Think cell-phone towers, credit-card payment systems, GPS chips and software, cloud data centers, social media connections, and more.)

The end result is an easy-to-use app that provides greater convenience, more flexibility, and better customer service than what was previously available.

Thanks to its ingenuity, Uber is not just transforming the taxi industry; it's transforming the entire transportation sector as a whole. (For a complete explanation as to how, see Chapter 8, "Governance: New Game in Town, Clear Rules Needed.")

So how did a company with a piece of software that some joke has about as much code as a printer driver revolutionize one of America's most mature industries? The pursuit of this answer started me on a journey of my own that ended up with the very book in your hands.

The short answer is the Uber app, a clever piece of software engineering if ever there was one. But the app is only what you see.

The long answer to how Uber emerged from almost nothing to a transportation powerhouse valued at more than $50 billion is a bit more complicated, because it involves a great deal of what you do not see or even consider. Uber implements many processes digitally by combining multiple technologies that, in and of themselves, do not constitute a revolution but collectively have the power to upend the competitive landscape of entire industries.

So what exactly are these technologies?

They are the very ones that you use every day. Think smart phones, social media, cloud computing services, software apps, and more. Never before in the history of technology have so many digital innovations made such significant advances at the same time and in conjunction with one another. It truly is a perfect storm of different innovations reaching maturity and ubiquity almost simultaneously. Consider the following:

- **Mobile phones:** In the past few years, smart phones have become as powerful as yesterday's supercomputers. Instead of a few, however, there are nearly 2 billion of these devices in the hands of global consumers.[1] In February 2015, according to *The Economist*, the penetration of smart mobile phones reached roughly half the adult population of the world. By 2020, the magazine reported, it will likely top 80 percent.[2]

- **Social media:** Few things have spread as rapidly as social media. Today there are more than 2 billion active social media accounts.[3] Every day, consumers spend more than two hours connecting with friends, family, and colleagues through

Facebook, Twitter, LinkedIn, and more. And every minute of every day, Twitter users send out 347,000 tweets. Just one day's worth of tweets could fill a 10-million-page book.[4]

- **Cloud computing:** Somewhere in the last five years, the idea that you don't need to touch something to feel its force took hold in computing. With cloud computing, consumers and institutions alike need only connect to the Internet to leverage compute, store, backup and other services that are made available "by-the-drink." Little wonder that more than 2 billion users have turned to cloud-based services.[5] Cloud democratizes technology and changes not just how it is consumed but how it is developed. Instead of waiting to upgrade to new innovations every few years, cloud technology companies can now introduce new versions of their technology every few days.

- **The Internet of Things:** In 2013, there were more than 10 billion things connected to the Internet, more than one for every person on earth, according to Cisco.[6] However, these represent just 1 percent of the items on earth. Put another way, 99 percent of the things that will be connected to the Internet have yet to join the global network. But they soon will. Come 2020, 250 new objects will be added to the Internet every second of every day. That might not like sound like much, but between the time that you go to bed one night and rise the following morning, 7.2 million things will have been added.[7]

- **Apps:** Tiny chunks of software functionality, created by millions of people, for everything from phones to tablets to watches and more. They allow you to do virtually anything you can conceive of—from transferring money to connecting instantly with your grandmother half a world away to repelling mosquitoes. (Yes, there is an app for that—several, actually.) Collectively, apps have been downloaded 75 billion times.[8]

- **Big data:** Data in the last decade exploded. Its growth was fueled by the more than 100 million apps we now have on our phones and computers and by the number of devices being connected to the Internet. According to Cisco, the amount of data generated monthly by mobile devices alone is nearly 30 times larger than the size of the entire global Internet in 2000.[9] IBM, meanwhile, says people generate 2.5 quintillion bytes of data every day—so much that 90 percent of the data in the world today has been created in the last two years alone.[10]

When I realized that these developments could be used in an almost infinite combination of ways to create new value, I began researching the impact of these mash-ups. In my role as Senior Vice President of Strategy for Worldwide Operations at Cisco, I talked with scores of customers from around the globe. What amazed me was how important digital transformation was becoming to some. I saw healthcare companies pushing the boundaries of informatics with social media, big data, and cloud computing. I learned of educators who were leveraging communication to not only increase their reach but also their relevancy. I also saw small businesses challenge the biggest brands in their markets. And I saw governments change how they govern cities and countries.

Equally amazing to me was how few people were talking about how they would be impacted by what was happening. And what they should do to prepare. This was so despite the fact that industries were being transformed, civil liberties were being threatened, and careers were being reimagined. A digital revolution was happening all around them, yet many could only see the status quo.

Why? Chalk it up to human nature, which can blind us to what is often happening right in front of our eyes. We see our children playing with their electronic devices and engaging with their friends in novel and creative ways. But do we think about the data that they produce or who uses this data for financial gain? Similarly, we take note when one of our friends connects with us through social media. But do we ever notice when a railcar, street lamp, or power grid is added to the Internet? Of course not. Yet these things now produce more data than people do.

So who will put this data to use?

Today, anyone can. While we see benefits that our businesses derive from these technologies and this data, we tend to overlook the disruptive business models that this digital revolution enables.

One day while driving home, I started thinking about the digital revolution. How far could it go? How would it touch people? How will businesses be propelled or disrupted by it?

While I sat at a traffic light drumming my fingers on the steering wheel and thinking about these questions, I was distracted by a car that pulled up next to me. It was a brand new Tesla Model S.

"Now," I said to myself, "there goes a revolution."

1

The Digital Revolution
Why You Should Care

The best ever.

Ask people to name the best of anything,—be it a sports hero, vacation destination, U.S. President, and so on—and they will no doubt volunteer an array of opinions. But if you were to ask car enthusiasts what is the most technologically advanced automobile on the road today—and quite possibly the best ever—they will most likely zero in on a single vehicle. The car?

The Tesla Model S.

If you live near a major metropolitan center, you've surely seen this car though you may not have heard it as it silently drove by. This is because the car is an all-electric vehicle built from the ground up not only to compete with the world's best carbon-fueled vehicles, but to beat them in every aspect of driving.

With a range of more than 250 miles, the car can travel three times the distance of other electric vehicles and rival some gas-powered vehicles in terms of driving range. And the Tesla can do so without producing any emissions.

As for performance, the Tesla Model S P85D, when used in "ludicrous mode," can accelerate from 0 to 60 mph in less than 3 seconds.[1] That's faster than a Ferrari F12 Berlinetta,[2] which is the fastest road car ever produced by the famed Italian sports car manufacturer.

When it comes to convenience, the Tesla is equally impressive. The entire vehicle, for example, can be controlled via a 17-inch touch-screen display that is handily mounted in the center console. Think of it as an over-sized iPad that can adjust everything from the temperature to the music to the stiffness of the suspension. When connected to your calendar on your smart phone, the touchscreen will automatically display a driving map to your next appointment, complete with up-to-the-minute traffic conditions.

By almost any measure, the Model S, which was unveiled in 2012, has become the most successful alternatively powered car of the last 100 years. Since its debut, the company has sold more than 50,000 Model S cars. Though priced at nearly $100,000 each, consumers buy them as fast as Tesla can make them (there is currently a waiting list to get one), while journalists heap on the praise.

In 2013, *MotorTrend* named the Model S its "Car of the Year"— the first in the 64-year history of the award to not feature a traditional gasoline engine.[3] Not to be outdone, *Consumer Reports* said the Tesla Model S sedan was "the best performing car ever tested" in the history of the magazine.[4] It gave the car a score of 100 out of 100 in a road test, a score that had never been achieved by any car. And car reviewer Dan Neil of *The Wall Street Journal* said, "The Model S is a daring public experiment in automotive vision that has the impudence to make the finest, fastest luxury cars feel like Edwardian antiques."[5]

Unquestionably, the Model S is the best electric car on the planet. But to its owners and inventors, the Tesla Model S is remarkable not only because it is *electric*, but because it is *digital*.

While that may not sound like a big distinction, it's literally the difference between 20th-century ingenuity and 21st-century innovation.

Virtually everything in the car that can be measured has an active sensor on it that is connected to the car's digital network. You can tell your Tesla Model S to park itself neatly into your garage, so you don't have to wedge your body out when finished. And with its mobile app, you can remotely check the cabin temperature on a hot day and tell the vehicle to power up the AC, so it will be at a desired temperature when you get to the car.

The car has dozens of other cool features that leverage digital technology. But there's one feature that sets it apart from virtually any other vehicle on the road. Aside from a handful of parts that need routine replacement—think tires and wiper blades—the bulk of the vehicle's components and functions were designed to be upgraded, not by mechanics wielding wrenches, but by software engineers working in Tesla's Silicon Valley research and development labs.[6] Like an iPhone, the Tesla S gets better every time the company releases a new software update over the Internet. They can make the car safer, more reliable, and even more pleasurable.

Take driving in San Francisco, which is something engineer and entrepreneur Robert Bigler, the inventor of the SmartMotor and Hoverboard, does quite frequently. Like a lot of successful people who work in Silicon Valley, Bigler was drawn to the Tesla Model S the moment that it was introduced. He bought one not long after it became available.

The more he drove the car, the more Bigler became a fan. But one thing bugged him about the vehicle, especially when he drove it around the streets of San Francisco, where street grades can exceed 30 percent.[7] When he drove his car over the famed hills of the city, he noticed it would roll back unnervingly when he stopped uphill at intersections for stop signs and street lights.

"It reminded me of driving an old manual transmission VW Beetle. Without a mechanical clutch, the Tesla wants to roll back on steep hills," Bigler says. Concerned about his safety, not to mention that of fellow Tesla drivers, he turned to Tesla for more information and discovered that other Tesla drivers had already alerted Tesla of the problem. A few days later, a message appeared on the touchscreen console when he started his car one morning. A fix, the message informed him, was automatically downloaded to Bigler's car (and every other Tesla) overnight while it charged in his garage.

Sure enough, when he next found himself stopped on an upward slope in San Francisco, the problem was gone. Tesla engineers had written some code that programmed the car to automatically engage the safety brake whenever it was stopped on a hill. When the vehicle begins to move forward now, the brake stays engaged for a few seconds until the motor can put sufficient torque on the wheels to give it the forward momentum it needs to prevent the vehicle from rolling backwards.

Much to the delight of Bigler and other Tesla drivers, the manufacturer has addressed other concerns and desires, too. He, for example, is excited that his vehicle's display can now show maps in the "track up" position. (As a pilot, he prefers his map to be shown in the direction that he is traveling.)

In addition to convenience, software upgrades have also improved safety. When one battery caught fire after being pierced by a piece of road debris, Tesla engineers made several changes. One reset the default height setting on the vehicle and raised it by a few inches with a simple software patch delivered wirelessly. No recall was required, and no fires have been reported since.

A recent software upgrade gave owners Blind Spot Warning and Automatic Emergency Braking. It also provided guidance for locating charging stations on road trips and improved the range monitoring while providing owners more options for safeguarding their cars, including speed restrictions when handing them over to parking valets.[8]

With its front-mounted camera, rear-mounted radar, and a phalanx of ultrasonic sensors, the car can start, stop, steer, drive, navigate, park, and avoid obstacles. With the AutoPilot software downloaded to the car recently, the Tesla can also operate like one of Google's much ballyhooed semi-autonomous driverless cars, leading Steven Colbert, host of *The Late Show*, to exclaim, "Tesla owners woke up to find that their cars could drive themselves." If and when the law allows for driverless cars, Tesla will be ready, much to the delight of its owners, who realize that the car they purchased is unlike any other.

"With my Tesla, I feel like I get a new car every time there's an upgrade. There are new features and new capabilities, and as a result the car just gets better and better," says Bigler.

A car that improves with age? That hasn't happened since *mechanical* cars were invented more than 100 years ago. But in the new world of *digital* transportation, this will become commonplace.

...

Look around you. If you haven't noticed, virtually everything is going digital. This includes *things* like cars, *industries* like transportation, and *careers* like driving. With each passing day, more of these are being connected to the Internet in ways we are only beginning to understand.

Unlike the first 14 billion things that were connected to the Internet, the remaining 99 percent of items on earth were never designed to be connected to the Internet. These atom-based things cannot be reduced to a "0" or a "1"—the DNA of all digital objects and devices—so easily and thus require a steep effort to connect them securely and efficiently. But once they go *digital*, the benefits to mankind will be transformational.

Why? Because everything that gets connected to the Internet has the potential to produce data, which can yield revolutionary insights about the world around us. This includes the whereabouts of a bus you're waiting for, the temperature of a donor organ in transit, or the level of methane gas underground in a mine. When you consider the potential value of every sensor update, every electronic medical record, and every Twitter tweet, you begin to realize how transformative this information could be when leveraged intelligently. And this is only a sampling.

Once *everything* is connected to the Internet, we will have at our fingertips data on every activity, interaction, and condition known to man. Translating this data into information, of course, will require an immense effort. But thanks to infinitely scalable resources now available to everyone via the Internet and cloud, we now have the power required to collect, store, and process this information. With better analytical tools now being developed, we increasingly have the capability to translate this information into actionable knowledge and insights required for solving our problems and addressing our aspirations.

Again, take driving, which is being transformed by a multitude of technologies, including the ordinary mobile device in your backpack or purse. The smart device that you use for taking selfies, responding to emails, or sending texts is also helping you get home faster and helping municipal planners reduce traffic congestion and improve highway safety. How? By providing insights into our world.

Unbeknownst to you, the GPS device inside your smart phone sends a signal to every cell tower you pass as you move along your daily commute. This information is aggregated and anonymized by technology companies including Google to determine how congested local thoroughfares are at any one moment. After crunching the data, these third parties send this information back to consumers' smart devices and connected cars, revealing where traffic congestion is worst, the whereabouts of construction hazards, and even the exact locations of traffic accidents reported on social media. With this information, which is often presented in the form of a color-coded map, consumers can reroute their courses, reducing fuel costs, emissions, and travel times. And city planners can ensure better traffic flow.

Although this might sound like a nice convenience to an individual commuter, it has the potential to be transformative to society as a whole. According to the 2012 Urban Mobility Report, the amount of fuel wasted in congested traffic each year would fill the New Orleans Superdome four times over. The cost of this fuel is estimated to be more than $120 billion annually, or more than $800 for every person who commutes daily in the U.S. For perspective, that total is more than the amount of revenue that United Airlines, Nike, McDonald's, and Starbucks generate in a year *combined*.

The implications of this example and other similar developments on transportation cannot be overestimated. The ridesharing company Uber, for example, is not only transforming the taxi industry, it is also influencing the automotive industry as a whole. In many cities, young men and women are not just asking themselves whether they want to drive or take Uber for a specific trip, they are wondering if they should take Uber for every trip. *Why own a car if a reliable service is cost-effective, ubiquitous, and safe?* many Millennials wonder.

For driving a transformation in their industries, these digital revolutionaries are being richly rewarded. For example, Tesla, as of this writing, has a market capitalization of approximately $32 billion, which is roughly half of what Ford and GM are each worth, despite the fact that Tesla commands less than 1 percent of the U.S. market. Similarly Uber, which is now valued at more than $50 billion, engages more than 1 million drivers worldwide and expects to double that figure to 2 million by the end of 2015.[9]

In this chapter, I've focused on automobiles, traffic, and getting around. But equally transformative changes are occurring in virtually every industry you can think of. In Part II, "Transforming Industries," I showcase several transformations underway in healthcare, education, retail, and government. In the examples, connected digital innovations are being leveraged to improve patient outcomes, increase access to learning, elevate shopping convenience, and support better living in smart cities.

The same is true when it comes to major business objectives. By connecting people, processes, and things, businesses are improving financial performance, enhancing customer experiences, and increasing employee engagement.

Add it all up, and you realize that we are in the early stages of a full-fledged digital revolution that will impact every industry, organization, business function, and career.

In terms of economic activity, the amount of commerce that will be generated from this digital revolution will be enormous. McKinsey's report on the Internet of Things estimates the potential economic impact between $4 trillion and $11 trillion a year by 2025.[10] Between 2013 and 2022, Cisco estimates that digital transformation will generate $19 trillion[11] in economic activity, nearly half of which will be from the replacement of activities or things that will simply fade away like the local travel agent, printed encyclopedia, and classified newspaper ad.

To put this into perspective, that's as much as the GDPs of Japan, Germany, UK, France, India, Brazil and South Korea combined—simply a staggering sum, in other words.

More than money, the digital revolution promises to have as big an impact on people's lives as their formal education, choice of careers, and physical activity. That's because digital technology will reshape virtually every facet of how we learn, work, and live.

While there are significant privacy, security, and regulatory issues to be sorted out, which I cover in detail in Part III, "Addressing Challenges," digital transformation may well turn out to be the single, biggest idea impacting humankind. The reason is simple: This digital revolution isn't just occurring in Silicon Valley or in long-overlooked nooks and crannies of our economy, such as the taxi and limousine industry. It's also happening in the industries and organizations that touch your life. This includes your bank, shopping mall, school, doctor's office, and more.

In the case of Tesla and Uber, the change is obvious. But in other instances, it is less apparent, at least for now. Take the work of GE, one of the oldest industrial companies on the *Fortune 500* list. Although the company has spent billions of dollars preparing to lead the digital revolution in the industrial economy, the company recognizes that few outside the world of heavy industry understand how transformative digital innovation could be to heavy industry. To increase awareness, the company launched a series of ads in the fall of 2015 depicting a fictional college graduate named "Owen" who struggles to impress his family and friends with his cutting-edge work. When Owen excitedly tells one group of friends that he is going to work on software that will transform machines such as locomotives, one puzzled friend wonders aloud if Owen has taken a job to "work on a train."

While the self-deprecating GE ads are funny, the message behind them is serious: The digital revolution has the potential to transform all parts of our world, including the operations, functions, and processes we rarely consider.

Which brings me to you. No matter where you work, the revolution is surely happening inside *your* industry. For better or for worse, whether you like it or not, it will affect your organization, if it hasn't already. Now is the right moment to join the digital revolution and help transform your own company and your career. How you think about digital innovation, leverage it, and master it will determine how you survive and thrive.

While some will be tempted to ignore or even thwart the advance of digital innovation where they work, they do so at their own peril. Widespread innovation will make it next to impossible to slow the digital revolution. By 2020, 75 percent of businesses will become fully digital.[12] Will yours be one of them?

This book will put you in the driver's seat of the digital revolution so you can transform your industry, company, and career.

Hop on for the ride of your life.

2

Healthcare
*The Patient Will See You**

Have you heard the good news about healthcare?

Spending growth, which drains resources and limits access to care on a global basis, has slowed from the alarming rates of just a few years ago, according to the Organization for Economic Cooperation and Development (OECD). In many developed countries, healthcare inflation has fallen to below 2 percent annually from historic norms of 4-7 percent.[1]

This is a wonderful turn of events for everyone from policy makers to practitioners to patients.

Now for the bad news: Healthcare is still "broken" across the globe.

In far too many places, quality is poor, access limited, and relevance scattershot. "Despite incredible improvements in health since 1950, there are still a number of challenges, which should have been easy to solve [but have not]," notes researcher and journalist Anup Shah. The data he presents on his Web site, *Global Issues*, paints a sober picture. Consider some of its findings:[2]

- One billion people worldwide lack access to healthcare systems.
- Thirty-six million die each year from non-communicable diseases, such as cardiovascular disease, cancer, diabetes, and chronic lung diseases.

---

* For their guidance with this chapter, I am grateful to Bernard Tyson, CEO of Kaiser Permanente; Dr. Charles Sorenson, CEO of Intermountain Healthcare; Dr. Martin Harris, Chief Information Officer of Cleveland Clinic; Vance Moore, Head of Operations at Mercy; and Greg Poulsen, Chief Strategy Officer of Intermountain Healthcare.

- More than 7.5 million children under the age of 5 perish each year due to malnutrition and preventable diseases.

- Nearly 7 million people die from infectious diseases—more than the number killed in natural or man-made disasters.

- And 164,000 people, mostly children under 5, die from measles even though effective immunization costs less than $1 and has been available for more than 40 years.

Not to be a downer, but there is more sober news to report. The slowdown in global spending growth highlighted above? It might be short-lived. Researchers know that a contributing factor was the economic crisis, which prompted millions worldwide to stop seeking medical treatment to save money. Eventually, they will need care. Given how long some have gone without, the cost could be significant.

Another contributor to the slowdown in spending might also have been a blip. This was the expiration of patent protection on several key drugs used worldwide, including Plavix, Lipitor, and Caduet. While other drugs are slated to lose protection soon, there will be nothing like the "patent cliff" experienced by drug makers for years to come.[3]

Then there are long-term challenges that seem to have no solution. This includes population growth and aging, which are expected to drive healthcare inflation for decades to come.

"This growth will place enormous pressure on governments, health care delivery systems, insurers, and consumers in both developed and emerging markets, to deal with issues such as an aging population, the rising prevalence of numerous chronic diseases, soaring costs, uneven quality, imbalanced access to care due to workforce shortages, infrastructure limitations and patient locations, and disruptive technologies," concludes professional services giant Deloitte in its "2014 Global Health Care Outlook."[4]

For a better understanding of how healthcare alone can influence a nation's agenda, look no further than the U.S., where per capita spending on healthcare totaled $8,508 per person in 2011—more than two-and-a-half times more than the average of OECD countries, according to Veronique de Rugy, a senior research fellow at George

Mason University. By 2013, the figure reached $9,255, according to the National Health Expenditure Accounts (NHEA).[5]

For comparison, the U.S. spends about 50 percent more than Norway—the next largest per capita spender, she notes.[6]

For that premium you'd think the country would enjoy *some* global advantage. But it doesn't. Americans, for example, don't live as long as citizens of Japan, Spain, Israel, and elsewhere.[7] In fact, the U.S. ranks number 26 on the global list of individual life expectancy by country, according to the OECD.[8] What is more, the additional money Americans spend on healthcare per capita does not result in lower rates of cancer,[9] heart disease,[10] diabetes,[11] and other conditions[12] that afflict people in others parts of the world.

Looked at from almost any angle, the premium paid is not an especially good investment. It does not produce better health outcomes and it puts an enormous strain on the nation's ability to invest in other parts of its economy. Think physical infrastructure, alternative fuels, and education.

Despite the enormity of the healthcare problem, policy makers are loathe to tinker. Of the leading candidates aligning themselves for a run at the Oval Office in 2016, none have made healthcare reform, as of writing, a cornerstone of their platform. Because they fear alienating those who profit from exorbitant spending or constituents who don't feel its pernicious effects, politicians wring their hands while healthcare literally sucks the lifeblood from other parts of the economy. Consider: When Ronald Reagan was elected President in 1980, for example, healthcare accounted for 9 percent of GDP. When Barack Obama was elected President in 2008, healthcare spending totaled 16 percent of GDP. By 2021, it will account for almost one of every five dollars of the U.S. economy.[13]

What makes that figure so alarming is the amount of healthcare that is literally wasted due to unnecessary procedures, inefficient care delivery, operational mismanagement, fraud, and other things. Greg Poulsen, Chief Strategy Officer at Intermountain Healthcare in Utah, points out that while the U.S. does get "rescue care"—the ability to salvage really sick, extremely premature, or horrendously injured humans—far better than anywhere else in the world, it turns out to be the most expensive way to extend life from a population perspective.

End-of-life (EoL) care, too, can be very expensive. Today, one-quarter of Medicare spending on healthcare in the U.S. is generated by the 5 percent of patients who die annually, according to the Centers for Medicare & Medicaid Services (CMS).[14] What is more, 28 percent of Medicare is spent on patients who are in the last six months of life.[15]

Are all of these procedures necessary or even beneficial? Experts have their suspicions. Physician Dr. Atul Gawande, an author and staff writer for *The New Yorker*, is among those who have questioned the efficacy and wisdom of certain end-of-life procedures, which not only put significant physical stress on patients but enormous financial strain on the loved ones they leave behind. Despite scant evidence that premium-priced, life-sustaining measures for dying seniors and terminally ill patients result in positive outcomes, the medical industry keeps piling on care until the very end. Today, nearly 1 in 5 Americans spend their final days in one of healthcare's most expensive situations, an intensive care unit.[16]

The total cost of pervasive inefficiencies and overtreatment is staggering. In September 2012, the nonprofit, independent Institute of Medicine in Washington released a landmark study on U.S. healthcare spending that pegged the number at $750 billion annually.[17] This is more than the entire budget for national defense, according to the Department of Defense,[18] and 2.5 times more than what the U.S. spends annually on public infrastructure, according to Moody's Analytics.[19]

Even if President Obama's signature healthcare law accomplishes everything it sets out to, the ACA will reduce the size of the healthcare problem in the U.S. only modestly, according to experts. The Medicare Hospital Insurance Trust Fund? It still has an estimated depletion date of 2030.[20]

From a financial perspective and more, healthcare *is* broken in the U.S. It will bankrupt America long before Social Security, interest on the national debt, or any other financial burden does. And it will do the same in other nations where care is piled onto those who don't need it and dribbled out sparingly to those who do.

That is, unless something radical is done.

The good news is that sweeping measures are being taken to remedy healthcare—both inside and outside the sector. Some of the most promising work is being done by industry practitioners who have teamed with outside reformers to develop new technology that leverages connected digital innovations, which we also refer to as the Internet of Everything (IoE). Their work has been shown to boost quality, improve access, and increase relevance for millions. For example, consider Dr. Basil Harris, an emergency room doctor from Paoli, Pennsylvania, and his brother George, an engineer who spent much of his career configuring data networks.

In 2011, the Harris brothers formed a team, Final Frontier Medical Devices, to build a medical device that consumers can use to monitor their heart rates, blood pressure, temperature, oxygen saturation, and more. With it, consumers will be able to decide for themselves when they need to visit a doctor or whether prescribed treatment is working as hoped.[21]

More than a dream, the company's product is one of 10 finalists in the running for the "Qualcomm Tricorder XPRIZE." If you're not familiar, the XPRIZE healthcare competition is one of several contests sponsored by the XPRIZE Foundation, a think tank comprised of entrepreneurs, inventors, and thought leaders devoted to kickstarting innovation. Board members include filmmaker James Cameron, media entrepreneur Arianna Huffington, Google co-founder Larry Paige, electric-car pioneer and space enthusiast Elon Musk, and Segway scooter inventor Dean Kamen.[22] The foundation's previous contests have led to the development of production-capable vehicles that "exceed 100 MPG energy equivalent" and "private, suborbital space flight."[23]

The Qualcomm Tricorder XPRIZE Competition is specifically aimed at jumpstarting healthcare innovation, personal diagnostic and monitoring instruments, in particular. If you're a *Star Trek* fan, you'll of course remember the "tricorder" device used by Dr. Leonard "Bones" McCoy to monitor patients and diagnose medical conditions on the "Starship Enterprise." Recognizing the fictional device's real-world potential, the foundation teamed with Qualcomm, the chipmaker from San Diego, to create a $10 million award that will go to the team that can build the most capable tricorder possible by early 2016.[24]

The real device must capture key health metrics and diagnose a set of 16 diseases, including anemia, atrial fibrillation (AFib), diabetes, hepatitis A, pneumonia, sleep apnea, and stroke, among others, according to the rules of the competition. "Ultimately, this tool will collect large volumes of data from ongoing measurement of health states through a combination of wireless sensors, imaging technologies, and portable, non-invasive laboratory replacements," the foundation says.[25]

A competitive entrepreneur, Dr. Harris would love nothing more than to win the prize with his brother, although they'll now have to share the prize with their other brother, Gus, and their sister, Julia, who have since joined the company. But what really motivates Basil Harris is the opportunity to contribute to an innovation that will help revolutionize patient care.

"I imagine a day when patients are coming in [to the ER] and saying, 'Hey, I have this tricorder device, and it's telling me that I have pneumonia.' And I want to be at a point where I trust that data," says Dr. Harris. Though several technological and regulatory hurdles—including blessing from the U.S. Food and Drug Administration (FDA)—remain, Harris expects the world will soon see a personal device that puts the insight of a physician into the hands of an everyday consumer.[26]

Imagine the possibilities: A reduction in the number of patients lined up unnecessarily in the nation's emergency rooms? Fewer seniors questioning end-of-life care options? A real tricorder could help achieve these outcomes and reduce annual healthcare spending by billions of dollars annually.

And that is just the beginning.

As in education, connected digital innovations can be applied liberally to healthcare to increase access by making medicine more affordable and convenient. It can also be used to improve the quality of healthcare by making it more replicable and precise. And it can increase the relevance of healthcare by making it more personalized.

Standing in the way of progress are a number of obstacles, including the rising price of medicines (for example, Sovaldi and Harvoni are approaching six figures) and devices, the exorbitant cost of malpractice litigation, the misaligned incentives that encourage waste and over-treatment, and a culture that is resistant to change. Despite these, dedicated professionals both inside and outside of healthcare are making gains. While some of their inspiration for curing healthcare's ills might be the stuff of fiction, the motivation propelling them is very real.

Here's why.

Access

Ask Bethany Stadeli what was one of the scariest days of her life and she can recall it as though it were yesterday. She has even seen a video of the day played out in all its chilling horror.

Her story begins in Silverton, Oregon, in April 2012. At the time, she was pregnant with her son. When her pregnancy took a turn for the worse, she was rushed to Silverton Hospital for an emergency cesarean section. The doctor on call that evening, James Domst, was alerted only minutes before and rushed to the hospital himself.

As reported by local TV station KGW, the baby's delivery came a month early and there were complications. After he was delivered, the boy was blue and unresponsive. Though Domst tried reviving the baby, the child did not respond. Realizing he had only minutes to save the boy, Dr. Domst brought another doctor, Katie Townes McMann, a neonatologist from Oregon Health & Science University (OHSU), into the room. With her guiding expertise, the team of physicians and nurses were able to revive the baby and turn one of the most frightening moments of Stadeli's life into one of her most joyous. Afterwards, her son was strong and healthy. And Stadeli couldn't be more grateful—or awestruck.

That's because Dr. McMann, the neonatologist from OHSU, never set foot in Silverton Hospital during the crisis. In fact, when Dr. Domst summoned her help, she was 40 miles away in Portland. Yet she was able to join him "in-person" at the press of a button instantly, thanks to a mobile two-way, robotic-telecommunication machine installed inside Silverton Hospital. From her vantage point, McMann could observe the patient and monitor the child's vitals as though she were in the room with Domst. She could zoom in for a tight focus or pull back for a broader look. She could even move her camera for a different perspective.

While Dr. McMann consulted with Domst that day in April 2012, a helpless Stadeli could only sit by and marvel.

"It was really hard to watch [my son] not breathing and [see] them doing chest compressions on him and everything," she told the television station afterwards. Of the technology, she said, "I'm just thankful for it. It's hard to grasp everything the machine can do. I don't know. It's crazy."

Though McMann uses technology routinely to practice medicine, she is also awestruck by the technology. "This to me is just so advanced," she told KGW TV. "I can't really imagine what else they're going to think of."[27]

Medical practitioners and technology developers have come up with plenty of new ideas since. This includes better communication and collaboration tools, improved diagnostic screening equipment, and even more capable robots that allow for the remote delivery of advanced medical care.

While first circumspect, the medical world is now rushing to embrace telemedicine, which is a subset of capabilities under an umbrella of care known as "connected health."[28] Connected health includes telemedicine, which is defined as remote doctoring via audio and/or video telecommunications; telehealth (education and patient management delivered electronically); and mobile or mHealth (various care services provided via a smart phone and/or wireless devices). According to the American Telemedicine Association (ATA), connected health can be delivered via two-way video conferencing, email, smart phones, wireless tools, and other forms of telecommunications technology to provide primary care, specialist referral services, and remote patient monitoring to adults and children alike.[29]

Kaiser Permanente, the nation's largest integrated managed care system (with almost 18,000 physicians and about 50,000 nurses), has been a leader in leveraging such technology to drive better outcomes for its patients. Bernard Tyson, the CEO of Kaiser, says that in 2014 alone, "the Internet through our electronic health systems has allowed us to now have a virtual visit between us and our members—about

20 million visits when the member never had to come inside Kaiser Permanente."[30]

While patient satisfaction of the interaction with the physician or the caregiver is similar to an in-person visit, in other respects, patients see the online interaction as more convenient—no driving, no parking, no waiting at the reception area, no undressing, no exposure to other patients, and so on. From a healthcare provider perspective, it allows a rebalancing of the cost structure because you need fewer parking spaces, fewer buildings, fewer receptionists, fewer examination rooms, and so on. However, online and in-office visits are not one-to-one direct substitutes of each other and major health systems are calibrating what this means for the total volume of visits, especially in the context of health outcomes rather than procedures done.

Since the launch of basic services more than 40 years ago, telemedicine technology has been used to treat an estimated 100 million patients worldwide.[31] This includes everyone from researchers and scientists working at the Amundsen-Scott South Pole Station in Antarctica[32] to displaced war refugees in Sub-Saharan Africa and the Middle East.

"We're estimating that 50 percent of all medical transactions will be done electronically by 2020," says Ronald S. Weinstein, M.D., professor of pathology at the University of Arizona College of Medicine and director of the Arizona Telemedicine Program.[33]

The reason for the sharp rise is understandable: today, more people have access to mobile phones than to a doctor or a toilet.[34] While potable water and the availability of more medical professionals would certainly advance health, the rise in broadband technology might be the next best thing. In fact, connected health represents one of the greatest expansions in medical care since the 1920s, 30s, and 40s, when governments around the world began immunizing entire populations to combat polio, diphtheria, yellow fever, and smallpox.

Since then, the world's population has more than doubled to 7 billion people.[35] Because it has grown so quickly, the world is short 7.2 million healthcare workers, according to the World Health Organization.[36] Given that the world's top producer of healthcare professionals—the U.S.—mints fewer than 18,000 doctors annually, it is unlikely that this gap will close anytime soon. In many countries, the shortage of care practitioners is especially acute. For example, consider Morocco, where there are just six doctors for every 10,000 residents, according to the World Bank. In Myanmar, there are only five physicians for every 10,000 people. And in Togo, there is just one for every 10,000 people.[37]

For millions of people throughout the world, getting to a doctor isn't a matter of making an appointment; it's finding someone who can treat you. For these millions, telemedicine is their best hope. This includes places like western Kenya, where the World Health Partners (WHP) and Kisumu Medical and Education Trust (KMET) have teamed up to provide critical health services to underserved communities. There, the two organizations are working to enroll dozens of village-level entrepreneurs and link them through a referral system to six clinics operated by nurses and clinical officers. Initially, the remote centers will connect to a hospital in Kisumu. Soon they will link to Nairobi and New Delhi. Tomorrow, they could connect to the world.[38]

To ensure that telemedicine provides high standards and reaches the greatest number of people possible, organizations including the ATA and The Virtual Doctor Project of the U.K. are teaming with local care providers, non-governmental organizations (NGOs), and other institutions dedicated to improving health around the world. They share technology tips, best practices, and other ideas that have improved lives in some of the most remote or dangerous places on earth. For example, consider The Virtual Doctor Project, which relies on a "store and forward" telemedicine system that creates an electronic link—be it simple email, video messages, or more—between care professionals and patients. This approach is often more successful in remote regions, where electricity and telecommunications services are expensive and signal strength weak or intermittent, says the organization.[39]

This simple method has proven extremely effective for improving health outcomes in Zambia, one of the poorest nations on earth. Life expectancy there is less than 50 years due to high rates of HIV and other diseases. In many parts of the country, there were simply no permanent medical facilities until The Virtual Doctor Project came to town. Now, tens of thousands of residents are getting professional treatment within single-room buildings in places like the newly formed Chilanga District, where The Virtual Doctor Project has installed computers, Internet communications gear, and other basic pieces of equipment. Thanks to these efforts, basic medical conditions can be treated professionally and without a doctor present before they become major health problems.[40]

The technology is also useful for increasing access where care is under-utilized or poorly managed. For example, consider the U.S., where Internet-enabled telemedicine is helping practitioners make better use of time and resources in one of the most technologically advanced places of all: Silicon Valley. In California's most expensive communities, access to first-rate medical care for working professionals isn't a financial or geographic challenge but one of time instead. Throughout the Valley, from San Jose to San Francisco, entrepreneurs and engineers are working impossibly long hours on "the next big thing." For many, this means sacrificing an active social life, exercise regimen, or vacations. Some of the very people working on advanced healthcare technology are routinely foregoing routine medical check-ups or consultations in the name of "focus."

To expand access for its employees, Cisco has developed a tele-medicine solution that combines high-definition audio and video technology to provide convenient access to high-quality patient care and clinical collaboration across any distance. Instead of jumping into a car and driving to visit healthcare professionals, Cisco employees can simply drop by one of the ExtendedCare stations located on the company's San Jose campus. If a care provider wants to consult with a specialist, he or she can dial up another practitioner at the press of a button for a second opinion—as several do, for example, with a dermatologist at the Stanford University hospital a few miles away.[41]

Connected digital technology is not only helping employers increase access to health services for working professionals, it's helping traditional care providers expand their reach. This includes physicians such as Bart Demaershawk of Mayo Clinic, who can review CAT scans on his mobile smart phone to make accurate diagnoses. Thanks to high-resolution screen technology, Demaershawk can see a clot in an artery or spot hemorrhaging from wherever he is.[42] Similarly, Dr. Victor Zach, director of Stroke and Neurocritical care at

John C. Lincoln Hospital in Phoenix, scales his expertise through the use of his iPad, which connects to medical offices and treatment rooms equipped with telerobots that feature high-resolution screens and cameras.[43] Dr. Zach says the resolution of these devices is so good that he can detect sagging lines in the faces of patients—a telltale sign of stroke. With the ability to move or swivel a camera-equipped robot remotely, he can pan to consult with in-room care providers or speak with a patient's family members from virtually anywhere.

"I carry a Wi-Fi hot spot with me at all times when I am on call, which allows me to do this anywhere there is a private room," he told KTVK TV in 2014. "I will find a private location; sometimes even if it is necessary, it can be done in a private vehicle."[44]

As practitioners push the boundaries of connected health further, they are finding new ways in which to apply it. Take teletherapy, which is greatly increasing access to mental health services in rural states like Indiana.[45] There, care providers are providing psychiatric care through an encrypted computer video system to treat mentally ill patients in rural locales. Elsewhere, the technology is being used to treat incarcerated criminals.[46] And the Veterans Administration is using it to remotely treat soldiers who suffer from Post Traumatic Stress Disorder (PTSD).[47]

What began as a way for therapists and other mental health professionals to stay in touch with patients outside of office hours has blossomed into one of the fastest growing parts of mental healthcare. It is especially effective for treating younger patients, who have grown up texting, instant messaging, and Skyping. Now when they need access to care, young patients don't have to wait until next Tuesday at 4 p.m. to get help with a crisis; they can dial up a care provider from wherever they are.

Given its promise, the Federal government has jumped into connected health in a big way. Among other things, it has authorized greater use of telemedicine throughout the U.S. by allocating more money for equipment and changing regulations governing what constitutes a legitimate, reimbursable medical consultation.[48] This includes loosening anti-kickback restrictions for the purchase of telemedicine equipment and requiring physicians to receive a separate license to practice in each state—a major barrier for doctors hoping to provide virtual care to patients across the nation—according to *Payers & Providers*.[49]

Of course, regulatory and technological advances won't mean a thing unless the public warms to the technology. Fortunately, there is good news to report on that front. In a recent survey completed by PwC's Health Research Institute, Ceci Connolly, managing director of the institute, notes that 40 percent of adults surveyed said they would accept an appointment with a physician via smart phone.[50] In fact, one care provider has found tech-savvy patients quite capable of handling thermometers, stethoscopes, and even otoscopes to transmit data to doctors at another location, according to Connolly.[51]

This brave new world of medicine is not only more convenient, it is better in certain instances. To lift quality for all, care providers are leveraging another pillar of digital medicine: data analytics. The results achieved from these efforts can be measured in the number of lives saved, says Marc Probst, the chief information officer at Intermountain Healthcare. The Salt Lake City health system is one of the nation's pioneers in evidence-based care, which is putting science behind as many clinical decisions as possible.

To look at how this data-driven revolution is changing modern medicine, we'll start with one of the most iconic figures in all of society: the Great American doctor.

Quality

If you think about the span of medicine, few images are more heroic than that of a physician—and for good reason: they save lives. The expertise and dedication of these professionals in the U.S. have produced some of the world's most advanced and specialized care. But the freedom and flexibility with which American doctors function has also led to wide differences in how the basics of medicine are applied. A patient with a particular condition is likely to be treated differently by different physicians based on myriad factors, including the age of the doctor, where he or she studied, the community in which he or she practices, and the doctor's own preferences. In medicine, these differences are known as "variance."

As you might imagine, there are widespread variances in U.S. medicine. But what you might not know is that variance isn't just a regional thing; it's a local one as well. As far back as the late 1970s, researchers at Dartmouth College began studying variance to a significant extent. What they discovered stunned the medical community: there was no such thing as "standardized" medicine. The number of tonsillectomies performed in a single ZIP code, for example, differed significantly from one practitioner to another despite no discernible differences in patients. The only plausible explanation for this kind of variance was doctor preference (and, to a lesser degree, patient preference).[52]

Played out across the entirety of the U.S., this variance contributes significantly to the quality problem in healthcare today. "Healthcare is actually in a pretty bad place today because we rely on expert opinion instead of real science," says billionaire philanthropist and Silicon Valley entrepreneur Vinod Khosla. To back this claim, Khosla likes to point to a study of cardiac specialists and their divergent, if not ephemeral, recommendations for treatment.

"...Cardiologist (sic) were given the same patient information and half recommended cardiac surgery whereas the other half did not," he wrote in a blog for the Web site TechCrunch in 2014. "Two years later with the same data, 40 percent of cardiologists reversed their recommendation."[53]

An investor in several medical technology startups, Khosla is taken seriously when he speaks on issues relating to energy, education, and, increasingly, healthcare—thanks to his track record. A founder of Sun Microsystems and a force behind several other technology companies and initiatives, he has studied healthcare extensively and even authored a 70-page manifesto on how to transform the field altogether through the widespread use of data analytics.

Khosla made a stir in the medical world in 2012 when he published a column in *Fortune* magazine that predicted that computers will eventually replace 80 percent of what doctors do. A predictable uproar ensued, but many people overlooked an important point that Khosla made in his essay: technology will not replace 80 percent of doctors, just 80 percent of what they do. Connected digital technology will "amplify their capabilities," he said, by giving physicians the right information at the right time and in the right place.[54] Computers, after all, are very good at processing information and storing large amounts of data—tasks that challenge everyday professionals in ordinary situations, let alone physicians under pressure to make life and death decisions. And computers can do these things without interference from prejudice, intuition, or ambition.

Connected digital technologies will make doctors better, in other words, by helping to practice more scientific medicine.

That's the theory anyway. Unfortunately, few medical practitioners are trained to think about variance in the same way as efficiency experts at big manufacturing companies or global service providers. Reducing variance requires an uncompromising level of discipline, dedication, and faith—in other words, belief in a single way above all others. This is an immense challenge in healthcare because opinions differ greatly over what constitutes "optimal" medical care.

This was certainly the case at Intermountain Healthcare of Salt Lake City for many years; at least until one Intermountain researcher took it upon himself to embed evidenced-based care into as many procedures as he could within the organization. His name is Dr. Brent James.

An Idaho native whose career took him to Harvard University before Utah, James is the Chief Quality Officer at Intermountain and the Executive Director of the organization's Institute for Health Care Delivery Research. His work has taken him to Europe and Asia, where he often lectures on healthcare reform, and to Washington, where he has testified to Congress.

Over the past several years, James has pored over patient data collected by Intermountain physicians who have determined the optimal way to treat Acute Respiratory Distress Syndrome (ARDS), pneumonia, heart disease, and other conditions. The protocols that Intermountain developed represented a true medical breakthrough, James thought. So why weren't more physicians jumping at the chance to leverage the information?

The answer has a lot to do with that freedom and flexibility I mentioned earlier and the heroic image that society has of its doctors. Despite data that suggests evidenced-based care produces better outcomes, many physicians bristle at the thought of treating patients with the same level of consistency used to build a Toyota Camry. Many have a personal bias against conformity, in other words. Consider obstetrics, for example.

According to the American College of Obstetricians and Gynecologists (ACOG)—the definitive voice of baby doctors nationwide—expectant mothers should not be induced until a child has reached the 39th week of gestation.[55] But many obstetricians ignore that advice. In fact, roughly one-third of mothers induced for no reason other than mere convenience are done so before 39 weeks.

Perplexed, researchers from Intermountain studied patient records going back decades. Unlike other researchers, they had a technological edge: data, and lots of it—thanks to a decision to embrace rudimentary computer decision support systems and electronic medical records (EMRs) as far back as the 1960s. Intermountain has 40 years worth of data at its disposal, which provides Intermountain with "more than two trillion unique medical data elements," according to the care provider.

When researchers at the organization analyzed their data on obstetrics, the findings astonished them. In Utah, home to the highest birthrate in the nation, a baby induced at 38 weeks was twice as likely to end up in an Intensive Care Unit (ICU) on a ventilator as a baby induced at 39 weeks. A baby induced at 37 weeks was five times as likely.

So why were some physicians ignoring the recommendations of the ACOG and other medical researchers? Because their individual experiences didn't reveal what Intermountain's population data did. Consider the country doctor who delivers fewer than 30 babies per year. Given that less than one percent of all babies born nationwide at 37 weeks wind up in intensive care, years could pass before he or she had an occasion to think about the macro impact of inducing mothers before 39 weeks. But to a care provider that delivers more than 30,000 babies a year, the numbers spoke loud and clear.

After it implemented an evidence-based protocol, the rate of premature inductions at Intermountain dropped from 28 percent to just 2 percent. As a result, 500 fewer babies born at Intermountain each year required an ICU ventilator. The change reduced Utah's health bill by $50 million annually. That's not chump change. If applied nationwide, the protocol could save an estimated $3.5 billion, according to James.

Believing it can achieve additional gains elsewhere, Intermountain has developed more than 150 evidence-based care protocols to reduce clinical variation. To help identify more, Intermountain has increased its investment in information technology and data analytics experts. Today, it employs more than 20 PhD-level medical informaticists and more than 200 data-mining experts to analyze clinical data stored in Intermountain's medical informatics system.

Their vision: Leverage technology that will greatly enhance the organization's ability to analyze large sets of clinical and research data. With it, Intermountain believes it can increase the volume and variety of the data it puts to use while increasing the speed and accuracy of its implementation. With better sensors and new tools, it could make better use of the data that its neonatal intensive care unit monitors produce. And with better tracking capabilities, it could more quickly identify community health issues that are trending on social media.

To ensure that it makes the most of new connected digital innovations, Intermountain teamed with Deloitte Consulting LLP in 2013 to "develop and provide health analytics insights to the medical community."[56]

"Health care is on the verge of realizing significant gains from big data, but it takes new tools and new approaches around collaboration to get there," said Jason Girzadas, a principal at Deloitte Consulting LLP. "This alliance will work to provide the health-care industry a destination center for the insights needed to change health care."[57]

Probst says he expects the alliance will help usher a new wave of innovation not just at Intermountain, but throughout the nation. "The use of our technologies will allow clinicians and researchers to more quickly discover practices that improve quality and keep costs lower," he said. "Research studies that previously might have taken years to complete could be conducted in just a few weeks instead."

Intermountain and Deloitte expect to engage other leading health systems to create "a community of medical researchers working with stakeholders across the health-care continuum," according to Intermountain.

What is more, the care provider joined several industry associations dedicated to the practice of evidence-based medicine. In 2013, Intermountain signed on with Dartmouth-Hitchcock, Denver Health, Mayo Clinic, and The Dartmouth Institute for Health Policy and Clinical Practice to form the High Value Healthcare Collaborative (HVHC). More than a feel-good partnership, members of the HVHC share best practices in nine different medical disciplines with the goal of reducing variance across multiple care systems. Since its formation, the HVHC has attracted 14 additional healthcare providers, including Baylor Scott & White, Beaumont Health System, Beth Israel Deaconess Medical Center, North Shore–LIJ Health System, MaineHealth, Providence Health, Sutter Health, UCLA Health System, University of Iowa Health Care, and Virginia Mason Medical Center. The members of the HVHC, which collectively serve 70 million patients nationwide, are working together to perfect the science of medicine.

The efforts have produced significant gains in many areas. In January 2015, for example, Intermountain was recognized by The Centers for Medicare and Medicaid Services for its work in a nationwide program known as the Partnership for Patients. Launched in 2011, the initiative is a coordinated national effort to improve patient safety in U.S. hospitals. Since its launch, the initiative has helped Intermountain avoid nearly 15,000 adverse events and helped it save an estimated $167 million, according to Intermountain.[58]

Nationally, collective efforts to reduce hospital-acquired conditions and readmissions resulting from urinary tract infections, bloodstream infections, surgical site infections, and other conditions have saved an estimated 50,000 lives, according to a report released by the Department of Health and Human Services. They have also saved an estimated $12 billion in healthcare costs nationally thru 2013.[59]

As for the number of lives being saved through the widespread practice of data-driven, evidence-based care, the numbers are growing. "I can document more than 1,000 [patients] per year in Utah that a few years ago would have died, but today they don't because of that approach," James told *Modern Healthcare* in 2014.[60]

New digital innovations, he and others believe, promise to save even more lives. In addition to improving quality, they will simultaneously reduce costs by helping practitioners make better decisions at the bedside, in the lab, and in the pharmacy. Intermountain is so excited about the possibilities that it even went so far as to change its mission statement in the Fall of 2014 for the first time in nearly four decades. By changing from an "Excellence in the provision of healthcare services" to "Helping people live the healthiest lives possible," the mission statement now takes a more holistic view and encompasses prevention, wellness, and shared decision-making with patients—a change that would not be possible without sophisticated information systems, according to CEO Dr. Charles Sorenson.[61]

"Having data systems that track clinical outcomes, cost outcomes, and service outcomes, and then showing [the outcome] to the doctors with a structure at Intermountain where we have a systematic way to implement best practices and improve outcomes in those three areas? That's been really critical to our new mission," he says. It begins to provide "transparency, which has been a huge barrier in healthcare."

Another care provider, Cleveland Clinic, is also pursuing care in new ways, thanks to advanced digital technology. Chief Information Officer and MD Martin Harris says care providers are looking beyond the four walls of their facilities and leveraging Internet and mobile technology to help patients manage chronic care conditions and stay better engaged with other members of the community to help improve their overall health. For example, consider diabetes patients.

"The way to provide optimal care for them is not by treating a patient in your office four times a year; the way to do that is to use technology to monitor their regular process, such as their glucose levels, and to make adjustments in the context of their daily living," says Harris.[62] This also has social aspects to it. For instance, Cleveland Clinic found that diabetic patients who were regularly monitored did better than those who were not because they felt more engaged with their doctor.

Helping care providers advance the quality of outcomes are new product developers who have turned their focus on this market. Several ideas combine the best from the world of medicine with the latest from the world of technology. For example, consider Kyron, a new start-up founded by the former chief of technology at AltaVista, one of the Web's first search engines. Its mission: uncover patterns in clinical data to help healthcare practitioners make better decisions. According to the company, its technology "enables researchers and clinicians to identify interventions that lead to differences in outcomes by conducting virtual clinical studies on similar patients." Like Intermountain, Kyron is mining patient data already being collected in medical facilities to identify patterns of care that lead to better quality outcomes.[63]

Lumiata, a company funded, in part, by Khosla Ventures, is also studying patient data to "optimize every health care interaction." The company delivers "real-time predictive analytics that help hospital networks and insurance carriers provide higher quality care to more patients in less time," it says.[64]

Although evidence-based care might sound like cookbook or paint-by-the-numbers medicine, it's more than that. When I went to Utah to meet with Intermountain executives in person, Dr. James, the care provider's chief quality officer, told me that for all the ways human beings are different—our sizes, genders, ethnicities, and so on—we are remarkably similar in how we respond to care. "The key to improving patient outcomes lies in the consistent application of medicine, not the occasional miracles we achieve practicing it," he said.

Rather than cookbook medicine, he sees evidenced-based care as by-the-book medicine—a form of medicine that data have proven to be superior in quality time and again. Intermountain's CEO, Dr. Sorenson, agrees. "If we could spend our time in this country focusing on consistently doing what we already know works, and doing that for everybody, there would be such a vast improvement in health outcomes and reduction in costs that it would be striking."[65]

After increasing access and improving quality through the power of connected analytics, digital technology promises to benefit healthcare in one more significant way: it promises to make it more personal. A prescription drug or medical treatment developed just for you? With new Internet-enabled devices and techniques for crunching unimaginably large sets of data, the next treatment you receive from a doctor could be as bespoke as a hand-tailored suit cut just for you.

In addition to making you look better on the outside, this care will make you feel better on the inside.

Personalization

In March of 2015, San Francisco 49er linebacker Chris Borland did what every professional football player must do: he hung up his cleats for good. Only Borland, one of the league's surprise stars of 2014, didn't retire at the end of a long, storied career; he did so at the beginning of one. Just 24 years old and with only a single season under his belt, Borland walked away from the game he loved and a $3 million contract.

Some fans and sports pundits wondered if Borland had lost his mind. Borland said he retired to save it. Like other gridiron athletes, he sustained a serious concussion while on the field. After weighing the odds of what additional concussions would do to his brain as the years rolled by, he decided to end his career while he still had his wits about him.

"I just want to live a long, healthy life, and I don't want to have any neurological diseases or die younger than I would otherwise," Borland told ESPN's "Outside the Lines."[66]

Other players who sustained concussions were not so lucky.

Scores of players have died from football-related brain injuries. "Outside the Lines" reported in March of 2015 that "more than 70 former players have been diagnosed with progressive neurological disease after their deaths, and numerous studies have shown connections between the repetitive head trauma associated with football, brain damage, and issues such as depression and memory loss."[67]

Though many athletes who suffer from depression recognized their deteriorating mental health, others had no real way to monitor or quantify their conditions. Despondent, several resorted to taking their own lives. One of those was Chicago Bears great Dave Duerson, who played on the 1985 Super Bowl Championship team. He committed suicide in 2011 after complaining to his family that his mental health was slipping. Hoping that researchers would find something amiss with his brain that would help medical professionals diagnose other players who suffered from neurological disorders, Duerson opted to take his life with a gunshot to the chest instead of the head. When researchers completed their autopsy, they indeed found that he suffered from chronic traumatic encephalopathy, the degenerative brain disorder that Borland so obviously hoped to avoid.[68]

Since his death, the National Football League (NFL), National Collegiate Athletic Association (NCAA), and governing bodies that oversee youth sports have taken concussions more seriously. So have technology developers. One company, MC10 Inc. of Cambridge, Mass., has teamed with shoe and clothing giant Reebok to develop the Checklight indicator, which uses multiple sensors to capture head impact data during play.[69] "Tucked under any helmet, this smart, sensing skullcap serves as an extra set of eyes on the playing field, contributing crucial information towards the assessment of each athlete," the company says.[70]

While stopping short of calling its product a diagnostic tool, MC10 says the technology gathers data on the number and severity of impacts, calculates their cumulative effect on an athlete, and then flashes a red indicator when a player needs medical attention. What's interesting about MC10's technology is that the same innovation that goes into the Checklight sensor can be applied to any number of wearable products that make healthcare more relevant by making it more personal. Its stretchable circuits can attach to almost any part of the human body. With these sensors, parents can continuously monitor the temperature of infants, for example, while care practitioners can use them to cost effectively monitor the heart rates of seniors from afar.

"It's our mission to extend human capabilities by making high-performance electronics virtually invisible, conformal, and wearable. We reshape rigid, conventional electronics into thin, flexible devices that can stretch, bend and twist seamlessly with our bodies and the natural world. And we're making them affordable for the everyday consumer," the company says.[71]

With technology like this, the long-promised era of personalized medicine, which the U.S. Food and Drug Administration (FDA) describes as "providing the right patient with the right drug at the right dose at the right time," is becoming real.[72]

"More broadly, personalized medicine (also known as precision medicine) may be thought of as the tailoring of medical treatment to the individual characteristics, needs and preferences of a patient during all stages of care, including prevention, diagnosis, treatment, and follow-up," says the FDA.[73]

Fueling the rise of personalized medicine are two different but complementary trends. First is the rise of wearable and ingestible products, which includes connected devices that will produce reams of individual data that can be analyzed to personalize the prevention and treatment of any number of medical conditions. The second is the transfer of medical data collection and even analysis from practitioners to individuals, which will result in the greater participation of patients in their health regimens, diagnoses, and treatment plans.

For a better idea of how these trends are coming together, look no further than the smart phone inside your pocket or purse. A recent study completed by the University of Pennsylvania concludes that the latest smart phones are as capable of tracking human activity as dedicated devices designed specifically to measure exercise. "Increased physical activity facilitated by these devices could lead to clinical benefits not realized by low adoption of pedometers," concludes researcher Meredith Case, one of the study's authors. "Our findings may help reinforce individuals' trust in using smartphone applications and wearable devices to track health behaviors, which could have important implications for strategies to improve population health."[74]

What this means in plain English is that the technology you use for texting and "showrooming" will very soon monitor your heart rate, calorie retirement, blood sugar, and cholesterol levels. When paired with new apps and devices, the technology will be able to help consumers test their own blood, DNA, and even urine.

To progress beyond the early stages, however, certain challenges will need to be overcome. Vance Moore, who heads Operations at Mercy, a non-profit U.S. healthcare system with more than 2,000 physicians and about 40,000 employees, points out that patients don't want to carry a tool belt of sensors, many of which become obsolete every year or two and sometimes offer conflicting data. However, he is optimistic that these issues can be solved.

"I truly believe that the future of care is very bright due to the potential of sensors, machine learning, and advanced analytics that will capture, interpret, predict, and even prescribe actions that will help individuals more actively participate in their care. It will also help providers determine the right paths of care based on predictability. Likewise it will allow provider, patients, family, care managers, advocates and other key players on a care team to interact responsibly. Care will be precision based once we truly understand all the variables and how they interact to render a condition. Bottom line: bright future, complex transition."[75]

Meanwhile, progress continues unabated. In January of 2015, San Francisco-based AliveCor received clearance from the FDA for two new algorithms for its $75 heart monitor, which attaches to your mobile smart phone and provides instant electrocardiogram (ECG) readings.[76] Another company called Scanadu is developing a phone-based urine test kit that can detect early signs of liver, kidney, or metabolism problems (such as diabetes).[77] Yet another, Cue, has developed an app and sensor that can monitor or detect inflammation, vitamin D deficiencies, fertility problems, influenza, and testosterone levels "via a swab of spit, snot or blood," according to tech site GigaOm.[78] Then there's Dexcom, a company that makes a wearable patch and accompanying pager-like device for monitoring Type II diabetes. Dexcom has developed a new app that will connect directly with an iPhone, eliminating the need for diabetes sufferers to carry a separate, single-purpose device to monitor their conditions.[79] Given that there are an estimated 400 million people in the world over who suffer from Type II diabetes,[80] the Dexcom app could make life easier for millions.

As innovative and advanced as these apps and sensors are, they are only part of the reason why the connected digital technology holds the promise of transforming healthcare into a more personal and collaborative experience. All the data these apps and devices produce, for example, will contribute to an ever-wider pool of information that will be crunched and analyzed for new medical insight. Instead of being available to only your doctor or healthcare provider, these insights will be available to you. This includes the information you collect on your activity and bodily functions, as well as the information that you amass from third parties such as 23andMe, the direct-to-consumer genetic-testing company.

For $199 and a spittle of saliva, 23andMe will provide you a detailed analysis of your unique genetic signature. This includes information on whether you carry genes that put you at risk for certain conditions, insights into your family ancestry, information about how your genes will react to exercise and diet, and discernments as to what makes you unique, "from food preferences to physical features," according to the company.[81]

Although 23andMe initially ran afoul of the FDA, which accused the company of providing medical advice without FDA approval—a major "no-no" in Washington—23andMe has since received approval from Washington to provide consumers with an overview of their DNA—all 23 pairs of chromosomes—through detailed reports, tools and more. Even before the company squared itself with the FDA, interest in the company developed almost overnight. Among other things, 23andMe received a $10 million infusion of cash from drug giant Genentech for further research. If it reaches specific commercial and scientific milestones, it could collect an additional $50 million from Genentech.[82]

That will, of course, depend on how negotiations with the FDA go (in February, the agency gave the company permission to market its "Bloom syndrome carrier status report"[83]) and, moreover, how many more people turn to it for help curating what has come to be known as the "quantified self." That's a term researchers and technologists have coined for the insights we can develop with new tools and analytics that help us better understand our health, fitness, and well being. According to *Forbes*, 23andMe has sold more than 800,000 genetic test kits and, more importantly, received the "okay" from 600,000 people to use their data for medical research, according to *Forbes*.[84]

This type of research "crowdsourcing" is growing quickly, researchers say, and will soon become widespread (if not commonplace). As it does, the one-way conversation that has taken place between patient and physician for more than 100 years will come to an end, says Dr. Eric Topol, a cardiologist at the Scripps Translational

Science Institute in La Jolla, California, and the author of the 2015 bestseller *The Patient Will See You Now.*[85]

In his book, Topol envisions a future in which a trip to the doctor for most needs will be unnecessary. Our smart phones or "tricorders" will be able to capture, analyze, and then transmit all our relevant physiological data to medical professionals on an ongoing basis. What is more, Topol says, the days of spending time in an overcrowded hospital are also drawing to a close. With the right portable sensors and smart apps, patients will be able to treat themselves at home better and for a fraction of the cost of most hospital stays.[86]

As for prescription drugs, technology will eliminate the guesswork of which to choose. "Genetic patterns will easily distinguish people likely to benefit from a drug from those likely to be poisoned," says physician and *The New York Times* contributor Abigail Zuger, who reviewed Topol's new book. "Drug selection will become safe enough that for some conditions, patients will prescribe for themselves."[87]

This is a radical departure from how medicines have been developed for the last 100 years. During this time, drugs were developed to treat the broadest population of consumers possible. This was so drug companies could recoup the money required to develop a commercially viable product, which amounts to an estimated $2.6 billion per drug, according to a 2014 report completed by the Tufts Center for the Study of Drug Development (CSDD). That's three times more than just a dozen years ago.[88]

Personalized medicine turns this economic model upside down. Instead of years of development, personalized medicines could be developed in months—if not weeks—for patients. And instead of being developed for broad populations, they will be targeted at just you. They will be formulated to your age, fitness, physical activity, and even genetic composition.

"Scientists are working to match specific gene variations with responses to particular medications. With that information, doctors can tailor treatments to individuals," says the Mayo Clinic.[89]

Given that 1.3 million Americans are injured each year by "medication errors," according to the National Coordinating Council for Medication Error Reporting and Prevention, this is likely to be a big deal.[90]

Personalized medicine accessible to all and of the highest quality?
That is the promise of the digital revolution for healthcare.

A Better System, A Healthier You

Greater access. Better quality. And more personalized care.

Could this really be the future of healthcare?

It can, experts agree, but it will require some changes.

For Internet-enhanced care to really take off, policy makers and regulators are going to have to rethink how their nation will pay for healthcare, what constitutes proper medicine, and what it means to dispense medical advice.

Tech companies, meanwhile, hoping to make a killing by saving lives, must think hard about their obligations to consumers when it comes to HIPAA compliance, security, integrity, and more.

Then there's the medical community. If practitioners are not on board with the changes that outsiders want to bring to them, there is little chance that new business models, technologies, and other conventions will gain traction in the field. For new ideas to gain acceptance, they must tightly integrate into the checklists, order sets, and clinical workflows that doctors and nurses rely on every day.

Finally, there is you. If you want a healthier life, then you too must be open to change. As we've laid out in this chapter, the system we have today is not sustainable. So it must evolve into something that is. What does this mean for you? It means some of the things you take for granted might not survive the modern healthcare revolution. As a result of cost-savings measures, you might not be able to see your preferred care practitioner without paying an expensive premium, for example. And you might not qualify for certain treatments based on your individual conditions and circumstances.

In exchange for parting ways with these benefits, which amount to unaffordable excesses in today's world, you can expect a healthcare system that provides greater access, higher quality, and more personalized benefits. Care in the future might come in the form of an electronic consultation, a data-driven diagnosis, and/or a personally inspired prescription based on your own DNA. While certain aspects might not be as appealing as before, the care you receive as a result of the digital revolution will be better for you and society alike.

And that's the real good news about healthcare today.

3

Education
*The Learner Triumphs**

"Think about every problem, every challenge, we face. The solution to each starts with education."[1]

Can you guess which famous person said these prophetic words? Hint: It's a former U.S. President.

Still stumped? Well, the answer is actually easy: almost every U.S. President has said something along these lines about education. For example, consider Thomas Jefferson, the nation's third President, who wrote in a letter to James Madison in 1787, "Educate and inform the whole mass of the people...[for] they are the only sure reliance for the preservation of our liberty."[2]

One-hundred and seventy-four years later, the 35th U.S. President, John F. Kennedy, said in a Proclamation celebrating "American Education Week, 1961": "Let us not think of education only in terms of its costs, but rather in terms of the infinite potential of the human mind that can be realized through education."[3]

As for the first quote in this chapter—about every problem and solution starting with education—it actually belongs to George H.W. Bush.[4] But it could just as easily have come from one of his contemporaries. This includes the South African leader and civil rights advocate Nelson Mandela, who famously said, "Education is the most powerful weapon which you can use to change the world,"[5] or former

---

 * For their guidance with this chapter, I am grateful to John Hennessy, President of Stanford University; Rick Levin, President Emeritus of Yale University (and CEO of Coursera); Geoffrey Garrett, Dean of the Wharton School at the University of Pennsylvania; Daphne Koller, Co-founder and President of Coursera; and Salman Khan, Founder and CEO of Khan Academy.

UN Secretary Kofi Annan, who once said, "education is the premise of progress in every society, in every family."[6]

Inspiring words, no question.

Despite all the rhetoric advanced by important thinkers over the past 250 years, however, cynics note that education has progressed at a very slow pace. Take the U.S., where performance has actually fallen compared to other nations in recent years. In 2012, for example, U.S. students ranked 36th on the global Program for International Student Assessment, or PISA tests—down several spots from four years before.[7]

Try as we might, the number of students who ace the nation's standardized, Scholastic Aptitude Test (SAT) remains stubbornly modest—less than one percent[8]—while the number of learners who land in the middle score roughly what their parents did a generation ago.[9] Similarly, student achievement has stalled or fallen in many developed countries, such as Sweden, France, and New Zealand, and in developing nations, including Jordan, Uruguay and Costa, according to the Organization for Economic Cooperation and Development (OECD).[10]

If the world were standing still, this would be troubling enough. But since it's evolving faster than ever, the gap between global needs and worldwide capabilities is not only stubbornly wide, it is getting wider. For all our affection for education, we have to conclude that we aren't getting from it what we need.

This is true despite massive outlays for public education around the world.

Public spending on education as a percentage of total GDP ranges between 1-10 percent worldwide, according to the UNESCO Institute for Statistics.[11] The total global education market today tops $4 trillion, according to IBIS Capital, a London-based investment bank.[12] In the U.S., annual spending on a per-pupil basis for students in public elementary, secondary, and collegiate schools exceeds $15,000, according to the OECD.[13] This is nearly twice what the U.S. spends annually on healthcare per capita,[14] and more than three times what it spends per capita on food.[15]

To improve outcomes, policy makers and practitioners alike have proposed all manner of reform. As a result, education is constantly "under construction." Each year introduces new standards, curricula, learning systems, schools, and more. And yet well-intended professionals do not make the gains in outcomes that they hope.

Some say the culprit is outmoded delivery models. Others insist it is inadequate funding or entrenched special interests. Even more point to the home, where parents struggle to create an environment of learning amid video games, social media, and extracurricular activities. Throw in population and demographic change, economic stagnation, and social strife in many places around the world and you have to wonder if we will ever get education right. What learning needs, many experts agree, is a revolution, one that embraces new strategies, cost structures, and technologies.

No doubt you've heard this before. Maybe you have even supported various experiments in education in your community. Despite the best of intentions, however, nothing seems to fundamentally change. The best we can hope from education, many believe, is basically what we have today. Anything more is just a dream.

Or is it?

While it is true that numerous attempts at reform have come and gone with mixed results, new ideas are being applied every day. This includes digitization, which has been shown to improve outcomes in the three areas that everyone from the World Bank[16] to the United Nations[17] has identified as top, global educational priorities. They are *quality*, *access*, and *relevance*.

While professionals, politicians, and parents wrestle over important issues such as school funding, teacher unions, charter schools, professor tenure, standardized testing, core curriculum, and more, I want to shine a light on the success that innovators have achieved integrating digital innovation into pedagogy. Among other things, it has improved quality by making education more collaborative, challenging, and personal. It has broadened access to learning by making it more affordable, available, and convenient. And it has increased the relevance of education by making it more flexible, immediate, and engaging. Simultaneous progress along each of these dimensions (quality, access, and relevance) is ushering in a digital-driven revolution that is transforming the classroom and the role of the teacher in ways not seen in more than a century. The impact is already being felt by millions of students worldwide and, one day soon, could reach billions.

For more on how, let's look at quality in education and the positive impacts that the digital revolution, or IoE—the Internet of Everything—is starting to have on it.

Quality

"Education is broken."

How many times have you heard that old saw?

Undoubtedly a lot.

If you enter the words "education is broken" into a Google search, nearly 300 million results pop up. Among these are critiques and insights proffered by people from all walks of life. This includes reformers, politicians, entrepreneurs, parents, and educators themselves. There are so many examples of people who promulgate the idea that there is even a Web site, "Edukashun is brocken," dedicated to "finding examples of the lazy 'education is broken' meme wherever they surface their squashy little heads."[18]

The Web site has a point.

Despite its shortcomings, education produces wonderful minds the world over. Take the oft-maligned education system in the U.S. If you were to rank the university affiliations of the Nobel Prize winners throughout history, you'd find that seven of the top 10 schools represented are U.S. institutions. There are three Ivies (Harvard, Columbia, and Yale), two West Coast powerhouses (Stanford University and the University of California at Berkeley), and two top-flight independent schools (the University of Chicago and the Massachusetts Institute of Technology).[19]

While the U.S. "higher-ed" learning system is considered to be the best in the world, it's misleading to view the entire system through the lens of its best and brightest. For all their accolades, remember that the eight schools that comprise the Ivy League, for example, educate only four of every 1,000 students enrolled in an undergraduate program in America.[20]

A better gauge of American education would undoubtedly be a measure of the quality achieved by the bulk of its learners. Judged by almost any objective standard along these lines—think test scores, worker-preparedness, or national competitiveness—you'd have to conclude that the U.S. does indeed have a quality challenge.

Who is to blame? Good question.

Educators certainly are a favorite target of some critics. But judging by the years they prepare, the hours they work, or even the personal money some spend on supplies for students, you'd be hard-pressed to make the case that American teachers are the problem with education—underachievers and malcontents notwithstanding. (I say this as a parent who has witnessed many sacrifices on behalf of my children, and as a guest educator at the University of California at Berkeley, where I've seen dedication that rivals that of Olympic athletes.)

So who then? Working parents with one or more jobs? Administrators who struggle with impossible social, financial, and security challenges? Maybe the blame should be heaped upon legislators, though some of them are legally obligated to cut spending to balance a budget?

When you step back and study the quality problem in the U.S., you realize the culprit isn't "who" as much as "how." We don't have a personnel problem; we have a modality one. In a documentary that debuted at the 2015 Sundance Film Festival, filmmaker Greg Whiteley, director of "Most Likely to Succeed," zeroed in on the problem. "The last major shift in education, if you can believe it, occurred in the 1800s when we went from one room school houses [and] a curricula that was largely designed by a teacher in a small town, a rural town usually, to this mass-produced, standardized, factory-like education system," he said in an interview with KUER Radio in January 2015.[21]

For much of the 20th century, this model produced graduates who were adequately prepared to take their place in the economy, not just in the U.S. but the world over. So long as a job didn't require an advanced, specialized degree, the traditional education patterned after the famed Prussian model helped make the 20th century worker the most productive in history.

"The problem is, in the 124 years since we instituted [the model], our economy has completely changed. It is not an industrial one any more, and yet our educational system is still rooted in this old industrial model," says Whiteley.[22]

Instead of turning out legions of factory workers who can follow instructions, our educational system should be preparing people to work in the information age, where decentralized, flat organizational work environments demand critical-decision making capabilities, collaborative social skills, and multidisciplinary subject matter expertise.

But it isn't.

One reason why is the traditional mode of knowledge transfer—the lecture—that amplifies the limitations of any one educator. As far back as the 1960s, futurists and thought leaders have identified the classroom lecture as a roadblock to reform. Philosopher Marshall McLuhan went so far as to decry the traditional classroom as "an obsolete detention home, a feudal dungeon."[23]

And yet every morning since then, students have gathered together to listen to a teacher deliver a lecture, much as they did in Medieval universities.[24] While the business world roiled with change, the classroom stayed static. This was true despite the fact that entire professions, including travel agents, switchboard operators, bank tellers, assembly-line workers, and data-entry clerks, were being eliminated from workforces everywhere.

Until recently, that is.

Inspired by development in the business world and innovations that have transformed consumer life, educators are now making more changes than at any time in the past 150 years. For starters, they have broken down the walls of the school. They have brought the world of knowledge into their classrooms and encouraged their students to think beyond their immediate environments.

As educators have done so, they have flipped the classroom; instead of standing before students and lecturing to them for an hour, they have begun to walk among them as students solve problems and use their mobile devices to research information from direct sources such as museums, universities, experts from around the world, and other sites devoted to advanced knowledge. Today, hundreds of thousands of students engage their peers around the world in a more collaborative manner. Doing so has exposed students to a greater diversity of influences and opinions, which has helped them develop better critical decision-making and social skills.

Teachers have also made learning more personal. While some students collaborate on group learning projects, teachers work with individual students on a one-on-one basis. This includes students who are ready to move ahead and those who are struggling to keep up. With so many tools available online, a teacher can easily provide a student with a recommendation to a remedial lesson that can help him or her move ahead or quickly catch up.

Add it all up—the flipping of the classroom, the breaking down of walls, the increased emphasis on collaboration, and the improved ability of an educator to provide a more personalized experience—and you end up with a better education delivery system. You end up with better quality, in other words.

One example of where this works in practice is in one of America's oldest centers of education, Philadelphia, which is home to the world's first collegiate business school, the Wharton School of the University of Pennsylvania. One of the finest schools in the country—it's routinely rated among the top three business schools in the nation by *US News & World Report*[25]—Wharton works like any other to provide the absolute best in terms of educational quality. What it's doing with IoE technology to overcome a particularly unique challenge serves as a model of what the future of education will look like in a mere few years.

For a better idea, imagine a scenario where you are a student enrolled in Wharton's "Macroeconomics and the Global Economic Environment" class. The purpose of the course is straightforward: prepare students "to think systematically about the current state of the economy and macroeconomic policy, and to be able to evaluate the economic environment within which business and financial decisions are made."[26]

On the first day of class, you arrive early and find a seat down front in the lecture hall. A few minutes later, you look up as a floor-to-ceiling screen descends. Suddenly, your professor appears in high-definition resolution and crystal-clear sound quality. After some perfunctory introductory remarks, he explains that he is in a classroom at Wharton San Francisco, which opened in 2001 to accommodate West Coast learners.[27]

Despite the distance, your professor assures you, he can see every one of you as clearly as you can him. And he can hear you, too. In fact, five minutes into the class you forget that your professor is 2,500 miles away. He appears life-sized and even clicks his heels as he paces across the floor in front of you. Then it happens: he cold calls you and asks what you think is the biggest factor driving growth in the economy today.

Because your background is finance, you craft a reasonable answer emphasizing the role of low interest rates and stable inflation. But one of your peers behind you challenges your answer. You swivel your chair and look at another massive screen over your shoulder. There, clear as day, is a Silicon Valley entrepreneur sitting among the students in the Wharton San Francisco classroom. His argument for "disruptive innovation" is pretty cogent but flawed, you believe. Before you can rebut, someone else chimes in on yet another massive screen. Instead of Philadelphia or San Francisco, this student is inside the Penn Wharton China Center in Beijing. The most important success factor, according to her, is "operational efficiency" made possible by data analytics and Internet efficiencies.

A heated debate ensues. Though your professor guides the dialogue, he lets it run for a few minutes. Then he tells the class that he has arranged for two guest speakers to join. As he speaks, the two individuals are projected onto two screens beside you. One is an official with the Securities and Exchange Commission (SEC) in Washington, D.C., and the other is finance legend David Pottruck, the former CEO of Charles Schwab.

"Yes," your professor assures once more, "they can see and hear every one of you—whether you're with me in San Francisco, on the main campus in Philadelphia, or in China." The discussion continues with the experts rendering their opinions and students challenging one another and your professor. When the class ends 90 minutes later, you are simultaneously exhausted and energized.

A static lecture taught by a lone educator? Not in Wharton's "Macroeconomics and the Global Economic Environment." In this class, walls are literally torn asunder. Collaboration with peers and guest experts is not only encouraged but expected. Instead of a textbook, you learn to read subject matter experts from the world of business, government, and academia regardless of where they are—or where you are, thanks to mobile technology.

So how is this possible? The answer is digital innovation, which Wharton uses to connect its West Coast campus in San Francisco and China Center in Beijing to its main campus in Philadelphia.

From a technology standpoint, the Cisco Connected Classroom leverages high-speed Internet communications, high-definition cameras, displays, and microphones to create an immersive experience in which students and educators separated by thousands of miles interact as though they were mere feet from one another. Professors can teach classes in more than one city simultaneously, appearing live in one classroom and virtually in life-sized, high-definition clarity in the other. Students now learn directly from experts who are no longer restricted by geography and students can attend classes on their smart devices no matter where they are being taught. What is more, students who are working professionals who cannot attend regularly scheduled classes can later review recorded lectures, lessons, and discussions in a searchable, indexed format after hours and from virtually any smart device.

The new style of learning beginning to take shape at Wharton and led by educators like Pottruck—a Wharton grad who routinely teaches one of the school's most popular classes—completely transforms the learning experience. Instead of the input of one, it leverages the contributions of many.

"It's not university education that's an endangered species," says Geoffrey Garrett, Dean of the Wharton School, "it's the lecture, and lecture halls."[28, 29]

This view is taking root far and wide, including places where the lecture and classroom experience is revered. Take Harvard Business School, which has taken the idea even further through its HBX Live. HBX is a "virtual classroom that connects 60 students from anywhere in the world to a professor in Boston for a dynamic and engaging HBS-style discussion." With 60 screens and 66 cameras, "participants from around the globe can log in and join real-time, case-based sessions with HBS faculty, who teach from the HBX Live studio," according to the school.[30]

"Perhaps the biggest surprise that's come out of HBX is how it is beginning to affect our thinking about the best way to teach live classes utilizing the case study method," says Dean Nitin Nohria. He once resisted online education but now sees the school's "HBX" online efforts as a transformative plus for education. "Five years after I said 'not in my lifetime,' I now believe that HBX could easily be one of the most important initiatives we undertake at Harvard Business School," he says.[31]

"Just as lecture-based programs are putting lectures online to 'flip the classroom' and deepen in-class discussion, we are exploring ways to use the technologies and methods pioneered by HBX to allow pieces of what we now do in our case discussions to take place online before class, opening up time for a richer classroom experience," Nohria wrote in a June 2015 blog for the school.[32]

The future of education? For tens of thousands of students at a handful of innovative institutions, it already is. And that's just the beginning. As technology matures and becomes more accessible, the insights and capabilities developed at Wharton and elsewhere are impacting other universities, colleges, high schools, and elementary schools nationwide.

Take Bellarmine College Preparatory, a high school in San Jose, California. There, educators including Science Chair Rod Wong use technology from a company called Nearpod to transform their classrooms into next-generation learning environments.

Nearpod, according to its developer, is a "device agnostic platform that allows teachers to easily create and share interactive lessons, receive feedback on student device use, assess knowledge in real time and personalize instruction for students based on powerful analysis and reporting features, all in a mobile learning environment."[33]

If that sounds too "Valley-speak" to you, then consider what Wong himself says of the technology: "With Nearpod, I can have my kids sit in a circle so I can have eye contact and a relationship with each kid. [A class] is a group setting and an interactive session. The kids are interacting. They are having a discussion. They are writing things down, typing things out. I can see exactly what the kids see. I can see exactly what the kids understand and what they don't understand so I can assess right where they are."[34]

Although he has a warm spot in his heart for the traditional lecture, he recognizes its limitations. The new IoE technology from Nearpod, he adds, is a superior way to deliver information.

Elsewhere, educators are leveraging other technologies to transform their classrooms. ExitTicket is a technology for increasing student participation. The technology, which is used by hundreds of thousands of students in K-12 settings, is a software app that students can download to their smart devices and use to answer questions posed by their teachers. They can also use the software to participate in classroom polls, take practice tests, and assess performance on Common Core curricula against their in-class peers and fellow students nationwide.[35]

The IoE-enabled software increases student engagement by introducing gaming, crowdsourcing, and other conventions into the classroom while providing immediate data feedback to teachers, including Jen Ciok, a middle school social studies teacher from Illinois. "Students know where they stand and can take charge of their learning when needed to understand a certain concept." says Ciok.[36]

Though very different, the connected digital technology used by Wharton, Bellarmine, and elsewhere is making education more collaborative, challenging, and personal. According to those who have leveraged it, it is contributing to a rise in quality for thousands upon thousands of learners. Additionally, real-time feedback improves teaching quality because teachers can modify their approach if it is not working.

But more than for a lucky few, the IoE technology has the potential to change the lives of millions more by breaking down the barriers that time, distance, and money have traditionally placed on education.

Quality, after all, means little if it is not widely available. So let's now look at how IoE is increasing access to learning for millions.

Access

If someone were to ask what you remember from 2012, what would you recall?

The riots and protests over austerity measures that erupted in Greece[37] and Spain?[38] The electrical blackouts of July that left more than 600 million in India without power for two days?[39] Or maybe President Barack Obama's victory over Mitt Romney to claim a second term in office despite a weak U.S. economy and jaded electorate?[40]

It was some year to remember for sure. There was the London Olympics,[41] Hurricane Sandy,[42] and the 2012 World Expo in South Korea.[43] During the year, the "Curiosity" rover began exploring the surface of Mars[44] and *Time Magazine* named President Obama its "Person of the Year."[45]

The New York Times, meanwhile, put its stamp on the year in November when it declared 2012 "The Year of the MOOC."[46] Remember? Probably not.

Unless you're a student or a professional educator, you likely have only a passing familiarity with MOOCs, which are formally known as Massive Open Online Courses. For the uninitiated, MOOCs are academic courses presented over the Internet for free or for very nominal charges by some of the world's leading educators and institutions. Think professors from Harvard, Stanford, MIT, and other institutions. Enabled by entrepreneurial startups—including Coursera, edX, and Udacity—that specialize in translating traditional curricula into online classes, hundreds of schools in the U.S. and abroad have embraced MOOCs. And so have millions of learners.

Why, you might wonder, would a leading center of academic advancement, one that typically charges tens of thousands of dollars to a select, limited number of consumers, put its most valuable product online and offer it free to anyone with a broadband connection? It's a good question since many institutions of higher learning warily eye MOOCs, which challenge—if not threaten—the way universities and colleges have delivered education for hundreds of years.

Yet those who have embraced MOOCs have a simple rationale for doing so: access. Broadening access to students around the world who otherwise would not have it is simply the right thing to do. It's also the key to increasing a school's influence, which has traditionally been constrained by basic physics. Take Princeton University.

As of August 2015, more than 27,000 students applied to the Class of 2019 at Princeton. But the New Jersey school had room for only 1,948 students—about 7 percent of the applicants.[47] At Stanford,[48] Harvard,[49] Penn,[50] MIT,[51] and other elite schools, a similarly large number of applicants apply for a similarly limited number of places. While slightly better, the odds of getting into a top public university are difficult as well. The University of California at Berkeley, for example, attracted nearly 79,000 applicants in 2015. It could admit only 17 percent of these.[52]

Today, there is a mismatch between the number of students who desire an education at a top-flight school and the number of spaces available to them. So what's the solution?

Expanding campuses isn't a viable option for most. Nor is hiring more qualified professors or taxing an already overworked faculty. One of the best answers to accommodate increased demand is MOOCs, which help schools increase access by reducing the physical barriers of time, distance, financial means, and even classroom size. Thanks to MOOCs, an almost unlimited number of students can attend a class at Harvard, Yale, Penn, Stanford, and hundreds of other institutions regardless of a student's geography, preparation, or means. If a mind is willing, a class awaits.

Rick Levin, President Emeritus of Yale University, believes that online education "has the potential to be very mission enhancing for universities."[53]

"If our job at universities is to create and disseminate valuable knowledge, this gives the dissemination function a vastly expanded set of capabilities," says Levin, who now serves as CEO of Coursera.

Not surprisingly, the rise of MOOCs has led to a massive increase in the number of learners who are interested in higher education. An early edX class offered online by MIT, Circuits and Electronics, attracted 155,000 enrollees from 160 countries.[54] That's more than 10 times the number of students enrolled at the vaunted school today[55] and more than the total number of living alumni from the school, according to MIT President Susan Hockfield.[56] And that was just one class.

Today, students from India, China, Russia, Chile, Australia, France, Fiji, and elsewhere regularly attend MOOC courses taught by leading educators at some of America's finest universities. They study everything from hard sciences to humanities. This expansion in access to advanced learning amounts to the single largest increase in the delivery of education since modern compulsory education was adopted in Europe and the U.S. in the 1880s.

This wouldn't be possible without the help that Coursera, edX, Udacity, and others provide in terms of course development, online enrollment and testing, and performance analytics. A combination technology platform provider and education advocate, these companies are staffed with some of the world's top academics. Coursera, for example, was co-founded by Daphne Koller, a top professor in the Department of Computer Science at Stanford University and a MacArthur Fellowship recipient.[57] Udacity, meanwhile, was co-founded by Sebastian Thrun, who was also a professor at Stanford.[58] Like many MOOC enthusiasts, they believe the key to increasing access is working hand-in-hand with the world's established education providers.

In addition to Stanford, Coursera, for example, works with Yale University, Johns Hopkins University, University of Edinburgh, Peking University, and others. As of October 2014, Coursera offered nearly 850 courses from more than 120 institutions worldwide. Collectively, they have attracted more than 10 million students from nearly 200 countries.[59]

More than enticing casual learners, Coursera and others have attracted serious students from every background imaginable. In fact, MOOCs have discovered that some of the world's hungriest minds aren't anywhere near the cherished lecture halls or hallowed libraries of top universities. Instead, many hail from Afghanistan, Syria, Sudan, Cuba, and other far-flung places. Despite their challenges, many of these students have proven themselves to be some of the finest learners of their generation. Consider the experience of Sebastian Thrun, the co-founder of Udacity.

In 2011, Thrun decided to offer his "Introduction to Artificial Intelligence" class at Stanford to anyone with an Internet connection. In 2013, *Fast Company* wrote about the results: "Over the next three months, the Professor offers the same lectures, homework assignments, and exams to the masses as he does to the Stanford students who are paying $52,000 a year for the privilege. A computer handles the grading, and students are steered to web discussion forums if they need extra help. Some 160,000 people sign up: young men dodging mortar attacks in Afghanistan, single mothers struggling to support their children in the United States, students in more than 190 countries. The youngest kid in the class is 10; the oldest is 70. Most struggle with the material, but a good number thrive."[60]

When Thrun tallied the scores from the final exam, *Fast Company* reported, he was stunned by the outcome: "None of the top 400 students goes to Stanford. They all took the class on the Internet."[61]

The outcomes that Udacity, Coursera, and edX have witnessed first-hand provide ample evidence that MOOCs constitute a revolution in learning. They also confirm how transformative connecting people, information, and things to the Internet of Everything can be. While MOOCs will never replace the education that traditional, on-campus learners get when it comes to social, emotional, and experiential enrichment, they have proven invaluable for increasing intellectual development.

For all their merit, however, MOOCs face several significant challenges. While a big believer in online education, Stanford President John Hennessy is keenly aware of the challenges with it. He told a gathering of the American Council on Education in March 2015 that the massive and open nature of MOOCs create a problem: testing and measuring student achievement. If classes are open to all, he wonders, how does an educator create an exam that challenges the best of students without "crushing" the rest of enrollees?

"When I think about MOOCs, the advantage—the ability to prepare a course and offer it without personal interaction—is what makes them inexpensive and makes them very limited," he said.[62]

In addition to testing, MOOCs have two other challenges. One is accreditation, the other is branding. Let's look first at the former and the measures people are taking to overcome it.

At the time of their launch a few years ago, no one was quite sure how MOOCs would evolve. Some thought they would emerge as the "international campuses" of elite schools. Others predicted they would become the libraries of seniors looking to fill their time. Still more thought they would become the next generation of community colleges and/or vocational schools.

Hennessy says the biggest misconception about MOOCs is that you can just "substitute" them for formal education.[63] They can be a complement to and extension of what a formal education system does, but not yet a substitute.

Daphne Koller, the co-founder and president of Coursera (the largest MOOC), says that only 15 percent of Coursera learners are college-aged. "We are only three years old," she says. "70 percent of our learners are outside the U.S., and most of our learners will never be college students. What we are is a lifelong learning initiative."[64]

What MOOCs have turned out to be is a whole lot more than originally envisioned. For example, when Coursera first launched, the company did not offer classes for academic credit; its founders even said it was not their mission. At the time, Coursera classes were all about learning for learning's sake. This was fine by many enrollees, including my friend, Cisco Senior Vice President Carlos Dominguez, who took a Coursera MOOC class simply to expand his knowledge. (He took "The Music of the Beatles" and absolutely loved it.)

As time went on and students put more effort into their classes, the pressure on MOOCs increased to give credit for classes taken. At first MOOC providers thought students would be content with credits earned through a rigorous but somewhat circuitous process known in academia as "prior learning assessment." According to *Inside Higher Ed*, it involves assembling a "prior learning portfolio" and then asking an academic advisor to approve it so that it can then be submitted to a third-party clearinghouse for official course credits.[65]

Because this process can be laborious and unpredictable, students want their MOOCs to count directly for college credit. MOOC providers and schools responded in a variety of ways. edX, for example, arranged for its students, "to be able to take proctored final exams at Pearson VUE's brick-and-mortar testing centers around the world, where their identity can be verified," according to *The New York Times*.[66] Colorado State University's Global Campus, meanwhile, told the *Times* in 2012 it would give three transfer credits to any student who completed Udacity's "Introduction to Computer Science: Building a Search Engine" and passed a proctored test thereafter.[67]

Then in February 2013, the American Council on Education's College Credit Recommendation Service (ACE CREDIT) recommended college credit for five Coursera courses. The classes included a pre-calculus course from the University of California, Irvine, and a course on genetics and evolution from Duke.[68]

Since then, efforts to increase the accreditation of MOOCs have increased. Levin, for example, was brought on board, partly to legitimize Coursera's work, which has been criticized for high dropout rates, among other things. In March 2014, *The Wall Street Journal* said, "Mr. Levin's appointment could represent a doubling down on Coursera's bid to win accreditation for its courses, a step which would open the door to significantly more revenue."[69]

A notable effort at Coursera is to create "specializations," which are collections of courses that have been specified by key employers, developed with key universities, and delivered through Coursera. The specializations have a completion requirement, essentially a mini-credential whose value might be better understood by the employers. Among the companies that Coursera is working with for these specializations are Google for software, Cisco for networking, and Nike for branding.[70]

Schools are also looking for help from other outside sources to help build accreditation for their online courses. Rutgers University, the University of Florida, and Arizona State University are working with publishing giant Pearson to help "run and promote the online degree programs," according to *Fortune Magazine*.[71]

While these efforts started helping students interested in pursuing a degree, they didn't do much to inform employers which MOOC students were ready for professional employment. Sensing an opportunity, a number of third parties stepped forward. This includes Aspiring Minds, a company founded in 2007 by two brothers, Varun and Himanshu Aggarwal.[72] "Our vision is to create a level playing field in education and employment by introducing credible assessments," the company says. "Our mission is to develop a merit-driven labor market where everyone has the access to talent and opportunity."[73]

From their base in Redwood City, California, the two entrepreneurs built a company of more than 300 employees distributed
over the U.S. and India. It offers online assessment tools for different industries to help employers find talent. Aspiring Minds is able
to gather reams of data on employability benchmarks and workforce
health and then craft its assessments accordingly. Today, the company
cannot only tell a prospective employer about a potential employee's
skills, it can also provide insights into a candidate's cognitive abilities,
domain knowledge, and even personality, according to the company.

Rather than distance themselves from an organization that gathers
so much information on them, many MOOC students have embraced
what the company does. Aspiring Minds gives legitimacy to the work
they have done online and, more importantly, provides them a path-
way to professional employment.[74]

Today, the company's emphasis is in India. Tomorrow, it could
be the world. (In May 2015, it announced the launch of its flagship
assessment test in the U.S.) The company's efforts to provide a bridge
between MOOC students and prospective employers who want an
independent assessment of their capabilities, especially as it is corre-
lated with on-the-job performance, is exactly what connected digital
education could provide.[75]

It's also seeking greater recognition, the kind that better branding
provides.

Universities have huge brands built over decades, even centuries.
These brands connote time-tested quality, and serve as an important
signal to employers. And online degrees just don't have this kind of
cachet.

But they are getting there. Consider Georgia Tech.

In 2014, Georgia Tech ranked among the nation's top 10 universities for graduate-level, computer science studies, according to *US
News & World Report*.[76] That same year, Georgia Tech unveiled its
Online Master of Science in Computer Science (OMSCS) program,
which is believed to be the first brick-and-mortar school in the U.S. to
offer online students a complete, post-graduate degree from a well-
regarded brand. In a blog that appeared on the "College" Web site of
the *Huffington Post*, Zvi Galil, the John P. Imlay Jr. Dean of Computing and Professor at Georgia Tech, took on critics who pointed out

that MOOC completion rates are generally under 10 percent. What critics miss, he notes, is that MOOCs can educate some students as effectively as traditional methods. This realization was the genesis of the University's OMSCS program, which the school developed with the help of Georgia Tech, Udacity, and AT&T, which contributed $2 million to help launch the program.

Galil says that the program's classes are delivered using MOOC technology, but with a key difference: The classes belong to Georgia Tech and lead to a university degree. "There would be no question among students, employers or other academic institutions as to the worth of OMSCS, because it would be the same Georgia Tech master's in Computer Science that is already recognized for its high quality and the accomplishment of its graduates," he wrote.[77]

When he says the same, he means it: The degree name in both cases is "Master of Science in Computer Science." The online degree, in other words, has no special distinction, other than being available for $6,600 instead of the traditional, on-campus cost of $46,000 for out of state enrollees.[78]

By offering access to name-brand curricula and accreditation that students want, and by offering assurances that employers need, MOOCs and other online learning options are transforming education for literally millions of eager learners. And not just those in higher education.

While distance learning has been around for years, new connected digital innovations are expanding access to virtual learning to more students than ever before. And the technology is making it possible for educators to produce the same, if not better, results than achieved in traditional environments—at least in some instances. Take the Florida Virtual School, which provides education to 200,000 students scattered across the state and beyond.[79]

Although the majority of enrollees take only a class or two, thousands of remote students rely on the virtual, online school for their complete education. The school leverages a technology platform from a for-profit company called Connections Academy, which provides educators with proprietary interactive web tools, online lesson plans, instruction guides, an email platform, secure community message boards, and more, according to the company.[80] With the company's

Learning Management System, educators can create "a virtual class-room experience where teachers and students work together in a supportive environment."

The school fills a void in Florida, where everything from immigration to military deployment to personal choice has created a vast need for alternative educational opportunities. In addition to students with unique circumstances, such as world-class junior athletes and musicians, schools like the Florida Virtual School provide access to learners who have fallen behind in their studies in traditional schools, giving them a way to make up credits during their summers, nights, and weekends so they might eventually earn their diplomas.

Though it is an outlier among online education providers, which have struggled in many instances, according to *NPR*, the results achieved at the Florida Virtual School speak for themselves, says *NPR* correspondent Anya Kamenetz, who examined the rise of virtual schools in February 2015. Florida Virtual School "is a very large online school with, by all accounts, good outcomes. On state end-of-course tests and AP exams, students do as well as, or better than, other Florida students," she reported.[81]

Whether it is the scaling advantages offered by MOOCs, the accreditation and branding problems that are being solved by Aspiring Minds and Georgia Tech University, or the void being filled by the Florida Virtual School, measurable improvements in access to learning for thousands of students regardless of their previous preparation, financial means, or geographic location are being made. That became clear to me from the experiences of two of Coursera's students.

My first story is one that Koller,[82] Coursera's founder, told me about a very poor woman in Bangladesh who ran away with a friend because she was about to be sold into indentured servitude. They opened a bakery but it floundered because neither of them knew anything about running a business. To learn how, the woman started taking Coursera business courses from Penn and Michigan. Today the bakery is successful and supporting not only her and her friend, but five other women who were saved from a life of slavery.

My second story is about one of my daughter's classmates in high school this year, Andrew Jin.[83] As a young boy, Andrew was always interested in science. Although he lived in Silicon Valley and attended an elite private school, it did not offer something that he wanted to learn about: machine learning. So he signed up for a Coursera class on machine learning taught by Prof. Andrew Ng, a Stanford professor who coincidentally helped to create Coursera. Jin took the course and applied what he learned to develop algorithms for identifying adaptive mutations in human DNA sequences. He then entered the Intel Science Talent Search, the nation's most prestigious science competition. He placed first in the nation in the competition, which rewarded the 17-year-old with a $150,000 prize and a trip to the White House to meet the President. At the time of this writing, Jin was a freshman at Harvard University in the fall of 2015.

From a woman in one of the poorest places on the planet fleeing a life of servitude to a teenager in one of the richest places on the planet winning the nation's highest science honor, digital education is changing lives profoundly.

But this might be only a fraction of the number of people who can benefit from the digital revolution in education.

By personalizing education to make it more relevant to the world's young people, the digital revolution can transform learning for billions of learners even more. Here's how.

Relevance

"Whoever you are, wherever you are, you only have to know one thing: You can learn anything."[84]

That's the promise of Khan Academy, a Silicon Valley company founded in 2008 that has embarked on a mission "to unlock the world's potential" despite having only 80 employees.[85]

If you're not familiar, Khan Academy produces short videos, typically 5-10 minutes in length, on academic subjects that anyone can watch for free. The company's videos cover everything from math to physics to biology, economics, art history, computer science, health and medicine, and more. Its 10:06 video entitled "The Beauty of Algebra," which was uploaded in February 2012, has been viewed, as of writing, more than 2 million times.[86] The Academy's highest-rated video, "Electron Transport Chain," has been viewed more than

1 million times and has attracted a legion of fans from around the world. "I'm a sophomore in high school and this really helped me solidify my understanding of this system for my AP Bio class!"[87] said one viewer. Said another, "Khan Academy, you da real MVP."[88]

Many outside education would concur. Though you might be familiar with Khan Academy, it's worth recapping its story. The company was founded by Salman "Sal" Khan, a former hedge fund manager, who began tutoring his niece, Nadia, over the phone in his spare time in 2006. When other members of his extended family began asking for similar help, Khan, who has degrees from both MIT and Harvard, started recording videos and posting them on YouTube. One video led to another and before long word of Khan's accessible and instructional videos caught on. Khan Academy was established thereafter. Soon, entrepreneurs and philanthropists—including Microsoft co-founder Bill Gates and Ann Doerr, wife of venture capitalist John Doerr—called to offer money and support. After word spread, Khan became the darling of both Silicon Valley and Washington.[89]

Since then, he's been invited to speak to hundreds of groups around the world. The media, most of it anyway, loves him. So do many of the world's most successful business and thought leaders. In an interview with television correspondent and physician Sanjay Gupta for *60 Minutes* in 2013, Google Chairman Eric Schmidt explained why he's a fan of Khan Academy.

"Google is very successful because of America, because of the American R&D system, because of the quality of our graduates, etc. America is not going to go back to be a low-wage, manufacturing country," Schmidt said. "We are going to be a country of advanced manufacturing, sophisticated services and global brands. All of those require higher-order reasoning skills, which might be better taught using the Khan Academy approach."[90]

Though an entrepreneurial inspiration to many, Khan has not lined his pockets to any significant extent. In fact, Khan is better known for the money he didn't generate from teaching people the world over than the money he did. Early on, Khan decided that a non-profit that paid modest salaries would likely stay more true to its mission than a highly leveraged venture that went public after a few years. When Michael Noer of *Forbes* asked Khan if he was looking to get rich from his work, Khan's response became an instant, journalism classic. "Being a billionaire is sort of passé," he told the publication. "It's ironic. When I used to try and describe what the Khan Academy was, I would tell people that if it were a for-profit I would be on the cover of *Forbes*."[91]

The next issue of Forbes carried a story with the title "One Man, One Computer, 10 Million Students: How Khan Academy Is Reinventing Education." On the cover was Salman Khan.

Without setting out to do so, Khan might have stumbled upon one of the greatest innovations in education in the past two hundred years. Per its own literature, Khan Academy "provides free online materials and resources to support personalized education for learners of all ages."[92]

In addition to "free," the key word to note is "personalized."

For hundreds of years, education has been an endeavor limited by fixed constraints, which has resulted in the need to embrace group learning. Think of your own experience.

Chances are your education was determined to a large extent by the fixed limits of the system you entered. This includes your school, your educator's knowledge, your school's class sizes, meeting times, lesson durations, and more. If you attended a school like most, your teacher was probably expected to follow a pre-determined agenda. That meant moving from basic concepts to more advanced ones as a term progressed, regardless of the academic achievement of individual students. Though you or some of your peers might not have been prepared for the next lesson, your educator had to plough ahead regardless. While you might not have realized it at the time, as Khan points out, this is the functional equivalent of putting a roof on a home regardless of how far along its foundation is.

Khan Academy, with its always on, ever-ready lessons available in nearly three dozen languages, turns the "fixed" world of education upside down. Instead of a fixed time-slot with an individual instructor's insights or abilities, Khan students rely on a variable world of expertise taught by subject matter experts. And they do so in their own time, at their own pace—not that of their school's calendar.

"One of the defining attributes of Khan Academy is just having access to hopefully great explanations and exercises, etc. The other aspect is mastery-based learning, which basically is the idea that you can take as much time as you need to learn something at a very deep level before moving on to something next," Khan told me. "This notion of using personalization to facilitate mastery-based learning is core of what we do."

Little wonder that Khan videos have been viewed more than half a billion times. Every month, students of all ages watch Khan videos more than 10 million times.[93] Thirty percent of these students hail from outside the U.S., where students in India, Brazil, Mexico, South Africa and elsewhere regularly log on. Khan students also solve problems—billions of them. In December 2014, Khan Academy celebrated the three-billionth problem answered on its Web site, which was one billion more than just one year ago.[94]

By almost any measure, Khan is transforming learning. And it's not the only one enjoying success doing so. Consider the experience of Dr. Carl Wieman. A scientist from Oregon, Wieman made a name for himself in the world of physics researching laser cooling and Bose-Einstein condensation. His work was so breakthrough that he went on to win the Nobel Prize in Physics in 2001.[95]

Although an acclaimed researcher, Wieman considers himself a teacher as much as a scientist. In fact, he was named the Carnegie Foundation's U.S. "University Professor of the Year" in 2004.[96]

With a resume like his, Wieman is welcome to teach at some of the finest schools in the world, including Stanford.[97] Though he gladly helps advanced thinkers, his passion is helping young students, including first year physicists, understand scientific principles. To aid them, he has developed dozens of free software simulations that demonstrate the basics of math, physics, and chemistry in an engaging and customizable manner. In fact, they are similar to the simulations that he created to explain his Nobel-winning work.[98]

Wieman's simulations for learners attracted an online following much in the way Khan's videos did. After receiving a National Sciences Foundation grant to create more, Wieman founded the PhET Foundation at the University of Colorado in Boulder.[99] His team there has created more than 125 interactive simulations for teaching and learning science. And, like Khan Academy videos, the simulations are free to anyone with an Internet connection. They also come with guides for teachers and students alike.

Now instead of using chalk and an eraser to explain Faraday's Law or "Energy Skate Park Basics," a teacher need only guide his or her students to a PhET simulation, the latest of which now support the Internet's HTML 5 standard, which means they work with touch or mouse input and run seamlessly on all of today's classroom technologies—from PCs to tablets to Chromebooks, according to the PhET Foundation.[100] Simulations have been translated into more than 75 languages,[101] including Turkmen, Sinhalese, Khmer, and Icelandic,[102] and have been delivered to students more than 200 million times.[103]

People who have used the simulations, including Dr. Stamatis Vokos, a professor of physics at Seattle-Pacific University, say they are unrivaled for teaching important concepts to anyone from middle-school children to graduate students. "The PhET suite of simulations are one of the most carefully thought-out simulations that we have employed in our instruction," says Vokos in a PhET educational video.[104]

If all of this sounds radical—if not antithetical—to traditional learning, note that neither PhET nor Khan Academy wish to undermine traditional education. Instead, the innovators hope to complement what professional educators already teach. This includes the lessons targeted at those struggling to keep up and high achievers who might have already mastered the basics in any one subject. In Los Altos, California, a community located in the heart of Silicon Valley that is known for its high-performing students, Khan Academy has teamed with several schools to pilot test programs that augment traditional in-classroom instruction with Khan Academy videos. In a blog posted on the Khan Academy site, the company reported on its progress there.

"[W]e could see amazing things happening with the 5th graders," the company said. "A majority of students were attempting early algebra, and many students were experimenting with trigonometry and calculus. These students were excited, engaged, and loved being challenged. Inadvertently, we highlighted a distinct but not often discussed problem with standardized, age-focused education. Students performing at high levels are often not sufficiently challenged.

Teachers shouldn't take kids who already know the material, and make sure they already know the material. Teachers should be pushing and challenging the students to their full abilities. Los Altos didn't think everything was perfect because their students were scoring well on standardized exams; they saw significant value in creating an environment that was engaging and challenging for all students."[105]

Why, you might wonder, are Khan Academy videos and PhET simulations so successful? The answer is twofold: dumb luck and advanced analytics. When Khan started making videos, for example, their length was largely determined not by design but by YouTube's posting limitations. At the time, YouTube would not accept any video longer than 10 minutes in duration. So Khan had to speak succinctly and quickly in his videos.

As luck would have it, there's a lot of scientific evidence that suggest young minds—as well as many older ones—have limited attention spans. In his 2014 best-seller *"Brain Rules,"* Dr. John Medina, a molecular biologist, writes that humans have developed over millennia a "10 Minute Rule" that basically says they will ignore anything after 10 minutes if it fails to stimulate them.[106]

Khan's videos, including the more than 3,000 that Sal Khan did personally, are not only visually stimulating, they are also clever and even funny. Despite YouTube's decision to end its moratorium on videos lasting longer than 10 minutes, most Khan videos remain under 20 minutes in length to this day. "The content is made in digestible, 5-20 minute chunks especially purposed for viewing on the computer as opposed to being a longer video of a conventional 'physical' lecture," Khan's literature reads. "The conversational style of the videos is the tonal antithesis of what people traditionally associate with math and science instruction."[107]

The other reason Khan Academy videos and PhET simulations are so popular is because they are field-tested. Each Khan video, for example, is rated, which provides Khan Academy producers with insights as to which videos resonate and which do not. As *Fast Company* reported in April 2013, "Khan Academy applies everything from graphical modeling to 'brute force empirics' and a/b testing to test tweaks that can make all the difference in students' learning."[108]

"Basically, Khan Academy is borrowing from the groundbreaking work of Stanford's Carol Dweck, who has found in a series of studies that inducing a 'growth mindset'—an awareness of the brain's flexibility and plasticity, based in neuroscience—has a lasting and positive effect on mental performance," *Fast Company* reported. In one example cited by the publication, Khan Academy added a single line of text to a video, "The more you learn today, the smarter you'll be tomorrow," that led to a 5 percent increase in the number of "problems attempted, proficiencies earned, and return visits to the site."[109]

"...Tracking each problem solved and answer submitted allows Khan Academy to map a literal 'learning curve' to model the acquisition of a concept such as fractions. They found that carefully matching the next problem offered to the student's demonstrated level of skill led to faster acquisition of a concept," *Fast Company* wrote.[110]

The benefits of this approach to teaching can be enormous. And not just for students. Better analytics can help educators make better use of their classroom time. They can also help teachers tailor lessons to individual learners. In time, this might eliminate the need for repetitive testing, which has come under fire from both sides of the political spectrum in the U.S. for the unwieldy cost and burden that it places on school systems and students alike.

Khan Academy and PhET are, of course not the only organizations doing this. Others include Lumosity (60 million members in 180 countries), Mastery Connect (22 million students covering 85 percent of school districts), Quizlet (15 million monthly users), Knewton (9 million students), Tynker (22 million students), WyzAnt (75,000 tutors), Edmodo (50 million students from 220,000 schools), and Class Dojo (35 million users).

While not perfect, these and other organizations like them are leveraging the digital revolution to deliver a more personalized educational experience, one that transcends the traditional, fixed limits of time, distance and capacity. Because they support a new, variable educational model that enables students to learn anytime and anywhere for free, they have made education more relevant. Not just to millions of students in the U.S. who regularly augment their studies with one or more of Khan Academy's videos or PhET's simulations, but to potentially billions of learners young and old around the world.

"In the middle ages, even in the fairly educated parts of the world, only 15 percent or so of the population—clergy, nobility, tutors and maybe the military—could read," says Khan. "But today a vast majority of the world can read. But what percentage understands calculus or has the wherewithal to become an engineer or write a great novel? I suspect it is on that same order, maybe just 15 percent. But what if you were able to give the kind of access to high quality education for much larger percentages and let them become exceptional at their one area? If 90 percent of people could get to a place where they could help push society forward in their field, that's a big deal."

Imagine the societal benefits that will result from this massive increase in educational relevance. The next JK Rowling? Stephen Hawking? Or Steve Jobs? He or she could come from anywhere—from Quito to Cambridge to Kolkata. With their input on global challenges and potential solutions, the world would almost certainly be a better place.

To help us understand how transformative a personalized education can be, Sal Khan points us to a video of one of the Khan Academy students, Charlie Marsh.[111] In the video, Marsh tells how he dropped out of high school not once but twice during his freshman year. When he finally went back to school, he was behind his classmates and was put in the lowest-level math and science classes. Then he discovered Khan Academy. With some effort, he was able to skip two years' worth of math just by using the site. When it came time for his final exams, Marsh scored at or near the top of his class.

"Khan Academy changed the trajectory of my entire life, because without it I don't think I ever really would have been inspired to learn and to love math and science," he says.

Marsh graduated as valedictorian from his high school. He went on to study computer science at Princeton University, with aspirations to pursue a career in technology. When he graduated with Highest Honors (Summa Cum Laude), Charlie got a highly coveted and lucrative job offer from Google to work in Silicon Valley.

Yes, he thought, technology was exciting. But changing lives was inspiring.

After careful consideration, he declined Google's generous offer.

Charlie Marsh now works at Khan Academy. And yes, for a lot less pay.

The Principal in You

Quality. Access. Relevance.

If properly leveraged, the Internet of Everything can help improve all of these without upending the many wonderful things that are happening in the field already. To us, the IoE is a tool that can be applied to enhance education—not a framework, doctrine, or instrument for replacing today's educational system.

Though we believe that education needs major reform and that technological innovations offer great promise, we also understand that technology alone is not the entire answer when it comes to transforming learning.

Stanford's Hennessy and Yale's Levin don't foresee MOOCs replacing the traditional educational experiences that undergraduates get from attending a full-time, four-year school where they mingle face-to-face with peers and educators. But they do foresee a time when they will become the staple of advanced and ongoing education for many. They also believe that online will become a blended part of traditional, on-campus learning everywhere, especially in more controlled and targeted environments.

Wharton Dean Geoffrey Garrett has likened MOOCs and other new forms of learning to digital music and iTunes, which revolutionized the recording industry but didn't diminish enthusiasm for live performances or musical appreciation. "iTunes didn't change the way music was made," he wrote in an essay for *The Australian* in 2013 with co-author and academic Sean Gallagher, "it leveraged iPod technology and revolutionized how people consumed music."[112]

People who think similarly are reshaping education for the better. And they are winning converts every day. Think Sal Khan, Carl Wieman, and others who embrace the transformative impact on education that the IoE provides *and* help introduce it to the practitioners who have already dedicated their lives to teaching. This includes the heroes who show up every day and make the world a better place, despite low wages, poor opportunities for advancement, and sometimes even dangerous work conditions.

Why do they do so despite the ongoing challenges they face and the new ones that technology poses?

Because they have a dream.

They want to tear down the walls of their classrooms and unleash the imaginations of their students. They want to expose learners to great thinkers and experiences not available in traditional settings. And they want to change their classrooms to foster a learning experience that is of higher quality, more accessible, and more relevant.

They strive for a world in which every teacher can become the Superintendent of their global classroom and every learner can become the Principal of their personal education.

Look around: learning isn't broken; it is outdated.

This includes the lecture, the unconnected classroom, and the isolated educators who must compete with the smart devices that their students bring with them into the classroom. As a result, our schools are not properly preparing graduates for competing in the new global economy. And they are not producing enough thinkers who can close the gap between the problems we face and the solutions we need for them.

This is why the digital revolution is so important. Only it has the power to reverse the decline we are enduring. Unquestionably it will lead to some disruption. Jobs will be lost and some schools might even be closed as a result of its implementation. But these negative impacts pale in comparison to what will happen if we allow education to degrade any further. If we move forward instead, we can change the world for the better.

Just imagine an education that is best in quality, accessible from anywhere, and personally relevant to all. Starting with thousands of learners, extending to millions, and finally reaching billions.

Thanks to the digital revolution ushered by the Internet of Everything, that dream is within reach.

4

Retail

Get 'Em In, Get 'Em Thru, Get 'Em Back*

Behold the all-new, third-generation 2016 Audi TT.

The technical marvel features a 211-hp turbo-charged engine, a quick-shifting six-speed S-tronic dual-clutch transmission, full LED headlamps, and a 12-speaker Bang & Olufsen sound system with AudioPilot noise compensation. Of all the advanced features crammed into the two-door sports coupe, the technology turning heads most is the 12.3-inch digital display that sits directly in front of the driver, where a traditional analogue dashboard normally goes. Developed in partnership with Nvidia, Japan Display Inc., and Bosch, and reminiscent of similar technology brought to market by electric car maker Tesla, the innovative computerized display "handles all the usual gauge functions to show speed, rpm, time, etc.," explains *AutoWeek*. "In addition, all infotainment and navigation features are shown there, too."[1]

Audi says the new technology underpins its new push to add "simplexity" to its cars.[2] That's the ability to pack more features into vehicles without overwhelming drivers with too many complications. Of the remarkable, technology-rich vehicle, *Car and Driver* says, "With the emphasis on a return to the TT's innovative design roots, Audi is looking to field a game-changer once again."[3]

This desire extends well beyond its vehicles—all the way to the showroom floor, in fact, where Audi is employing state-of-the-art

---

* For their guidance with this chapter, I am grateful to Suja Chandrasekaran, Chief Technology Officer and Chief Data Officer at Walmart Stores; Malachy Moynihan, Vice President of Digital Products at Amazon (Lab 126); and Rachael Antalek, Vice President of Concept Innovation at Starbucks.

technology to sell cars. Consider the carmaker's state-of-the-art show-room in London on Piccadilly Street. The facility is one of the first "all digital" showrooms in the world.[4] It's ideal for crowded urban places where retail space is extremely expensive. At Audi City London, there are only a few vehicles on display. But that doesn't prevent shoppers from exploring every possible combination of Audi products—all 120 million of them—"in a way never seen before," according to the company.[5]

Any model, color, or build is available for shoppers to peruse from touchscreen tablets, which project life-sized digital images onto floor-to-ceiling, high-definition screens. For those who want to get a feel for what an Audi vehicle is like on the open road or even on a closed track, which isn't practical from London's compact and crowded May-fair district, they can don one of Audi's Virtual Reality (VR) headsets and take a vehicle out for a "spin" without leaving the showroom.[6] Should they choose, they can even have a virtual version of Audi's senior product designer, Jürgen Loffler, accompany them on their test drive.[7]

"You can actually see how the car performs and what it looks like without actually being in the car," says Amit Sood, Technology Lead at Audi City London. This includes everything from how it drives, functions, and even sounds—thanks to the device's high-end head-phones, which were developed by renowned consumer electronics maker Bang & Olufsen.

Sarah Cox, Audi's UK Marketing Manager, says the Audi VR headsets, which were designed by Samsung around the Oculus Rift VR platform, are the latest in a long line of innovations developed by Audi to provide more compelling offerings, improve shopping effi-ciency, and enhance customer engagement.[8] Take its new financial offers, which were developed after crunching reams of customer data culled from surveys, online browsing habits, face-to-face interviews, and more. With new insights, Audi is exploring purchase options that will allow up to four different people to share a single lease, making it possible to extend offers to a significantly larger pool of consumers than before.[9] To increase shopping convenience, Audi is also taking the VR technology out of the showroom and into customers' offices and homes. And to improve customer experiences, Audi is assigning specially trained technicians to connect with consumers as part of its "Second Delivery Program." Their job: stay in touch via social media and other means to help with any technical questions consumers might have with their Audi vehicles. Studies have shown that these and other post-sale programs have increased customer satisfaction and brand loyalty significantly.

"We believe this is the future of car retailing," says Cox.

She might be right—and not just for automobiles, but all forms of consumer goods and services sold through retail, which today includes brick and mortar stores, e-commerce Web sites and, increasingly, mobile-enabled, on-the-go apps that support what has come to be known as m-commerce. After years of trying to strike the right balance between online and offline experiences, the world's retailers, product manufacturers, and service suppliers have adapted to a new world that is no longer bound by strict definitions or category distinctions.

Buy a product online and return it to a local store? Today you can in many stores. Tomorrow, browsing an entire chain's global inventory for a shirt in the color and size you desire from within an in-store dressing room will become commonplace. So will being greeted in a store by a sales person who knows not just your identity but your entire shopping history, including item preferences based on data you willingly share over your mobile smart device.

Just as Audi is doing, the world's retailers are retooling for an Internet of Everything-enabled world that is more tuned to the needs of the new mobile-equipped, socially active, and information-savvy consumer. With new data analytics tools and insights, retailers have developed customized financial incentives and offers, remodeled and retooled stores to increase shopping convenience, and created engaging individual experiences that combine the best of consumer education with personal entertainment. The result of all this work has produced a new "hyper-relevance" for consumers that is transforming shopping.

"Such hyper-relevance implies delivering value—whether greater efficiency, savings or engagement—to the consumer in real time throughout the shopping lifecycle," says Cisco. "This requires an analytics-driven approach that incorporates data from sensors, beacons, smart phones, and other sources to apply intelligence to the context of the consumer (i.e., where he or she is, what he or she is looking to accomplish in that moment) and dynamically providing the experience that best suits that context."[10]

Before getting into how, let's look at the state of retailing today. We'll start with the U.S., where retail sales account for nearly one-third of the nation's total Gross Domestic Product (GDP).[11] According to the latest figures available from the U.S. Department of Commerce, which is the official bookkeeper of the nation's retail output, retail sales topped $5 trillion in 2013.[12]

According to the U.S. Bureau of Labor Statistics, the industry employs approximately 15.7 million people directly nationwide. This figure is growing roughly 10 percent per year. Retail workers typically earn between $19,070 (the mean annual wage for a cashier) to $37,670 (the mean for a retail manager or supervisor).[13]

While retail comprises a sizable percent of the nation's workforce, the National Retail Federation notes that retail indirectly supports many more jobs—42 million in all.[14] This includes professionals in insurance, healthcare, real estate, technology, and other fields who focus specifically on retail trade. These employees work in or support roughly 3.8 million retail establishments nationwide.[15]

Thanks to the rise of warehouse retailing, online shopping, store consolidation, market saturation, and other factors, the total number of retail establishments nationwide has been trending downward for the past several years. In 2011, the last of the Borders bookstores began shutting their doors in the U.S.[16] Just two years later, Barnes and Noble began to close one third of its stores.[17] And in early 2015, JC Penney announced plans to shutter 40 stores. Radio Shack, meanwhile, moved to shutter more than 1,700 stores but was given a reprieve in the summer when Sprint stepped in to keep the struggling stores open—at least temporarily. Radio Shack's luck notwithstanding, a number of retailers decided to shut thousands of retail stores throughout 2015. The list of those shuttering locations includes many once high-flying companies, including Office Depot, Abercrombie & Fitch, Target, Wet Seal, Chico's, and Children's Place.[18]

In addition to individual stores, entire malls have shuttered or otherwise disappeared from the retail landscape. Since 2010, "more than two dozen enclosed shopping malls have been closed, and an additional 60 are on the brink," reported *The New York Times* in January 2015.[19] Green Street Advisors, a real estate and REIT analytics firm, predicts that 15 percent of U.S. malls will fail or be converted into non-retail space within the next 10 years.[20] Afterwards, as many as half of the nation's approximately 1,000 retail malls will fail through 2035, says retail consultant Howard Davidowitz.[21]

Early casualties, including the Randall Park Mall of Cleveland, once the world's largest shopping mall, have already been torn down or repurposed.[22] Their space has since been converted to other uses, including light industry, office space, and, in one example in Nashville, even a medical center.[23] For insights into why, consider a report published in the February 2015 edition of the *McKinsey Quarterly*. It concludes that the digitization of goods and services (otherwise known as "Digital Darwinism") is having a significant impact on retail, though the impact varies across different industries and their retailers:

"Some notable variations among industries lie across this spectrum of journeys. In the software, airline-booking, and utilities industries, consumers are more likely to be fully digital. Autos, insurance, and food have similar numbers of digital consumers in the consideration and evaluation stages, but fewer who purchase digitally. Telecommunications, banking, and appliances have relatively strong numbers of consumers considering and evaluating products and services digitally but more modest numbers making digital purchases."[24]

By creating hyper-relevant experiences for consumers, many retailers have repositioned themselves for better days ahead. Not surprisingly, several of the nation's top property owners, including Simon Property Group, have seen occupancy rates and sales-per-square foot at rates not seen since the beginning of the 2008 recession, according to *CNBC*.[25] Opportunities to engage modern consumers in the physical world have even prompted e-tailers (including eBay and Amazon) to venture into the world of brick-and-mortar retailing.[26] As they experiment with pop-up stores and other retail concepts, their counterparts from the physical world (including Nordstrom and West Elm) have become increasingly adept at Web commerce.

The net of all this activity is a new "omni-channel" world of retail where distinctions between online and offline sales blur. Today, "where" a transaction is completed is not as important as "how."

"Omni-channel retailers can define the unique shopping experience of the future," concludes PwC, a global management consulting and strategy company. "Some stores will focus on in-store amenities. Sophisticated algorithms can identify meaningful relationships to shape this approach. Others will bolster online tools that allow a seamless transition from in-store research to purchase and fulfillment."[27]

The bottom line for retailers is this: no matter their business model, the Internet that once threatened to imperil retail is looking more and more like the innovation that could save it. A study completed in 2013 by Cisco concluded that retail has the largest opportunity of any industry to capture the value of the Internet of Everything (IoE).[28] Not to put too fine a point on it, but Cisco believes the average retailer could increase profits by more than 15 percent simply by leveraging the IoE in an effective manner.[29] This will require a transformation in three key areas: customer acquisition and retention, transaction efficiency and convenience, and consumer engagement and experience.

For more insights into how, let's begin with the first area: how retailers are developing compelling offers to attract and retain customers.

Capturing Your Attention and Never Letting Go: Offers That Compel

Christmas Eve is always a big day for retailers, Amazon.com included. But 2013 was especially big for the company, not because it broke sales records that day, but because of what a patent clerk in Washington, D.C., decided before shutting things down for the day.

On Monday, Dec. 24, 2013, the U.S. Patent Office issued Amazon a patent, No. 8,615,473, for developing a "method and system for anticipatory package shipping."[30]

What is "anticipatory package shipping?" That's the ability to predict when customers are about to buy products and then send them to their area *before* they actually make their selection and complete a transaction. In the world of retailing, that's as good as having a crystal ball, says journalist and market watcher Lance Ulanoff. In 2014, he wrote an article entitled, "Amazon Knows What You Want Before You Buy It," that explained how Amazon uses predictive analytics to determine when to ship products to a forward-situated warehouse to reduce delivery times on goods eventually ordered by consumers.[31]

Customers have no idea that Amazon does this. All they know is not long after they hit "Place Your Order" on Amazon's Web site, UPS, FedEx, or some other carrier knocks at their door. How does this actually work? Math, of course, is the simple answer. But better algorithms than what other retailers use is the real answer.

Amazon loves algorithms. The more sophisticated, the better. Like no other company, Amazon is able to take reams of disparate data and combine them to make compelling offers for consumers. For example, Amazon routinely collects customer data on shopping preferences, browsing histories, and financial means and then blends it with economic information, consumer insights, and even atmospheric data to predict retail behavior.

If there is unseasonably sunny weather in Las Vegas in December, for example, Amazon knows who among its more than 250 million customers worldwide[32] is likely to want new evening clothes, sun screen, and concert tickets for a visit after Christmas. Thanks to its sophisticated algorithms, which it keeps improving continuously, Amazon can even predict which electronic books and digital movies customers will rent to pass the time flying to the destination city.

Talk to anyone at Amazon and they will tell you that while Amazon is in retail, they are all about data. Malachy Moynihan, who led the design of digital products such as Fire TV and Echo at Amazon, believes that Amazon is "the most instrumented company on the planet."[33]

Amazon's connected digital innovations are enabled by the thousands of data scientists that they employ. From the time that you are on the Amazon Web site, whether you click to purchase or not, Amazon can see your actions (including where you went last time) and continually compares them with the aggregated knowledge of all their users. Every second that there is a delay in you getting what you want at the Amazon Web site is a definitive and measured metric that correlates to the likelihood that you will proceed to purchase eventually.

Because Amazon knows these things about us, it can create unique and personalized offers that keep us coming back to it again and again. Little wonder, thus, that an estimated 30 to 40 million Americans have an Amazon Prime membership with the company, which guarantees free shipping on virtually any product bought on Amazon's site for just $99 per year.[34] Be it an 85-inch Samsung Ultra-HD LED television,[35] a dual-suspension, 26-inch Schwinn mountain bike,[36] or a queen-sized, Sleep Innovations SureTemp memory foam mattress,[37] you can have it delivered for free if you're an Amazon Prime customer.

Thanks to its use of big data, Amazon has taken over from Walmart as "the catalyst for changing retailers' behavior," according to Guy Courtin, vice president and principal analyst at Constellation Research, a retail research and consulting firm. Writing in a guest column for the tech site *ZDNet* in February 2015, Courtin said, "Amazon is now the force that is driving behavioral changes. It is no longer simply about low prices; it is about access to apparently unlimited options for products. The name of the game is availability of that inventory via any device anywhere, anytime through flexible fulfillment."[38]

This goes for retailers of all size and ilk, including Stage Stores, a $1.6 billion, Houston-based specialty department store that operates under the Bealls, Goody's, Palais Royal, Peebles, and Stage names.[39] Since 2010, the company has invested millions of dollars into tools for improving price optimization, inventory management, and product personalization. The investments have helped the company achieve a rare feat in retail: the ability to compete toe-to-toe with a much bigger rival—Macy's, in this instance. Stage Stores did so with predictive analytics that have enabled it to create specialized offers for consumers that are more relevant, attractive, and timely than before.

"We knew we couldn't put as many feet on the ground as Macy's," Stage's CIO Steve Hunter told *Forbes BrandVoice* in early 2015. "They had thousands of people in geographical areas who fed numbers to corporate, which had a lot of people to crunch those numbers. So we decided to leverage technology and analytics to get us to the same place."[40]

First up for the company: markdown optimization, which is the art of selling goods at the highest price possible. With a hot-selling product, markdown optimization is easy so long as stores have sufficient product inventory. But the task becomes more difficult when products begin to languish in back room inventories. Correctly determining when to cut prices and by how much can mean the difference between a profit and a loss on a certain item.

Stage Stores implemented store-level markdown optimization and launched plans to develop and implement "size-pack" optimization to better tailor assortments on a more localized level. Today, Stage Stores' markdown optimization tool can help set prices style-by-style based on up-to-date inventory levels and customer sales history.

For the most part, the technology has proven to be a game changer. But getting everyone behind it took some convincing. When Stage Stores first tried implementing its own data analytics, its suppliers and own staffers scoffed, *Forbes* reports, believing that they were the ones best suited to determine when to cut prices. Hunter told the magazine that people initially preferred to trust their intuition and emotion instead of the data. He, however, believed there was a better way.

"Traditionally, retailers lower prices enormously at the end of a season to make way for new merchandise. Analytics suggested they would do better by selling items at a lesser discount earlier, when demand was starting to sag, but before it hit a low point," wrote *Forbes* contributing editor Teresa Meeks on markdown optimization. To prove its assumptions, Stage initiated a six-month pilot program, pitting its computerized analytics against those of a control group comprised of merchants and in-store managers.[41]

In nine out of 10 trials, the suggestions generated by the computer proved more profitable than the recommendations of frontline staffers. Today, all of the company's more than 800 stores rely on computer-generated analytics to create offers and set prices for customers.

Additionally, the company is working on a recommendation engine that will provide sales associates with information about a customer's past purchases, as well as the buying habits of similar customers, to suggest recommendations for accessories. Instead of offering an opinion out of the blue, Hunter told *Forbes*, Stage Store employees will be able to make insightful recommendations on the spot and even craft specialized offers while customers shop.

At many Palais Royal stores and Peebles, the question, "Can I help you?" is giving way to "A new shirt just came in that would go with the jacket you bought last month and we have it in your size. Would you like to try it on?"

"We're going towards retail being a science instead of an art," Hunter says. "We'll always have to buy the right merchandise. But the way we do it, and the way we leverage technology, will continue to evolve."[42]

Thanks to success stories like these, the entire retail industry has stepped up its collection and analysis of data. Today, retailers routinely collect information generated by Web searches, smart devices, connected digital consumer goods, medical appliances, and more. A report from the Platte Retail Institute says retailers are combining this data with information collected from barcode and RFID systems, point-of-sale systems, and finance and inventory control systems to create new offers.

"The challenge retailers face," the Institute concludes, "is to quickly and accurately evaluate the data in order to determine the best ways to get existing customers to spend more on products while also attracting new customers to the retailer's offerings."[43]

This is a far cry from the days of yore when collecting "cutting-edge data" was done in rudimentary ways. "In parallel with improvements in technology applications, there has been significant improvement in retail market research. This discipline has advanced from mystery shoppers and exit interviews to current techniques including observational and ethnographic research, online surveys, virtually instantaneous social media comments, and anonymous analytics gathered by way of video cameras and mobile phones," says the Institute.[44]

The result of all this analysis should be offers that better appeal to consumers. This goes well beyond mere transactions. To get shoppers to come back to the mall, for example, some retailers have mined their data for ideas as to what appeals to consumers most. Some have found valet parking, free babysitting, and a free lunch as enticing as a discounted coupon or an extended warranty.

The key to these offers is relevancy and transparency. Any time consumers begin to think that personalized offers targeted toward them infringe upon their privacy, they begin to recoil. This is a difficult lesson that several retailers have learned the hard way. In 2012, for example, *The New York Times* called out Target for mining browsing data, purchase information, and other data to determine who among its shoppers was pregnant so that it could send special offers on diapers, baby wipes, and prenatal vitamins their way. (The behavioral research led to one unfortunate situation in which a suburban Minneapolis father discovered his teen daughter's pregnancy after berating a Target store manager for the baby-oriented coupons that the company sent to the family's home.)[45]

Another company that has both benefitted and suffered from mining customer data to develop personalized offers is Tesco, the U.K.-based grocery giant. In the 2000s, Tesco earned a well-deserved reputation as a data-mining pioneer for its clever use of customer research, analytics, and loyalty programs. The Clubcard loyalty card launched in 1995 literally changed not only Tesco's fortunes but the entire industry's as a whole, says author and MIT Research Fellow Michael Schrage. But since then, the company has struggled to make its personalized offers sufficiently better than what other retailers now offer.[46]

Believing Tesco has used its Clubcards to manipulate customers rather than reward them for their loyalty, some U.K. shoppers have taken their business to other retailers, much to Tesco's disappointment.

Although data management can be a competitive differentiator for retailers, knowing when and where to apply insights will be critical for developing a sustainable differentiation. If retailers apply data in ways that consumers consider to be creepy, such as the way Target did, or irrelevant the way that Tesco has done, such efforts could backfire or fall flat. "The shopper of the future will almost certainly use retailers' effectiveness at data management as a filter for where to shop and spend. Savvy online shoppers already do this today, knowing that many too-good-to-be-true Web site offers are simply generators of new email lists for marketers," sums up PwC.[47]

In addition to personalized offers, shoppers are eager to engage with online and brick-and-mortar retailers that understand their wants *and* their needs—be it help closing a transaction more efficiently or locating a product more quickly. Given the technology available, no one today should have to drive to a store to find out if a product is in stock. Nor should they have to wait in an interminably long line simply just to check out.

At a growing number of retailers that leverage connected digital technology effectively, they don't have to. Here are some examples.

No Time to Waste: Streamlined Shopping Efficiency

Since 1994, the American Customer Satisfaction Index (ACSI) in Ann Arbor, Michigan, has surveyed consumers about their satisfaction with numerous major retailers. Think Kroger, Kohl's, Macy's, Target, Nordstrom, and Dollar General.[48]

In the U.S., consumers say retailers, even the best of them, consistently stumble in one facet of their business. Can you guess which? It's not prices, selection of merchandise, or even friendliness of staff. It's the checkout.

Commenting on the ACSI survey for *The Consumerist* Web site, writer Chris Morran said, "For both the retail and supermarket categories, 'Speed of Checkout' was the category in which stores fared the worst, meaning retailers could probably make customers a lot happier just by opening up a few more checkout lines."[49]

Alternatively, they could make customers more satisfied by simply borrowing a page from retailers who have eliminated the checkout aisle altogether. After Apple ditched checkout aisles in 2010, sales increased 40 percent over the next two years. Newer and more advanced merchandise obviously played a major role. But customers really liked the shopping efficiency of the Apple stores once they got used to not queuing up to pay. Not surprisingly, other retailers followed suit. High-end clothing purveyor Barney's has launched a plan to ditch cash registers.[50] So has Anthropologie[51] and Urban Outfitters.[52] JC Penney, meanwhile, announced plans in 2012 to eliminate checkout aisles by 2014. (It didn't achieve its goal, but it made headway and hopes its ACSI scores will improve as a result.)[53]

Nordstrom, already the top-ranked company in the ACSI survey,[54] is also working to eliminate checkout aisles that force shoppers to line up like schoolchildren. It is equipping all of its Nordstrom Rack discount stores with Apple tablets that customers can turn to throughout the store to pay quickly and exit more efficiently.[55]

With IoE-connected smart phones and tablets, sales associates in more and more retail settings are completing sales from any place in their stores, including dressing rooms. With the cash register gone, the world's retailers have set their sights on transforming shopping efficiency even more. Again take Apple, which has launched a number of initiatives to make shopping more pleasurable. In February 2015, for example, the company announced plans to leverage big data and customer smart phones as part of an effort to overhaul its customer service department. With overwhelming demand for better service at its Genius Bars, the company has developed new algorithms for prioritizing service requests. Now when a customer requests an in-person appointment, Apple's algorithms analyze the request more carefully and determine whether a particular inquiry can more efficiently be handled in another way—be it a telephone call or email with a link to a Web site with information, for example. If Apple's software determines that a customer does indeed need a technician, Apple will make an appointment with the customer and then send him or her a text when a technician is available.[56]

The result of these and other efforts is a more fluid, convenient experience that is heavier on shopping, lighter on transacting and problem solving. This goes well beyond retail clothing stores or general merchandise shops to all forms of retail stores. Take big box hardware stores, where customers' chief complaint isn't trying to pay for merchandise, but trying to find it instead.

To help shoppers find its wares, hardware giant Lowes introduced a robotic shopping assistant at its Orchard Supply Hardware store in San Jose, California, in November 2014. Developed in conjunction with Fellow Robots, a Mountain View, California, startup, the Lowes OSHbot "will greet customers, ask if they need help and guide them through the store to the product," according to *The Wall Street Journal*. "Besides natural-language-processing technology, the 5-foot tall white robot houses two large rectangular screens—front and back—for video conferences with a store expert and to display in-store specials."[57]

Need a specific screw or pipe coupling? Just hold it up to the built-in 3-D scanner and the robot will tell you in which aisle you can find the product and how many are in stock.

In addition to digital robots, retailers are investing millions of dollars to buy digital signs to help consumers navigate big-box stores, which are often larger than some indoor sports arenas. Retailers are also pouring sizable sums into augmented reality applications that consumers can download to their smart devices to help them locate merchandise. The apps can even create a visual "route" through a store for consumers based on their digital shopping lists. These tools not only help consumers navigate physical stores, they also reward them for their patience and patronage with on-the-spot offers.

Several companies are trying to marry "the conveniences of the online world" with "the tangible excitement of in-store shopping." This includes Hointer, a Seattle technology developer that has developed an IoE innovation that takes the hassle out of a frustrating aspect of everyday life: trying to find a pair of pants that fits. You can see its technology for yourself at its men's jean shop in Seattle, where it is installed along with its end-to-end software platform and hardware devices.[58]

Instead of poring through racks and shelves of inventory to find an item in their choice of style, color, and size, customers simply scan the Q-codes with their mobile devices (or company-provided tablets) that are affixed to every item on display and then step inside a dressing room. Within minutes, desired merchandise appears inside the dressing room from a chute above. Customers can try on as many jeans as they like. Should they want a different size, color, or style, they can browse the store's inventory from their smart devices and order more products to be delivered to their fitting rooms.

"We offer an amazing digital experience that turns customer smart phones into remote controls to the physical store so they can get what they want, when and how they want," says Hointer founder and CEO Nadia Shouraboura, a PhD in mathematics from Princeton University and the former head of Supply Chain and Fulfillment Technologies for Amazon.[59]

Though relatively new, consumers are warming to these kinds of innovations. Consider the results from a survey completed by Cisco. More than three-quarters of consumers surveyed said they would willingly use "optimized checkout" stations instead of traditional checkout aisles. Sixty percent, meanwhile, said they would gladly use scan-and-pay systems, while half said they would be interested in using mobile payment services. As these technologies proliferate, familiarity and utilization are likely to only increase.

Kathryn Howe, a Cisco retail industry consultant, says in a company report, "Imagine a scenario in which a shopper is hurrying through a store. Sensors in the store can determine that one particular shopping cart is traveling 20 percent faster than the average. Through the application of analytics, the retailer could even know that the shopper is a mother who usually buys diapers and baby formula. Yet in the real-time context of that moment, a coupon for diapers might not be relevant—and might even feel intrusive. In this context, it is best if automatic processes simply help the shopper find the fastest way through the store. Thus, automated processes respond to the context that is relevant to that shopper at that specific time."[60]

Howe says the preceding illustrates how connecting people, data, and things to the IoE can take the inefficiencies and hassles out of shopping. Additional measures that involve adding tags and sensors to merchandise, which makes supply chain and inventory data readily available to sales associates and consumers alike, go even further. At German clothing giant Gerry Weber, for example, every single garment has an RFID tag sewn into the label. Instead of running around a clothing store like a track athlete looking for different sizes and styles, sales associates at Gerry Weber simply tap their smart devices to determine where an item desired by a customer can be found—be it across the sales floor on a display rack or halfway around the world in a shipping container.

Since 2011, Gerry Weber has put more than 26 million RFID tags in its clothes. Doing so has helped the company reduce loss and theft, lower security costs, more quickly replenish shelves, and increase sales. Instead of performing a manual inventory of clothes once a year, the company can now perform one weekly with the simple press of a key. And it can do so with 99-percent accuracy. What is more, the RFID tags sewn into garments at time of manufacturing mean Gerry Weber sales associates do not have to spend time painstakingly affixing or removing traditional electronic article surveillance (EAS) security trackers to every garment in their stores.[61]

From an industry perspective, you have to wonder what the future of single-purpose security devices, which cost roughly $0.45 each, will be now that RFID tags, which can enhance retail efficiency in several ways, cost just $0.12 each. You also have to wonder about the fate of retailers that make checkout, navigation, and product search difficult. This goes for both on-line and bricks-and-mortar retailers.

When given a choice, consumers are demonstrating that they prefer spending their money with retailers that provide them compelling offers and convenient shopping efficiencies.

They like buying burgers with the mobile app from Five Guys, for example, which asks that they enter their credit card data only once and lets them skip the counter and go right to the head of the pick-up line at a time they choose. They also love the Home Depot Pro app, which helps contractors, painters, plumbers, roofers, and other construction professionals save time, according to the retailer. Instead of leaving a job site in search of a particular product, professional tradesmen can search for items online for the closest Home Depot store that has them in stock. They can also buy products directly from their mobile devices and have them bundled and waiting for them at a special in-store pick-up counter.

As significant as convenience and efficiency are to shoppers, they aren't everything. Nor are compelling offers, as important as they may be. From time to time, shoppers of all ages and income brackets want something more from the world of retail. They want *experiences*, the kind that dazzle and delight.

When shopping for high-end items like a car, or special-occasion merchandise like a wedding gift, or even personal indulgences like an evening bag, today's affluent and tech-savvy shoppers want a retail experience that's as memorable as the item they purchase.

These experiences may include the décor that consumers immerse themselves in, the amenities they enjoy or, increasingly, the technology they showcase. In a growing number of places online and off, retailers are using IoE innovations to transform everyday transactions into something more meaningful—something consumers cannot forget easily or do without.

For a better idea, let's take a trip to New York's trendy SoHo neighborhood, where the future of shopping is already on display in one store on Greene Street.

A New World of Possibilities: Experiences That Resonate

"Toothbrush not included."[62]

That's a line you don't forget easily. But unless you're a certain kind of consumer—female, stylish, outgoing, and not hurting for money—the words probably aren't familiar to you. They are part of the promotional copy that New York designer Rebecca Minkoff uses to market her popular "M.A.B." handbags. For the uninitiated, M.A.B. stands for "Morning After Bag." To fashionistas, the M.A.B. bag is the signature item that helped the clever clothing designer expand into accessories.[63]

Cheeky? No doubt. But innovative, too, just like the rest of Minkoff's approach to fashion. Take the New York City flagship showroom in SoHo that she created with her brother, Uri. There, shopping isn't just a leisurely pursuit, it's an immersive interactive experience. If the styles don't dazzle you (or the complimentary champagne somehow leaves you feeling flat), the video mirror will surely inspire you to see shopping in a whole new light.[64]

More a giant tablet computer than a mirror, the interactive display showcases all of Minkoff's designs and inventory. Customers can browse looks, send items to a dressing room, and even check on merchandise availability. Should they wish, customers can do the same from within their dressing rooms. In addition to a floor-length touchscreen mirror, each fitting room is equipped with an antenna that can read RFID tags affixed to every item in the store. When a customer takes a bag or blouse with them into the dressing room, the store's computer instantly records the items the customer has selected. Should they wish, customers can then ask the computer to display additional items that pair well with pieces they have chosen. They can also tap the mirror to see what other shoppers have said about the merchandise on Twitter and Instagram. If a customer is feeling a bit parched, he or she can even ask a sales associate to bring a bottle of sparking water from their touchscreen display.

When it comes to creating a truly memorable shopping experience, Minkoff has thought of everything.

"Try on your favorite styles in our personalized fitting rooms featuring mood lighting (we're not vain, we're just conscientious) and easily swap out colors and sizes with the tap of the mirror," the company says. "You'll also get recommendations based on your preferences and be able to save your fitting room session (in case you're feeling indecisive)."[65]

Even if you're not in the market for an "iconic satchel [that] is perfect for staying out till sunrise," you have to admire what Minkoff has created: a fully immersive shopping experience that shows off her company's entire stock list of clothing (and in-store inventory) complete with third-party reviews in a tiny retail environment that doesn't ask guests to traipse about in their underwear.

More than a convenient customer engagement, Minkoff has created an emotional consumer experience for her shoppers.

The future of retail? Many in the business think digitally-enhanced experiences like these are. Take Italian eyewear giant Luxottica, the world's largest maker and retailer of glasses and accessories.

Luxottica produces spectacles for premium fashion brands, including Armani, Burberry, Chanel, Oakley, Oliver Peoples, Prada, Ralph Lauren, Tiffany, and Ray Ban.[66] It also owns retail outlets, including Sunglass Hut and other stores.[67] To increase its reach and improve customer experience, the company bought the online retailer glasses.com and developed a unique eyewear app that allows customers to "try on" glasses from the privacy of their own homes and offices.[68]

After downloading the app to their smart phones or tablets, consumers make high-definition scans of their faces with the camera found on their devices. After uploading these images to the glasses.com Web site, consumers can literally sample thousands of eyewear products. From within the app, they can sample different brands, peruse different styles, change frame colors, swap lenses, and compare multiple 3-D images at once. Should they desire, consumers can even share saved images with their friends over social media to get a second opinion on how certain designs look on their faces.

After selecting a design, glasses.com customers can then print out a pupillary distance ruler directly from the company's Web site to ensure a proper fit and upload a photograph of their prescription for ocular clarity.[69] If they need to, they can even ask glasses.com to obtain a prescription for them.[70]

From almost any vantage point, glasses.com has tried to transform the experience of selecting new eyewear less opaque and more enjoyable.

"You don't need to have 20/20 vision to see the appeal of the new and free glasses.com app for iPad," wrote *USA Today* columnist Marc Saltzman in a review.[71] Added former *The New York Times* tech columnist David Pogue, "Without question, the glasses.com app represents the state of the art in virtual style shopping. It's superb technology that really works and could save a lot of people a lot of embarrassment."[72]

While saving "people a lot of embarrassment" might not be a priority in some industries, it's a huge thing in retail, where—like entertainment and travel—image counts for a lot. Because of this, retailers are exploring new ways to engage customers with holographic ads, virtual shopping assistants, and more. In the market for a watch or a pair of earrings but don't have the time or resolve to visit an upscale retail establishment in person? With holographic displays that project virtual items onto a hard surface such as your wrist or face, you can shop from the privacy of your home for as long as you like and never worry about taking too much of a salesperson's time.

The key to making modern retail experiences successful, says Luxottica group CIO Dario Scagliotti, is ensuring that they make the most of the unique capabilities of offline and online experiences without compromising either.

"We have been investing in ecommerce and omni-channel for the past four years, like everyone," said Scagliotti in an interview with the tech Web site *Diginomica* in January 2015. "Our presence in the e-retail space is relatively recent. But we have decided to rapidly invest in making the online experience a differentiating factor—customizing your frames, engraving, whatever you want—an online experience that gives you exactly what you are looking for."[73]

To achieve this, Luxottica has examined data culled from 100 million transactions completed through its Web sites and retail chain stores. Its goal? Create unique eyewear offers for consumers that combine the convenience of on-and-offline shopping with the excitement of virtual reality. "The data captured from those interactions constitutes a massive trove of potential product, marketing, sales and customer intelligence," says its technology supplier, IBM.[74]

For its effort, the Italian eyewear giant anticipates a 10 percent improvement in marketing effectiveness. And for its customers? The ability to see the world in a whole new way.[75]

Like a growing number of retailers and merchants, Luxottica recognizes that digitization offers an unprecedented opportunity to create new experiences that are long lasting. The idea that a retail experience ends with the swipe of a credit card is antiquated. The relationship retailers have with customers extends well beyond the showroom or browser and into almost every facet of life. Because IoE tools and applications provide an opportunity for consumers to interact with their favorite brands in ways not imagined just a decade ago, their expectations have grown considerably. Just ask anyone that has visited Disney World and tried the entertainment giant's MyMagic+ wristband, which changes "how visitors do everything from enter their hotel rooms to ride Space Mountain," according to *The New York Times*.[76]

Disney spent $1 billion on the technology, which allows consumers to shop freely at its stores, order food without paying via a traditional credit card, and prebook front-of-the-line access to rides, parades, and character meet-and-greet events. People who have used the devices say they have improved the theme-park experience in many ways. Though Disney is still working out some kinks associated with wait times for rides, many consumers say they could not imagine going back without having the wristbands. Said one consumer on Disney's review Web site, "If you are planning your first trip to Disney don't fret, the MyMagic+ system works very well and is designed to cater to you and make your stay as carefree as possible."[77]

A lot of tech-savvy consumers feel the same way about other experiences that have been improved by a retail pioneer. If a brand lacks a significant presence in social media, for example, a tech-savvy consumer is likely to think less of that company. Take Audi. For all the accolades that Audi receives for its quality interiors and innovative digital showrooms, some buyers are off-put by its feeble mobile apps, which consumers and reviewers alike say don't quite match what rival Mercedes or BMW offer. At least, not yet.

Does being a technology laggard that cannot provide the immersive experiences that others do translate into lost business? Unquestionably it has, say retail analysts, especially among younger buyers who value different qualities than older customers in a number of different product categories. In addition to cornering capability, shelf life, or hem length, Millennial buyers, in particular, desire brands that understand their desire for 360-degree experiences that last long after their credit card bill has been paid.

While some attempts to create lasting experiences are destined to flop, connected digital technology is unquestionably ushering in a new era of experimentation and re-imagination in retail. Thanks to the IoE innovations, retailers can take bolder steps to establish or reinvent themselves without taking on the financial risks that would normally accompany new experiments. Armed with new ways to manage inventory and display products, big box retailers can explore smaller footprint stores that never would have suited their business strategies before. Boutique sellers like Rebecca Minkoff, meanwhile, can dazzle customers as thoroughly as larger companies that have greater marketing resources or greater sales breadth.

Those who cannot adopt are destined to struggle. But those who understand that they are in the "experience business" as much as they are in the "merchandise trade" have an opportunity to compete like never before.

The World of Hyper-Relevancy

To say that the world of retail has been turned upside down is an understatement. Buying an entire Christmas's worth of presents without setting foot into a single store? Tens of millions of consumers do it today even though it would have been unthinkable a decade ago.

So is buying a car without test-driving it. Yet, one in six consumers never test-drive a vehicle before buying one today, according to research from DMEautomotive (DMEa).[78] In fact, the number of trips consumers make to a car dealership before purchasing a vehicle has dropped significantly in recent years. A decade ago, car shoppers made an average of five trips to a dealer showroom before purchasing. Today, they make just 1.6 trips on average, according to a study completed by McKinsey & Co. The reason, of course, is the information they collect online before ever setting foot into a showroom.[79]

A Google study, for example found that consumers now connect with 24 "research touch points" before deciding upon the vehicle they choose.[80] The average car buyer knows a vehicle's technical specs, average sales price, and consumer ratings before they ever speak with a salesperson. This explains why car makers like Audi and others are putting so much money into making consumers' online experiences as memorable as the ones they get within their showrooms.

Customized offers developed through real-time data analytics? Improved shopping efficiency enabled by mobile checkout devices and automated robots? Dazzling experiences made possible by virtual reality shopping apps and touchscreen mirrors? That's what hyper-relevance is all about.

More than that new car smell, firm handshake, and free cup of coffee, these are the things that are driving retail sales today.

For cars—and anything else that moves you.

5

Smart Cities
Bustling with Activity,
*Brimming with Opportunity**

Ah, springtime in New York. Leaves on trees. Flowers in bloom. Colors in every store window.

If you've been to the city, then you know it's a celebrated time of the year that almost everyone adores.

"Pre-Spring," on the other hand, is a period that is universally loathed. It's a time *The New York Times* describes as when "the sins buried beneath February's snowstorms reveal themselves in March's squalid muck."[1] Think cigarettes, candy wrappers, lottery tickets, soda cans, and worse.

The unsightly display chronicled by the newspaper in March 2015 inspired one reader to muse about the city's under-appreciated sanitation workers. "Every year when this happens, I think of them," 'Jon' posted online, "and how disease-ridden this city would be if they stopped cleaning after the lazy and inconsiderate that make up a sizable portion of our neighbors."

Other readers weren't so broad-minded. "Yuk!" said one. Wrote another, "My mind is still boggled that everyone here seems to think that this is normal human behavior."

Whether you think littering is an abomination or "normal human behavior," you have to sympathize with the professional urban

---

* For their guidance with this chapter, I am grateful to Prof. Carlo Ratti, Director of Senseable City Laboratory at MIT; and Dr. Anil Menon, President of Smart Connected Communities at Cisco. They co-chair the World Economic Forum's Global Agenda Council on the Future of Cities.

planner whose job it is to make sure that trash is taken away efficiently; it's a tough job. And so is fighting crime, providing power, managing traffic, and more. Every day brings a new challenge and another reminder that familiar tasks need more clever solutions.

In Barcelona, Philadelphia, Helsinki, and elsewhere, smart thinking has led to the installation of IoE-enabled trash cans equipped with wireless sensors that send out alerts when they are full. The bins are being deployed in parks, city centers, and more. With these receptacles on their streets, city leaders don't pick up trash the way other municipalities do. Instead, they deploy their fleets more efficiently. Instead of routine missions to collect trash, smart cities only pick up trash when bins are full or have foul-smelling odors. This helps civic leaders reduce litter, fight pollution, and ease traffic, among other things.

After installing 1,100 solar-powered Bigbelly trash bins, for example, the city of Philadelphia saved $1 million a year on trash cleanup.[2] The covered bins can compact five liters worth of trash into one and send out messages when they are full. According to city officials, they not only help the city reduce weekly collections (from 14 to three on average), they also help make its streets cleaner.

Other cities—including El Paso, Texas; Bath, U.K.; Viborg, Denmark; Arnsberg, Germany; and even New York—have invested in Bigbelly cans.[3] The Big Apple is running a pilot program in Times Square and lower Manhattan to see if the devices are a fit for its trash needs.[4]

Another company, Helsinki, Finland-based Enevo, has developed an entire IoE-based system that it claims can help municipalities save as much as 50 percent on trash collection.[5] Unlike the specially designed Bigbelly bins, Enevo's technology works with "any type of container and any type of waste," according to the company. Enevo's technology leverages wireless-enabled sensors, which collect data on bin volume, temperature, and more. The data can be analyzed and modeled to design optimum pick-up routes and even help determine staffing needs.

If all of this "trash" talk is making you hold your breath, consider for a moment the impact of waste on urban centers worldwide. According to a report from The World Bank, the world's 3 billion urban residents generate 2.6 pounds of trash per day each.[6] That's 1.3 billion tons per year.

The cost for hauling away this frightful mess is enormous. The City of New York alone spends $1.6 billion annually to remove 3.8 million tons of trash from the city, according to *The New York Post*.[7] Worldwide, solid waste management costs total more than $205 billion, according to The World Bank.[8] That's as much as the amount of damage extreme weather events (including hurricanes and tornados) cause annually around the world.

Why is waste management so expensive? A big reason is the cost of equipment and manpower required for hauling it away. In many urban centers around the world, trash is removed by trucks that cost upwards of $250,000 each.[9] The men and women who operate these vehicles earn more than $50,000 annually in several U.S. cities.[10]

Sadly, much of the time these trucks and workers are deployed to collect trash is wasted. Regardless of need, they follow pre-determined routes created by administrators who lack data on actual trash levels. The problem isn't just a first world one, either.

In the Philippines, Peru, Kenya, and elsewhere, urban administrators can handle only a fraction of the waste that their urban centers create. The rest is collected by "waste pickers," who collect half, if not more, of the trash produced in cities around the world, according to a UN Habitat 2010 report.[11] As employment opportunities for these pickers improve and they get better jobs but trash volume increases, developing cities will need smarter solutions.

Whether you live in a rich city or a poor one, trash is an unrelenting problem that never takes a holiday. This is doubly so if you're the mayor of one of these municipalities. Trash collection not only weighs heavily on your city budget, it weighs heavily on your mind. Like road conditions and bus service, waste removal is one of a number of municipal burdens that do not generate good will when handled capably and engender an inordinate amount of outrage when managed poorly. This is as true in Beijing as it is in Boston.

The world over, there is trash to contend with every single day. And traffic. And crime. And pollution, energy waste, water consumption, parking shortages, and more. This is why simple, IoE-enabled innovations like the smart waste receptacles have captured the attention of so many urban planners the world over, including mayors who, unlike a nation's statesmen, are expected to produce tangible results for their communities and citizens.

Speaking to a roomful of mayors at the 2015 National League of Cities, President Barack Obama expressed a mix of appreciation and envy over the duties of mayor. "You all have something in common, and that is that every day you wake up ready to solve problems, and you know that people are depending on you to make sure your streets are safe and your schools are strong, trash gets picked up, roads getting cleared," Obama said.[12]

Free from the burdens of law making, trade negotiations, or foreign relations, most mayors relish the opportunity to roll up their sleeves and implement pragmatic solutions to community problems. When they look around their municipalities today, they see literally thousands of places where smart ideas could make a big difference when it comes to energy consumption, pollution, crime, and traffic. Take the lowly street lamp, for example.

In Europe, as much as 40 percent of energy used by local governments goes to powering street lamps.[13] One Dutch designer, Chintan Shah, is determined to change this. After glancing down at the world from an overnight flight one evening, he was shocked by the display of artificial illumination below. So he dedicated himself to reduce the energy being wasted. His work led to the development of Tvilight, an LED lighting system that uses wireless sensors embedded into street lamps to preserve energy. When Tvilight lamps detect human movement below them, they come to life and provide illumination for a passerby. When they sense that activity beneath them has passed, they turn off. What makes these smart lights unique is that they can determine the direction of a pedestrian and send a signal to a lamp ahead to turn on gradually so that a citizen can be assured of illumination as they travel along a city street without disturbing residents with excessive flickering.

Some basic calculations suggest that Europe could slash its street lighting bill, which totals $13 billion annually, by as much as 80 percent with Shah's invention, according to *CNN*.[14] Because the lights can be programmed to alert managers when a bulb needs to be replaced, the new technology can help reduce maintenance costs by as much as half. Add it all up—the money, labor, and so on—and you begin to realize how transformative IoE technology could be to cities worldwide.

Given how rapidly cities are growing, the arrival of this technology has come not a moment too soon. The raw numbers from a 2014 United Nations (U.N.) report on "World Urbanization Prospects" provide a compelling explanation as to why.

According to the U.N. report, more people live in urban areas than rural ones today. For perspective, less than one third of the world's population lived in cities in 1950;[15] by 2050, two thirds will.[16] Today, the percent of people in North America, Europe, Latin America, and the Caribbean who live in cities already exceeds 70 percent. Africa and Asia, which today account for 90 percent of the world's rural population, will be 56 percent and 64 percent urbanized, respectively.[17]

In terms of raw numbers, the urban population of the world has grown to nearly 4 billion from just 746 million in 1950.[18] By 2050, this figure will grow by another 2.5 billion.[19] To put this into some perspective, imagine a basketball arena filled with 10,000 fans. Every hour of every day, urban centers around the world are growing by this many people.[20] While you might not notice the increase where you live, cities around the world are collectively adding the rough equivalent of the population of present-day London to their ranks every month.

All this growth is creating unimaginably large urban centers—and more of them with each passing year. In 1990, for example, just 10 cities had populations of 10 million or more. The list included familiar names such as New York, Tokyo, and Mexico City. By 2030, the world is projected to have 41 mega-cities.[21] Some of these urban centers are places you likely have never heard of before, including Dhaka, Tianjin, Dar es Salaam, and Luanda.[22] But every hour, they are growing by the arena-full just the same. So are the world's "large" cities that have a population somewhere between 5 million and 10 million inhabitants. By 2030, the number of large cities is expected to grow to 63 worldwide—triple what the number was in 1990.[23]

The strain on the world's urban centers to accommodate all of these residents will be enormous. Roads, bridges, and sewer systems will be pushed to their limits. And access to education, government services, and healthcare will be tested. By 2025, cities will consume 40 percent more energy than they do today, according to British Petroleum, and at least 30 percent more water, according to the U.N. How will cities source these resources? Or provide necessary clean water, housing, public safety, and even simple trash removal to citizens?

In almost every corner of the globe, questions like these will come to dominate the agendas of city planners and civic leaders, who are beginning to realize that growth will only compound the dilemmas they face today. To these questions, there are no easy answers. But there are smart solutions.

These solutions combine sensors that are capable of capturing data on everything from parking space availability to water purity. They also leverage data analytics to reduce crime and improve traffic flow in urban areas. And they depend on an engaged citizenry to make use of their smart, mobile devices to report problems and make recommendations for improving urban life. When combined over the IoE, these smart solutions can have a transformative impact on quality of life. They alone won't cure poverty, eradicate crime, or eliminate traffic woes. But they "have the potential to be the most significant catalysts for change during this century," says Dr. Anil Menon, President of Smart Connected Communities at Cisco.

For more insights into why, let's look at several smart ideas that are being applied to enhance citizen services, increase economic opportunity, and improve environmental sustainability, among other things, in the world's urban centers. Let's start with how "Smart Cities" provide better services to citizens.

Social Development and Enablement

One hundred and one.

That's how many murders are committed every week on average in Guatemala, according to the figures collected by the U.S. State Department's Overseas Security Advisory Council (OSAC).[24] With a homicide rate of 116.6 per every 100,000 residents, the capital, Guatemala City, has the third highest murder rate in the world, according to the U.N. Office on Drugs and Crime.[25] (For comparison, Los Angeles has a murder rate of just 6 people per 100,000 residents.)[26]

There are many reasons why Guatemala City's murder rate—as well as its rates of theft, assault, rape, and kidnapping—are so high. In its annual report for the State Department, the OSAC said, "violent crime is a serious concern due to endemic poverty, an abundance of weapons, a legacy of societal violence, and weak law enforcement and judicial systems."[27]

Locals, of course, know this only too well. For three decades, they endured a bloody civil war between dueling political factions. When it ended in 1996, residents hoped for a lasting peace. Instead, drug dealing, theft, and prostitution took root in the capital. When they did, street violence climbed even higher. Fed up with the level of crime in their country, Guatemalans elected Otto Pérez Molina as president in 2011. A retired military officer turned politician, he vowed to restore law and order with a "firm hand, head and heart."[28]

After being sworn into office in 2012, Molina surprised some with his aggressive moves. Among other things, he called for the legalization of drugs,[29] the reform of the capital's police force, and new legislation to reduce street crime. Try as he did to stem street violence, however, law breaking continued much as it always had. Recognizing that Molina's firm hand needed some smart thinking behind it, Guatemala City committed $150 million in June 2014 to install 1,900 video surveillance cameras around the capital.[30]

More than tough rhetoric, the action put local criminals on notice. Knowing that their deeds could be seen from far away and captured for perpetuity, the city's pimps, thieves, and drug dealers changed their behavior after the cameras were installed. Since then, violent crimes have dropped by up to 40 percent in the capital, according to a report published in *Dialogo*, the digital military magazine of the Americas.[31]

From central police stations, police agents now monitor video feeds and direct officers on patrol to potential conflicts when they occur. "Police forces have more 'eyes' for surveillance, which prevents criminals from committing crimes," said Carlos Argueta, Deputy Minister of Technology of the Ministry of the Interior in *Dialogo*. "It's such a novelty that agents patrolling the streets have support from the center. This has allowed them to make some captures red-handed."[32]

The images that the cameras in Guatemala City produce are so precise that they can even read vehicle license plates, which has led to a reduction in car theft and carjacking.[33]

While exemplary, the results achieved in Guatemala City have not been universally enjoyed. In fact, some attempts to reduce crime with video surveillance technology have produced only modest gains. But experts believe newer technology, better training, and smarter placement of cameras can lead to the kind of results that cities such as Guatemala City have enjoyed. An independent study completed by the Campbell Collaboration confirms as much. It found that video surveillance systems are most effective when deployed in parking lots and on public transportation systems.

With better analytics capabilities, mapping tools, and visualization training, city leaders around the world are confident that they can reduce crime and lower policing costs with video surveillance. Guatemala City is so confident that is has committed to 2,100 more cameras in the city, in addition to the 1,900 cameras it purchased in June 2014.[34]

Other metropolitan areas have taken video even further. Take Songdo, Korea, one of the world's smartest cities. Located 25 miles from the nation's capital, Seoul, Songdo is a new city being built on land reclaimed from the Yellow Sea. The city is being built from scratch with the express purpose of easing congestion in the rapidly expanding capital nearby. To make sure that the community is as attractive to area residents as possible, Songdo leaders have embedded IoE technology into almost every facet of the community. Songdo's streets have sensors to help improve traffic flow. Its buses have WiFi connectivity to provide residents the latest in amenities and conveniences. And almost every major building in town is equipped with video communications and surveillance technology to help make the city as safe, efficient, and environmentally friendly as possible.

Each apartment block in Songdo has its own integrated operations center that manages the advanced video surveillance systems. These centers not only monitor crime, they monitor fires, water leaks, and more. Almost every public space and piece of infrastructure—from a building to a road to a park—can be monitored remotely via video camera in Songdo.[35] Not surprisingly, it is one of the safest cities in all of Korea.[36]

Songdo is an outlier—and not just because of its extensive use of video. It is one of the only cities in the world where trash isn't collected curbside but instead sucked out of apartment and office buildings through pneumatic tubes that deposit refuse into massive receptacles located inside sorting centers. There, Songdo's refuse is sorted and treated before being sent to its final destination.[37] What is more, Songdo is the first city in Asia to comply with Leadership in Energy & Environmental Design (LEED) standards for water, waste management, and green IT infrastructure.[38]

That said, Songdo offers a glimpse of what the future of city living could be with smart innovations. In addition to surveillance video, each home there is equipped with Cisco TelePresence, a real-time video communications system that enables residents to use remote services such as home tutoring, distance learning, and tele-health and citizen services such as Driver License renewals. The same video network that can alert officials of a criminal attempting to steal a car from a parking lot in Songdo can also support communications between a patient and a doctor, a consumer and a merchant, or even a student and teacher.

With fewer reasons to get behind the wheel of a car, Songdo promises residents a cleaner, less congested, and safer living experience than what other municipalities can offer. That's a big deal in today's world, where the young and upwardly mobile have choices when it comes to where they want to live. More and more, they are choosing to cluster in municipalities that are clean and safe and that promote sustainable businesses, non-profit organizations, and academic institutions.

Knowing this, more cities around the world are looking to leverage IoE at every turn. They are even inviting citizens to come up with new ways that the technology can be put to use to enhance urban living. In 2013, tech researcher IDC released a report on smart cities in which it analyzed how different municipalities leverage data collected from security footage from video cameras, transponders collecting highway tolls, and sensors attached to bridges, parking spots, water pipes, street lights, and more to provide new data about city operations. "Big data and analytics will turn the vast amount of data into valuable and usable information and knowledge. Cities that have opened their data to the public have spurred the creation of new business; these businesses develop applications using city data and provide innovative citizen services while creating exciting new jobs," IDC concluded in its 2013 Digital Universe Study.[39]

One place you can see this in action (if you can divert your gaze from the "pre-spring trash") is New York City. There, city administrators working with the New York City Economic Development Corporation hold an ongoing competition to reward entrepreneurs for developing smart apps that put city data to use.[40] Launched in 2010, the NYC BigApps initiative has awarded more than $500,000 to third parties. In 2014, the competition gave $25,000 to two companies, Heat Seek NYC and Explore NYC Parks. The former created a hardware and software package that includes an Internet-connected sensor that records temperatures in private dwellings such as apartments and condos and then captures that information so renters and city officials can make sure that landlords are providing private citizens the heat they are entitled to. The Explore NYC Parks team, meanwhile, has developed a mobile-friendly Web application that helps users to find information on parks in their proximity and events and adventures scheduled there.

Boston is also using IoE technology to help its citizens in other ways. NationSwell reports that the city was among the first in the U.S. to develop a "citizen engagement app," which is a modern twist on the 311-hotline that many cities in the U.S. established in the 1990s. A citizen engagement app enables residents to report problems, including road hazards or nuisances such as graffiti, to the city directly from their smart, mobile devices. With Boston's Citizens Connect app, for example, residents can take a picture of a hole in road pavement, tag its location, and then send that information to city transportation authorities. When they submit a request or complaint, residents receive an incident tracking number that allows them to monitor when remediation work on their submission is completed.[41]

After Boston rolled out its citizen engagement app, other cities (including Oakland and Philadelphia) followed suit. Smaller municipalities have deployed third-party apps such as Cityworks, a Government Information Systems (GIS) application developed by Azteca Systems of Sandy, Utah. The app has helped smaller munici-palities such as Hendersonville, N.C., provide the same level of engagement that bigger cities with greater resources do. When they see a problem within their community, Hendersonville residents can snap it, tag it, and then submit it for remediation.[42]

Thanks to new IoE-enabled innovations, life in the big city is get-ting better, one video camera, communications systems, and citizen engagement app at a time.

From city services designed to address residents' basic needs and provide for their modern desires, let's turn our focus to how cities are leveraging the deployment of smart, IoE-enabled technology to foster economic growth and vitality.

Economic Viability

Ever ask yourself while stuck in traffic, "Where are all these peo-ple going?"

It's a question millions of commuters in major urban centers ask every day. Is everyone off to the dentist? To work? Shopping? Where *are* all these people going?

While experts who study urban life for a living cannot say for cer-tain where "everyone" is going, they know where roughly 30 percent of big-city drivers in certain cities are headed at key times of the day. The destination will undoubtedly surprise you: they are actually look-ing for a place to park, according to experts such as Donald Shoup, Professor of Urban Planning at the University of California at Los Angeles (UCLA).[43] Among other things, Shoup is famous for a study that he did around the Westwood, Calif., campus in which he found that people looking for parking in and around UCLA alone racked up the equivalent of 38 trips around the Earth each year.[44]

Because parking in a big city is often a game of chance that some-times feels as random as a spin of the roulette wheel, drivers go round and round until fate smiles upon them and presents a place where they can park their vehicles. The cost of this parking roulette in big cities is enormous. Each day, commuters spend 15 minutes looking for places to park their cars, according to Fastprk, a developer of smart parking solutions.[45] This translates into billions of dollars in lost productivity and millions of tons of additional pollution pumped into the air. It also translates into billions of dollars in terms of lost city revenue.

While citizens might not consider the latter to be a big deal, urban planners certainly do. That's because money generated from parking is the third-largest source of revenue that municipalities collect, after property and sales taxes. In the U.S. alone, municipalities collect $430.3 million annually from parking. Worldwide, the sum is almost $2 billion.

What's interesting about parking, in addition to the wasted man hours people spend looking for it, is the number of people who don't pay for it. Some simply prefer to take their chances with parking authorities while others push their luck to the limit by failing to return to their vehicles before their fares expire. In Los Angeles, for example, for these and other reasons, as much as 40 percent of parking places are not generating the revenue they could for municipalities.[46]

Given the amount that cities miss collecting, it is literally true that the people who are responsible for parking collections in major urban areas are as frustrated at the state of parking as many of the drivers in their cities. What is especially infuriating to urban planners is that supply is infrequently the reason why drivers circle block after block looking for a place to park. MIT professor Eran Ben-Joseph, the author of *ReThinking a Lot: The Design and Culture of Parking*, says the U.S. has plenty of parking spaces for cars. His estimate of 500 million spaces[47] suggests that there are two parking places for every one vehicle registered.[48] In some cities, parking lots cover one-third of all the land in metropolitan areas.[49]

Yet drivers circle round and round in an uncoordinated fashion. Instead of more spaces, they need better information to help them find places for their cars. And in more and more cities, they are getting the help they need, thanks to increased investments into IoE technologies. Take Barcelona, a city with 1.6 million residents and an estimated 600,000 cars.

In 2012, the city launched a massive project to inject smart technology into as many civil administration functions as possible. This includes public safety, energy consumption, water management, trash collection, traffic flow, crime prevention and, of course, parking.

Working with Cisco and other technology and consulting partners, the city installed thousands of sensors next to municipal parking spaces in 10 heavily trafficked districts. The sensors connect wirelessly to a central computer whenever there is no car adjacent to an assigned space near them. The information is then made available to any driver who has downloaded the city's free mapping application onto their smart phone or tablet. From these devices, motorists can identify an available space that may be a block behind or a block ahead of them and pay for it right from their smart device. The meters that accompany each space display when a space has been reserved.

Should someone rudely park in their spot before they arrive, they can request a refund—and alert authorities of the exact location of a parking scofflaw, who can be imposed a hefty fine.

Although questions abounded when the service was first offered to area residents, the system has proven popular among Barcelona's residents. As they have become accustomed to using the IoE-enabled application, residents have adopted a new respect for parking. They don't park without paying as often as they did before because finding parking and paying for it is easier than ever. What is more, the ritual of leaving a restaurant or community event to refill a meter is now a thing of the past in many Barcelona neighborhoods. Now diners can linger over dinner and add time to a meter directly from their smart devices.[50]

"Putting sensors in parking spots results in less traffic," says Tony Vives, previously deputy mayor for Urban Habitat, Barcelona City Council. The new technology "makes the city more livable, and makes people happier."[51]

This includes some of the administrators who work in city hall. When all of the city's traditional meters are converted to smart ones, Barcelona is expected to increase parking revenue by an estimated $50 million annually while simultaneously cutting down on traffic and pollution caused by drivers circling the block looking for open spaces.[52]

Another city using smart technology to transform parking is San Francisco, which has taken the concept of IoE-enabled parking one step farther. Working with a $19.8 million grant from the U.S. Department of Transportation's Urban Partnership Program, the City of San Francisco and the local Mass Transit Authority (MTA) launched a pilot program in 2011 to put IoE-enabled meters and data analytics to work in the city.[53]

The program, SF*park*, uses sensor technology and data analytics to count the number of spaces available in key city neighborhoods and then adjusts the price of parking in these areas as demand increases or decreases. The city launched the program with the hopes that variable pricing would inspire drivers to avoid congested areas, where prices can climb as high as $6 per hour, and instead seek parking in less congested ones, where rates can go as low as $0.25 per hour.[54]

"This innovative project will reduce circling and double-parking, help make Muni faster and more reliable, reduce congestion, and create safer streets for everyone," said SFMTA Executive Director/CEO Nathaniel Ford in a press release from 2011.[55] The City also hopes that the program will improve the utilization of parking so that on-street and off-street spaces don't sit unused, resulting in greater parking revenue for the City.

After installing more than 8,000 sensors, meters, management software, and more, the City began testing the program in 2011. In June of 2014, it released a progress report that found that times when no parking was available fell by 45 percent in key test areas. The program proved effective, in other words.

"While the SFpark pilot project had many goals, its primary focus was to make it easier to find a parking space. More precisely, the goal was to increase the amount of time that there was parking available on every block and improve the utilization of garages," the report said. "Even as the economy, population, and overall parking demand grew, parking availability improved dramatically in SFpark pilot areas."[56]

In addition to Barcelona and San Francisco, Mumbai, Bangalore, and Paris are also benefitting from smart parking technology. This includes technologies implemented by the municipalities themselves and those developed by independent third parties that promise to help ease traffic congestion and spur economic development. Take the app SpotOn, which is used by scores of parking lot and driveway owners to rent their spaces out whenever possible. This includes

Preston Turner, chairman of the board at Third Baptist Church in San Francisco. He uses SpotOn to rent out his church's overflow parking area when it's not used for church services and other events. In 2014, he was featured in an article on the Web site *SFGate* in which he said the app was "a win-win for our neighbors and our church."[57]

"The 'donations' from renters help fund church programs. More importantly, the church is 'networking and building a rapport' with people who might never come through its doors," wrote reporter Kathleen Pender.

Like SF*park*, apps such as SpotOn, Parking Panda, and SPOT that allow people to rent out private parking spaces have proven effective at easing congestion and spurring economic activity. And because users must report the income they make from renting out their spaces to the IRS as well as their state and local governments, they can also increase local tax revenue for urban municipalities.

More controversial are the apps that help beleaguered commuters find parking in *city-owned* spaces. This includes MonkeyParking and other apps that locate available parking on city streets and charge fees for reserving the spots. Community organizers and municipal leaders have cried foul over these apps, which profit from city-owned property. In January 2015, the Los Angeles City Council voted to ban these apps within city limits, according to *The Los Angeles Times*. "Councilman Mike Bonin, who asked for the legislation, likened it to 'pimping out public parking spots,'" reported the *Times*.[58]

Weeks after, San Francisco followed suit. Other municipalities have taken a wait-and-see attitude. While they don't like the idea of someone profiting from community assets, they are desperate enough to give entrepreneurs some leeway to prove their worth in the name of reducing congestion and citizen frustration.

Smart parking, of course, isn't the only innovation that urban leaders are leveraging to stimulate economic growth and reduce costs in their cities. In addition to IoE-enabled parking solutions, lights, and waste bins, they are also investing in smart sensors embedded into roadways that connect with bridges and toll systems that provide feedback on road conditions. When necessary, traffic engineers can reprogram traffic lights on the fly to improve traffic flow in many cities.

Urban planners are also installing smart grid systems and meters to better manage energy consumption in their communities. They are even looking at experimental technologies such as smart sidewalks from companies such as Pavegen, a U.K.-based technology company that is developing specialized sidewalk tiles that can store kinetic energy generated from foot traffic that can then be converted to electricity for street lights and more.[59]

From the economic benefits of smart cities, let's turn to environmental sustainability and how IoE technology can help improve it in an era of rapid urbanization.

Environmental Sustainability

When it was first proposed, the Emirates Golf Club in Dubai seemed like an absurd idea. An all-grass championship golf course built in the middle of the Arabian Desert? It had never been done before in the Middle East.[60]

As with a lot of things in the United Arab Emirates, however, the words "never been done before" didn't prevent the construction of the facility, which boasts not one but two golf courses at the club. To pull off this miraculous achievement, the city of Dubai allowed the Emirates Club, which opened in 1988, to use as much water as it needed to keep its fairways lush and its greens emerald. But the decision came at a steep environmental cost.[61]

The water used by the club, all 700 million gallons of it annually (enough to fill 14 million bath tubs), was the same as the total amount of water that flowed through residents' taps in Dubai.

Devoting that much potable water to golf course watering when the city had only 500,000 residents was one thing; it was an altogether different one when the city's population hit 1.5 million, which it did when course director Craig Haldane arrived in 2007. He knew the water consumption rate was unsustainable. In a 2015 article that appeared in the English UAE newspaper *The National*, Haldane said, "When you come [to] a new site you see things with a new pair of eyes, and it did not take me long to see things needed to change if we wanted to move forward and improve."[62]

Since his arrival, the club has turned to more salt-resistant grass seeds and treated sewage water to reduce usage. Then in 2012, it installed a high-tech, IoE-enabled sprinkler system that uses moisture sensors and analytics to monitor usage. It can control water flow to more than 2,000 individual sprinklers used by the club and analyze the data these devices generate to determine the most efficient watering locations, times and amounts, which can be based on wind, temperature, humidity, and so on. Since the measures were put in place, water usage has dropped by half at the club—a very good thing now that Dubai's population is well more than 2 million residents.[63]

"Prior to having [the new sprinkler technology] it was a bit of a guessing game," Haldane told *The National* in 2015. "We have a lot more information at our fingertips today than we did back then, so as an industry we really are in a fortunate position in that we can put out only what we need to put out."

Saving water is a noble aim. So is making recreation more environmentally friendly. People in big cities, after all, need diversions and golf certainly brings joy to millions. But simple sensors and basic data analytic tools used to reduce water consumption on golf courses are hardly the only way IoE technologies are helping municipalities conserve and improve water quality. Water crises, according to the *Global Risks 2015* report from the World Economic Forum (WEF), are the world's number-one global risk in terms of impact—ahead of infectious diseases, weapons of mass destruction, and climate change.[64]

In 2014, researchers at the University of Bath's Department of Chemical Engineering in the U.K. unveiled a potentially life-saving, IoE-enabled, low-cost sensor that can detect pollution levels in water supplies.

"Working in collaboration with Bristol Robotics Laboratory at the University of the West of England, they made the sensor using 3D printing technology that can be used directly in rivers and lakes to help monitor water quality," reported *Consumer Business Review*.[65]

"The biosensor also contains bacteria that produce an electric current as they feed and grow. If pollutants in the water come into contact with the bacteria, the electric current drops, which indicates the extent of toxins in the water," the newspaper reported.[66]

The advantage of the technology is that it can instantly tell its users whether water is safe enough to drink or bathe in. More traditional technology requires water samples to be sent to a lab for testing and analysis. Given that 840,000 people the world over die from water-borne illnesses each year, it is not hyperbole to say that the value of the time savings that the IoE-enabled biosensor provides will be measured in the number of lives it saves.[67]

Less immediate but no less important is the technology that is being applied to help Beijing reduce its notorious air pollution, which has been called everything from a menace to an embarrassment to residents of the Chinese capital. Unfortunately, there are no simple answers to the problem there.

"The city is flanked on three sides by smog-trapping mountain ranges," writes Gwynn Guilford in the tech and business Web site *Quartz*. "There are numerous sources of foul air, and a multitude of subtle ways the chemicals interact with each other, which make it hard to identify what problems need fixing."[68]

To mitigate the problem, Chinese officials have declared "war"[69] on air pollutants and vowed to take extreme measures to mitigate their impact. This led to the creation of massive area-wide initiative in collaboration with IBM called "Green Horizon."[70]

For help making Green Horizon a success, officials turned to IBM, which is applying its famed Watson cognitive computing, data sensing, and data analysis technology to fight the problem. The company is installing its latest generation of optical sensors in and around the Chinese capital to capture on the ground and in-air data on pollution levels there. It is taking that data and marrying it with meteorological satellite data. The information is then being fed into Watson, which has been tasked to help Beijing officials identify where pollution is coming from and anticipate when levels will rise to unhealthy levels.

"[The] initiative will also see IBM use big data analytics and weather modeling to forecast availability of renewable energies like wind and solar, power sources that are notoriously intermittent. That should limit the amount of that energy being wasted. The third layer of the plan involves a system that IBM is developing to help industrial companies manage their energy consumption," *Quartz* reports.[71]

While the air in Beijing has yet to improve to desired levels, the technology shows promise. Moreover, it says volumes about China's interest and commitment to applying IoE technology to improve the quality of life in the world's most populous nation. It will undoubtedly lead to greater use of sensors, mobile technology, data analysis, and personal devices there.

This includes innovations that everyday citizens can put to use, such as the Air Quality Egg, which is an IoE-based "sensor system designed to allow anyone to collect very high resolution readings of [nitrogen dioxide] and [carbon monoxide] concentrations outside of their home," according to the loose coalition of developers, technologists and scientists who've pooled their resources to create the technology.[72] Their goal: develop a "community-led air quality sensing network that gives people a way to participate in the conversation about air quality."

The technology, which can be easily installed on the exterior of a home, is simple to use and costs less than $300.[73] The data collected by the devices will lead to new insights about how, where, and when air pollution is created.

This is also the idea behind a new personal, wearable technology called "Breathe." Invented by serial entrepreneur and inventor Samuel Cox, Breathe is a small, wearable sensor that is roughly the size of a bar of soap. (Cox is the man behind a number of smart devices, including the water-level monitoring device known as "Flood Beacon" and the keyless Bluetooth-enabled "BLE Bike Lock").[74]

When worn by a consumer, Breathe will monitor the air quality around its user. If the sensor detects a contaminant or high level of pollution nearby, it will alert the wearer with an audio sound. The device will also record the level of pollution and its exact location using GPS technology. When connected to a smart device app, the device will upload its information and help its user make smarter decisions for avoiding pollution. Should the user wish to, he or she can upload the information into a central Breathe database that collects data from all Breathe users who opt to share their personal information. Once there, data scientists working with Breathe can analyze the data to help create pollution maps that provide insights that consumers can apply in their daily lives. Among other things, the crowdsourced information can help consumers determine when air quality is the best for exercising. It can also help them determine when to reduce their use of a car or not use a wood-burning stove or fireplace.[75]

Carlo Ratti, MIT professor of Urban Studies & Planning, believes that the real solution to this in the longer term will likely come from shared self-driving cars. He points out that, "a recent paper by the Massachusetts Institute of Technology's SMART Future Mobility team shows that the mobility demand of a city like Singapore—potentially host to the world's first publicly-accessible fleet of self-driving cars—could be met with 30 percent of its existing vehicles. Furthermore, other researchers in the same group suggest that this number could be cut by another 40 percent if passengers traveling similar routes at the same time were willing to share a vehicle—an estimate supported by an analysis of New York City Taxi shareability networks. This implies a city in which everyone can travel on demand with just one-fifth of the number of cars in use today. Such reductions in car numbers would dramatically lower the cost of our mobility infrastructure and the embodied energy associated with building and maintaining it. Fewer cars may also mean shorter travel times, less congestion, and a smaller environmental impact."[76]

In the meantime, armed with the knowledge that solutions like Air Quality Egg, Breathe, and other devices provide, we will have our best opportunity yet to fight a problem that impacts us all, whether it is in the air we breathe or in the water we drink.

This is vitally important because everyone contributes to pollution in some measure or another. Reducing its harmful effects, thus, benefits all.

Bright Lights, Big Cities

Big data and analytics. Mobile technologies. Wired and wireless broadband infrastructure. Sensors. As much as roads, bridges, and sewers, these are the pillars of the modern global city. In fact, these technologies might be as important as leadership and policy when it comes to making a city work. And because of this, urban planners and community leaders are rethinking what it means to be not just a big city, but a great one, too.

In addition to looking sharp, great cities must operate efficiently. Population growth has made this an imperative—so much so that civic leaders now realize that steel and concrete alone won't help them achieve their aims. Instead of bigger and brawnier, great cities must become *smarter*.

"Smarter" in terms of how they collect trash more resourcefully, how they light streets more efficiently, generate tax revenues more wisely, share information more beneficially, and use natural resources more sustainably.

So how do cities get smart?

Technology researcher and urban planning expert Ruthbea Yesner Clarke of IDC suggests they start by developing a comprehensive plan that includes all civil departments and citizen constituencies. Many cities have multiple Smart City initiatives, but they are ad hoc and not well coordinated across multiple departments, says the research director of smart cities strategies at IDC.[77] Her advice to civic leaders is to take an inventory of all needs and objectives, build a comprehensive Smart City strategy, and then begin implementing a converged technology infrastructure.[78]

If that sounds a little obvious to you, then let me provide some context why it is not. Big cities looking to become great cities have a lot of options. And they are very excited about the benefits that can come from investments into smart technology. But they need to be shrewd about where they commit their money. A lot of solutions today don't talk to each other or run on the same information and communications network. Nor do they produce data in the same format. In fact, they don't make it possible for third-party innovators to build on top of them. Thus they are destined to be islands of ideas in a sea of needs.

That's why Yesner Clarke recommends cities coordinate planning and investments that span all city departments and citizen constituencies. This starts with a common technology platform that provides not only for multiple capabilities and third-party applications, but also anticipates demands not yet fully understood today.

With such a platform, a city can roll out one network that connects all of its people, processes, data, and things seamlessly, says Wim Elfrink, previously executive vice president and chief globalization officer with Cisco. The unified, interoperable platform, he and others believe, is the critical enabler for the new digital revolution that is occurring in municipalities all around the world.[79]

The Port of Hamburg, Germany, is one place where you can see this in action today. The city has deployed a unified platform that connects its street parking with traffic control, which connects to port arrivals, which connects to bridge operations, and more. Now when a ship arrives, traffic can be rerouted to avoid drawbridge openings to keep things moving. And instead of driving around and around, drivers can easily click their city apps to find parking. As for port operators, they now equip every shipping container with a WiFi-enabled chip so they more efficiently move freight on and off ships and onto trucks that are dispatched all over Europe.[80]

With its investment into smart technology, Hamburg officials are confident that they can double the amount of container traffic they handle *and* improve quality of life.

And that's only a few ways that smart technology can improve urban living. Once they have developed a common technology platform, cities can pile on an almost infinite number of new benefits onto it. The IoE-connected LED lights that Sensity Systems of Sunnyvale, Calif., has developed for urban use are one such example. They work with existing light poles, don't require additional power or need to be hard-wired to a network. Because of this, they can lower energy consumption and improve public safety without a massive investment of time or equipment. Moreover, once installed, the sensors on these lights turn every lamp post into a wireless smart node that can be remotely controlled and individually upgraded with cameras that can detect illegal activity beneath them and automatically alert authorities to potential crimes. When linked together, these "nodes" form a de facto high-speed wireless, mesh network that citizens and city employees alike can use to connect to the Internet.[81]

MIT's Carlo Ratti believes that the solution needs to also engage citizens directly through "bottom-up" dynamics. "It is important to get people excited about creating apps and using data themselves. If we can develop the right platforms, people can be the ones to address the key urban issues—from energy, traffic, health care, food distribution, and education. What is happening in the world of urban apps is an example of this bottom up approach."[82]

Technology, of course, is only one piece of the solution to creating smarter cities. Astute, forward-thinking leadership is another. Well-informed leaders understand the difference between closed, proprietary systems and flexible, open standards. They also recognize the benefit of reaching across all city departments and constituencies, and coordinating investment with other members of local and global ecosystems. It also means looking for new and alternative ways to generate good ideas or fund investment. This is where citizen engagement apps, third-party innovations, and new partnerships come in.

What happens when cities pursue this agenda? They discover that the benefits they derive in one area spill over to another. Better city lighting, for example, not only reduces energy consumption, it also reduces crime in places as diverse as Kansas City, Rio de Janeiro, Adelaide, Bangalore, and Toronto, just to name a few.

Smart trash solutions, meanwhile, save dollars *and* improve environmental sustainability. They can also support new public-private partnerships (PPPs), which can generate new sources of revenue and/or savings for city officials. Those WiFi-enabled trash bins now being installed in urban centers around the world? They can now be outfitted with digital advertising displays. Instead of being a cost center for cities, waste bins can now be revenue generators. And they are only one example of the types of PPPs that can transform urban economics. The multiplier effect from embracing smart technology can literally transform the math that urban planners have had to calculate for decades.

Don't need to spend as much on trash collection? The savings for a city could be used to help feed the poor. Or beautify public spaces. Or buy more fuel-efficient buses.

Smart technology is literally providing city planners a new way to provide for urban needs. It's as true in Barcelona as it is in Boston, Beijing, and Bangalore.

When burdened with the same social, economic, and environmental problems that exist elsewhere, these varied and vibrant urban centers lose their distinction and differentiation. They become a muddle of traffic, crime, and pollution that looks (and smells) roughly the same the world over.

But freed from these burdens, cities can rise above everyday challenges and be the cultural beacons for millions that they have always been—distinct in their own way, destined like no other.

6

Privacy
Wait, Am I the Product?°

"We Experiment on Human Beings..."[1]

If you had to guess where this disclosure was made, would you choose:

a. The Trials of Nuremberg

b. A heavily redacted Department of Defense memorandum

c. A science fiction novel

d. A blog post from a popular online dating Web site

Though "d" may not be the obvious choice, it is the correct one. Why an online dating site would choose to disclose this takes a little explaining. The story starts with a similar confession made by another social media site, Facebook.

In June 2014, the social media giant attracted the ire of millions of subscribers when it admitted that it had secretly manipulated the news feeds of more than 600,000 Facebook users in an attempt to see if depressing stories diminished their enthusiasm for the Web site. (They did.)[2]

"Unethical," said some of the Facebook research project on "emotional contagion."[3] "Cruel," others opined.[4] When the media weighed in, such as CNN with a story entitled, "Facebook Treats You Like a

° For their guidance with this chapter, I am grateful to David Hoffman, Global Privacy Officer at Intel; Michelle Dennedy, Chief Privacy Officer at Cisco; Professor Alex "Sandy" Pentland of Massachusetts Institute of Technology (MIT), Co-creator of the MIT Media Lab and Chair of the World Economic Forum's Data Driven Development Council; and Mark Chandler, Chief Legal Officer at Cisco.

Lab Rat," the Menlo Park, California, company recognized that it had a public relations debacle on its hands.[5] While traveling in India, Facebook COO Sheryl Sandberg tried to quell the issue. "This was part of ongoing research companies do to test different products, and that was what it was; it was poorly communicated," she said at a public gathering. "And for that communication we apologize. We never meant to upset you."[6]

Instead of deflating the issue, the careful parsing of phrases further infuriated millions of loyal social media fans.[7] And not just of Facebook, but of other social media sites. This includes the aforementioned online dating site, OkCupid. Did the industry really view consumers of online services as lab rats the way that CNN suggested? Many wondered.

Absolutely, said the author of the "We Experiment on Human Beings!" blog, Christian Rudder. Rudder is the outspoken CEO and co-founder of OkCupid, one of the World Wide Web's most popular dating services. The best-selling author of the book "Dataclysm," Rudder is known for his provocative stances and straight talk. Amid the backdrop of the Facebook debacle, he decided to speak out on the issue of testing live humans to fine-tune web services.

"...[I]f you use the Internet, you're the subject of hundreds of experiments at any given time, on every site," Rudder wrote without apology in July 2014. "That's how Web sites work."[8]

While his candor was refreshing, the disclosure was nonetheless unsettling to those who didn't realize what should have seemed fairly obvious: if you use a free, online service such as Facebook, Twitter, or OkCupid, *you* are the product that these organizations sell.

By "you," I mean the individual digital footprint you leave behind on the Internet. While you might not think about it, the data you create from your online activity is gold to others. This includes the "likes" you click on Facebook, the tweets you send out about your interests, and the Google searches you craft carefully.

Ever wonder how the same hotel you researched on Yahoo winds up being advertised on your Facebook page? Or why that new Honda you "liked" on Facebook is miraculously recommended afterward anytime you type the word "car" into your browser? It's because a commercial organization somewhere is tracking your every move online. And while people often talk about Internet giants like Facebook, Google, and others, it isn't just a handful of technology giants following your every move, it's also thousands of other companies big and small.

A growing industry of data brokers has arisen in the past few years, amassing billions of dollars with your personal information. Data brokers buy and sell your information to various third parties who are hoping to make money off you. This includes merchants and retailers, manufacturers and product developers, and even charities and not-for-profit organizations. By and large, this industry operates with minimal oversight. Partly as a result, it has developed incredible capabilities and sophistication. In March 2014, Federal Trade Commissioner (FTC) Julie Brill told *60 Minutes* correspondent Steve Kroft that Americans have essentially "lost control of our most personal information" to commercial interests.[9]

While the FTC does have some powers to combat what it perceives as abuse, it urged the U.S. Congress in May 2014 to create tougher laws that would make industry practices more visible to consumers and give them greater control over how their personal information is collected, shared, and used. This followed the release of a scathing FTC report entitled, "Data Brokers: A Call for Transparency and Accountability," which concluded that "many of the purposes for which data brokers collect and use data pose risks to consumers."[10]

While it is easy to point fingers at aggressive industry profiteers, some of the "blame" for the current state of affairs falls directly on consumers. Why? Because the more we use and become dependent on the Internet to search, browse, review, and eventually pay for goods and services, the more we share about ourselves.

When the Internet was limited to desktop PCs and notebook computers, the amount of "gold" that could be mined from our activity was relatively modest. But as people who worked at Web-based companies got better at business analytics, they realized that more of our online activity could be put to use. When smart devices went mobile and people went social in the early 2000s, the value of your online activity increased dramatically. And it could get exponentially bigger once more when the majority of the devices in our homes, workplaces, and communities get connected. This is because each device will capture ever-increasing amounts of data about us and the world around us. In many cases, this data will ultimately be used by third-parties—so much so that some experts wonder whether the concept of privacy as we know it will even exist in a decade or two.

"Over time there will be fewer people who recall pre-Information Age privacy, [and] more people who will have grown up with few expectations of privacy. While a backlash against the erosion of privacy is possible, it is more likely that people acting on their fear of big government and big corporate data will be a minority," wrote Richard Clarke in *The Wall Street Journal* in July 2014. The former White House Cyber Security Czar under Presidents George W. Bush and Barack Obama worries that privacy might one day be available only to the rich and tech-savvy among us. "Privacy advocacy groups will probably be overwhelmed by corporate interests, the security industrial complex, and by a public that perceives benefits from the, frequently free, data-yielding devices and applications."[11]

In Europe, however, the prevailing opinion is we will need to have a clear set of privacy measures in place that secure consumers while allowing the data analytics market to grow.

When you look at privacy from a global perspective, you note that individual attitudes about privacy are not uniform; they differ significantly across geography, socio-economic status, and demographics. These differences underlie some of the key challenges faced by companies and governments that struggle to balance interests and satisfy diverse constituents.

For example, some view privacy as principally a *property* right that can be exchanged for value, freely transferred and even trumped by other rights, such as free speech. Others view privacy as a fundamental *human* right that cannot be sold or taken away at any price. To these people, individual privacy is as sacred as freedom of religion.

Partly because of their passion, partly because of their world views, the people who see privacy differently can both pull at your heart strings and appeal to your best thinking. One way to understand the two sides, albeit simplistically, is to think of privacy in terms of potential transgressions against it.

If you view privacy as a property right, then taking it away is like trespassing—intruding on someone else's property without permission. In these instances, privacy is about economics. To those that view privacy in these terms, individuals should be able to freely trade away their property rights for money or other value.

In contrast, if you view privacy as a fundamental human right, then taking it away is more akin to kidnapping, which can evoke a more visceral response and conjure up even worse crimes, such as organ harvesting. For those who see privacy in these terms, debates on it raise profound ethical questions and draw lines that corporations and governments simply cannot cross.

Many people would say that the U.S. is more aligned with the economic/property rights point of view, while the EU is more aligned with the fundamental human rights perspective. That may be *generally* true—though not universally so. The assessment is blunt and overly simplistic. In reality, there are a number of factors that influence an individual's perspective on privacy, including a person's world view, political leanings, education, economic status, and more. These influence the attitudes toward opting-in versus opting-out, about the importance of privacy within the home versus in public places, and about the value of privacy for private individuals versus public figures. That being said, views toward privacy across geographies are gradually starting to converge.

What's interesting about digitization and the Internet of Everything (IoE) is this: no matter how you perceive privacy—as a piece of property or a fundamental human right—innovation is upending its traditional definition. As it does, the current balance between personal privacy and broader, societal considerations tips unnervingly out of its traditional place.

In this chapter, I examine three constituents this impacts: commercial companies that want a return on the free services they provide, social organizations that value public disclosure over personal confidentiality, and government institutions that struggle to balance collective security with individual liberty. You can think of these three struggles as privacy versus profit, privacy versus free speech, and privacy versus security.

Let's start with the pressure that commercial interests are putting on personal privacy and some of the inconvenient truths and policy challenges that exacerbate this stress—one in particular: when it comes to the Internet, everyone lies.

The Con of Consent: The Monetization of You

Question: When you mindlessly click the box next to the words, "I have read and agree to the terms and conditions" of a commercial Web site, do you always tell the truth?

Of course not.

Estimates vary but the percent of people who even attempt to read the terms and conditions of their iTunes account, Box subscription, or Twitter agreement are thought to be in the single digits at best. Who can blame them? The latest version of the iTunes agreement updated June 30, 2015, after all, is more than 20,000 words—or roughly one quarter the length of the book you are currently reading.[12] It's almost twice as long as Albert Einstein's *General Theory of Relativity*.[13]

While you might not think twice about the user agreements of Facebook and other commercial Web sites, the little white lie you tell them comes at a steep cost. The price is your individual privacy. (In a scandalously funny episode of Comedy Central's *South Park* devoted to the fine print of the iTunes user agreement, the cost is far more.)[14]

Take your browsing habits. Deep in the text of Facebook's terms are some things that you might not so readily agree to if you took the time to think them through. For example, beginning Jan. 1, 2015, Facebook informed users that their use of its service gives the company "permission to use your name, profile picture, content, and information in connection with commercial, sponsored, or related content (such as a brand you like) served or enhanced by [Facebook.]"[15]

While that might not sound ominous, the terms also include this disclosure: "This means, for example, that you permit a business or other entity to pay us to display your name and/or profile picture with your content or information, without any compensation to you."[16]

In addition, users also agree that Facebook can "suggest that your friend tag you in a picture by comparing your friend's pictures to information we've put together from your profile pictures and the other photos in which you've been tagged."[17]

Not many people realize that signing up for Facebook gives the organization permission to track your browsing history and mobile app usage. The same goes for your movements, which can be tracked via GPS. Facebook does say that it does not "share information that personally identifies you...with advertising, measurement or analytics partners unless you give us permission."[18]

That said, the unsettling reality for many (though not all) is that the company often knows where you are, what you're doing and, quite possibly, whom you are with.

Facebook likes to say that you own the data you put onto Facebook but downplays one inescapable truth: it does what it wants with your data unless you specify otherwise. For certain things, such as your name, profile photo, gender, and network, you do not even have that option.[19] In Europe, Facebook has been required to introduce certain means for the users to control Facebook's use of their data. Improvement has been made but certain reports claim that it is not fully compliant yet.

Facebook, of course, is just one company of many that puts your digital information to use. The list of others is endless. And so is the amount of data they collect every time you visit a Web site or engage a mobile app. Take Acxiom, one of the aforementioned data brokering companies. Based in Little Rock, Arkansas, Acxiom is one of the largest marketing companies in the data collection and dissemination industry. The company has, according to *The New York Times*, "information about 500 million active consumers worldwide, with about 1,500 data points per person." This includes data on the majority of adults in the U.S., including 11 of 19 hijackers who participated in the terrorist attacks on 9/11, according to the newspaper.[20] And remember that 9/11 happened in 2001, when Google was a small private company,[21] and Facebook did not exist because Mark Zuckerberg, its founder, was still in high school.[22]

What can third parties do with all of this information? You'd be amazed.

In the hands of a capable data-mining specialist, your online activity will reveal plenty about you—including your financial net worth, political leanings, sexual orientation, social affiliations, community involvement, and shopping preferences. Data specialists know where you live, which car you drive, and which car you want next. They know your tastes in film, music, and books. They even know if you have an aversion to pornography. Or not.

What else? Data collectors know how many kids you have and their ages, what medical conditions you might have, and even the ones you might not know of—yet. In one case that made headlines in 2012, data scientists working for Target recognized that a teenage girl in suburban Milwaukee was pregnant before her own father knew. After analyzing her Internet activity, the retailer determined her medical condition and began sending the high school student promotions for baby clothes and related merchandise. Incensed by what he found in his mailbox, the girl's father stormed into a local Target store and demanded to speak to the manager. "Are you trying to encourage her to get pregnant?" he complained.[23]

If all of the preceding makes you want to ditch your smart phone and move to a desert island, hold off on that until you consider all sides of this complex issue. In many instances, you may *want* Target and others to access your digital footprint, even if they profit handsomely from it. With access to your information, retailers and other commercial interests can reward you for loyal patronage, help you make more informed purchase decisions, and even save you money. For these benefits, you might choose to give up certain personalized data on yourself.

In other instances, such as occasions where sharing personal data could improve your health or even save your life, you might opt to share additional information. Take everyday wearable fitness devices, for example.

Because these products automate measurements and tests that are otherwise performed manually, the amount and accuracy of data they produce is far greater than ever before. In the right hands, these data could help scientists discover new medical breakthroughs, run care facilities better, and help healthcare professionals make more informed and timely decisions, concludes Saviance Technologies, a New Jersey-based IT service provider focused on the healthcare industry.[24]

In exchange for insights that could improve your health, wouldn't you give up some personalized information? Most of us would gladly say, "Yes."

Now imagine the benefits your data could provide to researchers in other fields, including transportation, energy, and government administration. If individuals and institutions lowered their guard and approved broader use of their personal data, the benefits to the economy, public safety, environmental sustainability, and more could be enormous.

While you ponder this, consider another question: when was the last time you wrote Facebook a check? The answer, of course, is never. For all the privacy concerns that Facebook and other companies like it create, it's important to remember that they typically do not charge consumers for using their services. Unless you have a premium account, Google doesn't expect you to pay for its services. Neither do Yahoo, Twitter, LinkedIn, OkCupid, and a whole lot of others. Providing these services is hardly cheap. In fiscal 2014, for example, Facebook's total costs and expenses, which include wages, property leases, equipment investments, and so on, totaled $7.5 billion[25]—more than seven times as much as in 2010.[26] In 2014, the company spent $2.7 billion on research and development, fully 21 percent of its revenue.[27] That's a pretty hefty percent, even by Silicon Valley standards, just to enhance a service they don't charge for.

From Facebook's perspective, no one forces you to use its service; but if you choose to do so, your right to privacy should be balanced with its obligation to responsibly turn a profit.

So, maybe it's not just *any* collection or use of data that should worry us, or even the use of it in ways tailored to specific individuals; perhaps we should instead ensure the use meets the *reasonable expectations* of the end user and the end user is not surprised by its usage. Both how and why our information is used matters. For personalized healthcare, it's the clear benefit to the individual and society that stands out. For Facebook, it might be that we think the free service offered is worth the data shared.

If it's the expectations and decisions of the end user that determine whether use of their data is okay, then we need to ensure they are able to make such choices in a meaningful way. The key is providing users with *transparency* and *control*. At the same time, we need to shoulder some of the responsibility to educate ourselves, too. And once we're informed, we need clear options for allowing our data, or subsets of our data, to be used.

Unfortunately, transparency and control are not always easy to implement in a new Internet of Everything digital world where sensors are embedded in everyday objects. Not all things have the types of user interfaces we are used to on laptops or smart phones. On these devices, we can read terms and check boxes on our screens easily. But should we expect that a street lamp ask us if we are okay with it increasing its brightness levels as we walk past? Would we want it to, given it might be irritating to be pestered by thousands of such sensors when walking around cities in the future?

The answer to these questions isn't bombarding consumers with an unwieldy number of requests, says Chris Gow, Senior Manager of Government Affairs with Cisco; the answer is in simplifying information, aggregating decision points in a transparent manner so that we're not overwhelmed. And where consent becomes unwieldy or inappropriate (for example, for the common good, such as public safety), we have to make sure other privacy protections are in place to allay valid concerns of citizens.

"To improve transparency, companies need to think about layered privacy policies that complement detailed terms with easy to digest summaries. To improve control, they need to think about ease of use for the consumer—can they make a single decision that captures their expectations for a range of uses or services? To strengthen privacy they need to think about techniques and principles such as anonymization and aggregation, security measures and engraining privacy into the culture of the workforce—including the engineers who may be developing new products and services, i.e., privacy-by-design," says Gow.

In other words, what we need is a tool belt of privacy practices that can be applied to the use case at hand. For example, anonymization can't always be used—there's little point treating a disease if you don't know who your patient is—but in cases where a company doesn't have a reason to identify you, why should they retain that option?

The tension between control over one's information and the value that can be derived from its use that we have discussed in this section is not, however, the only privacy dilemma that the IoE creates. Another way in which the IoE tests privacy is by pitting your individual privacy against society's collective right to free speech.

Throughout history, these two rights have battled. With the advance of new technology and the rise of IoE, especially, these liberties will be in greater conflict than ever before.

For a better understanding of how, consider the case of Texan Frank Rodriguez.

Never Let You Go: The Right to Be Forgotten

Frank Rodriguez of Caldwell, Texas, is many things. He's a devoted husband, a loving father, and a dedicated worker. He's also a registered sex offender and has been for nearly half his life. Before you jump to conclusions, note that Frank is not *that* kind of sex offender, but a new one that is wholly the creation of the Internet age.

When he was 19 years old, Frank consummated his love for his girlfriend of one year, Nikki Prescott. Though the sex was consensual, Frank had committed a crime because Nikki was not yet 17 years old, which is the age of legal consent in Texas.

In an article entitled "The Accidental Sex Offender" that appeared in *Marie Claire* magazine in July 2011, Frank's nightmare was detailed: "Nikki's mother, worried that her daughter's relationship with Frank was getting too serious, reported Frank to the police. She expected the cops to issue a warning, but instead she set in motion a legal nightmare from which Frank would never recover. He became a registered sex offender—for life."[28]

After his name was added to Texas' sex offender list, Frank faced a litany of challenges and hurdles. He also struggled to find his rightful place in his community. Although he married Nikki when she turned 17, and then had four beautiful daughters with her, he cannot coach his girls' soccer teams. Nor can he accompany them to playgrounds, public swimming pools, or anywhere else where other children gather.

Frank is not alone.

Nationwide, there are approximately 650,000 people on registered sex offenders lists. While many are perverts and predators, more than a few are like Frank—former young men who fell in love with younger, equally smitten girlfriends. When Frank met Nikki, for example, he was the 18-year old star of his local high school football team, she the bashful, 15-year old freshman cheerleader.

Ironically, Frank is a big believer in sex offender lists. He's a father, after all, who, like the parents of Megan Kanka, the murdered victim for whom the national 1996 sex offender act known as "Megan's Law" is named, believes in the community's right to know who is living among its residents.[29] So does Nikki. Regarding the sex offender list that informs parents and children in Texas of sex offenders living within their communities, Nikki told *Marie Claire*, "It's a good thing. It's just that Frank shouldn't be on it."[30]

So long as there is an Internet constituted as it is in U.S., he likely will be. This is true even if the State of Texas, like other states before it, starts treating youthful offenders differently than hardened criminals.

It is because the Internet never forgets.

Frank may one day be taken off the list of official sex offenders. But the Internet will always remember that he was on it.

If Frank lived in Europe, things might be different. That's because The European Court of Justice decided in the Spring of 2014 that an individual has the right to ask search engines to take down links to information deemed "inadequate, irrelevant or no longer relevant, or excessive in relation to the purposes for which they were processed and in the light of the time that has elapsed."[31]

The case that put the issue front and center involved a Spanish attorney named Mario Costeja González who had fallen behind on some property payments. In 1998, the Spanish newspaper *La Vanguardia* published notices that properties owned by González would be auctioned off to pay his debts. Although González cleaned up his finances, Google searches of his name years afterward turned up links to these stories, as reported in *The New Yorker* magazine.[32] The mentions, González claimed, hurt his reputation long after he cleared his name in the courts. Despite raised eyebrows in certain quarters regarding the perceived expansionist interpretation of Europe's privacy law, in a landmark ruling, the EU court agreed. It demanded that Google and others create a way for people to ask to have information linked to them hidden from Web searches.

In a powerful story published in *The New Yorker* magazine in September 2014,[33] legal scholar and television commentator Jeffrey

Toobin said the EU's move to increase personal privacy at the expense of broader free speech stands in stark contrast to what is happening in America, where personal liberties are giving way to government intrusion and commercial exploitation on a regular basis.

"In recent years, many people have made the same kind of effort [as González] from actors who don't want their private photographs in broad circulation to ex-convicts who don't want their long-ago legal troubles to prevent them from finding jobs. Despite the varied circumstances, all these people want something that does not exist in the United States: the right to be forgotten," Toobin wrote in *The New Yorker*.

In the age of IoE, this "right" is only going to get more difficult for authorities to provide. If you buy a movie ticket with your smart phone, for example, third parties are going to not only know your cinematic tastes but also your whereabouts. If you tell your friends what you thought of the film via social media, the producers of said film are going to know about it. And if you left before the credits rolled, GPS tracking technology will take note.

Not just for a while, but possibly forever.

Is this a good thing? Many social scientists and legal scholars wonder. There is room for debate. On one hand, people have a right to know who among them has a history of predatory behavior. But that right seems out of balance if it infringes upon the individual liberties of Frank Rodriguez and thousands like him. Isn't Frank entitled to a little privacy after all these years?

The answer in cases like Frank's seems clear.

But what about other instances? In the immediate aftermath of the EU's ruling, the *DailyMail.com* reported that among the first to file requests to be forgotten with Google and others were a scandal-prone politician who was running for reelection, a man convicted of possessing child pornography, and a doctor who had received some bad reviews from patients.[34] In each instance, most people would agree that the significance of this is too valuable to sweep under the rug.

Free-speech advocates are alarmed. Cisco's Chief Privacy Officer, Michelle Dennedy, points out that "we have never had the 'right to be forgotten' since the beginning of time."[35] She says that we have many legal mechanisms for protection already, such as fraud, slander, and libel laws, that can be used to address the issue.

Writing in a blog on behalf of Wikipedia, Lila Tretikov, the executive director of the Wikimedia Foundation, said, "the European court abandoned its responsibility to protect one of the most important and universal rights: the right to seek, receive, and impart information. As a consequence, accurate search results are vanishing in Europe with no public explanation, no real proof, no judicial review, and no appeals process. The result is an Internet riddled with memory holes—places where inconvenient information simply disappears."[36]

Her point about "no judicial review" is particularly vexing to transparency supporters. Right now, it is up to search engine companies to decide what they will link to and what they won't. While they are independent arbitrators, critics of the current process for requesting to be forgotten note that tech companies are not subject-matter experts qualified to make delicate decisions about content.

But that's not the half of it. Since the initial ruling, European regulators have discovered that European citizens wanting information about their communities, history, and fellow citizens don't limit their searches to Google.fr or Google.es, which are the domains for Google France and Google Spain, respectively. Instead, they routinely look for information on Google.com, which is the global Web site of Google Inc. based in California. So adamant are European regulators that European citizens not find information determined "to be forgotten," that they have asked that Google Inc. remove any such search findings, not just on the company's European Web sites, but the American, South American, and Asian ones as well. In essence, European regulators are trying to limit not only what their citizens can reasonably find online, but also what citizens of virtually every other country on earth can find as well. And technology companies that run search engines or social media sites are having to be arbiters and implementers.

David Hoffman, Intel's Global Privacy Officer, believes that a centralized obscurity solution is needed to address this. His proposal: Companies like Google, Facebook, and Twitter could contribute a proportional amount of money each year to set up and run a centralized non-profit center, trained and approved by the regulators, that serves as the arbiter of what can be deleted, with the liability of participant companies limited so long as they are compliant with the rulings of this centralized entity.[37]

In an editorial that appeared in *The New York Times* in February 2015, the *Times* editorial board blasted the European Commission's heavy-handed approach to enforcing this decision by the EU Court of Justice. "The European position is deeply troubling because it could lead to censorship by public officials who want to whitewash the past. It also sets a terrible example for officials in other countries who might also want to demand that Internet companies remove links they don't like," the board concluded.[38]

Speaking at the Mentor Group Vienna Forum in September 11, 2014,[39] U.S. Federal Trade Commissioner Julie Brill noted that reasonable solutions can emerge over the "fullness of time." She illustrated this with the example of the Fair Credit Reporting Act (FCRA) in the United States, which contains a relevance requirement. "After a certain period of time—seven years, in most cases—information about debt collections, civil lawsuits, tax liens, and even arrests for criminal offenses become 'obsolete' and must be taken out of consumer reports." This type of policy judgment, coupled with "specific obligations to allow consumers to exercise greater control over information about their lives, present and past," could begin to form the basis of a solution.

In a perfect world, of course, technology would help balance conflicts between privacy and free speech. But as you can see, digitization creates new challenges.

Nowhere is this truer than the clash between the First Amendment to the U.S. Constitution, which guarantees free speech, peaceable assembly, and more, and the Fourth Amendment, which protects individuals from unlawful search and seizures. Thanks to new innovation, it has never been easier for a government to violate the privacy of its citizenry in the name of protecting them.

Safe but Not Secure: The Contents of Your Head

People have a right to privacy.

So says Apple CEO Tim Cook.

In the Fall of 2014, his company was challenged by the security community for equipping its latest innovation, the iPhone 6, with end-to-end encryption. For the uninitiated, end-to-end encryption is technology that essentially makes a device impossible to compromise. With the technology, third parties cannot unlock the phone or view its contents.

One of those who objected to Apple's decision most vociferously was FBI director James Comey, who complained that it would take "more than five-and-a-half years to try all combinations of a six-character alphanumeric passcode with lowercase letters and numbers" to crack into the phone, according to *Time Magazine*.[40]

That's exactly the point, said the Apple chief executive.

When told that his company's devices were aiding pedophiles and terrorists, Cook took the moment to remind everyone of the right to be left alone that is enshrined in U.S. law. In an interview with PBS and CBS correspondent Charlie Rose, Cook established where Apple stood on the issue of government intrusion. "People have a right to privacy," he said bluntly. "And I think that's going to be a very key topic over the next year or so."[41]

Throughout 2014, security interests and civil libertarians battled over the government's need to protect its citizenry and an individual person's rights to privacy. In November and again in January 2015, one of the staunchest, pro-security legislators in the Utah House of Representatives threatened to sponsor legislation that would have essentially cut off the water supply to the super-secret, $1.7 billion data center that the NSA built in the Utah desert in the aftermath of 9/11. When he learned that workers at the facility had the capacity to listen in on every telephone call and email conversation in the country, he became outraged.[42]

Anger over governmental oversight came to a head in June 2014 when the U.S. Supreme Court ruled on whether local law enforcement officers could compel individuals to divulge the contents of their personal devices the way they can force suspects to surrender the contents of their pockets. In a rare, unanimous 9-0 decision, the court ruled in the case of Riley versus California that the government cannot search a suspect's mobile phone without permission or a warrant.[43]

While civil libertarians celebrated, security professionals fumed. At a news conference after the decision was handed down, FBI director Comey expressed his concerns in the strongest of terms.

"What concerns me about this is companies marketing something expressly to allow people to hold themselves beyond the law," he said. "The notion that someone would market a closet that could never be opened—even if it involves a case involving a child kidnapper and a court order—to me does not make any sense."[44]

In the days before Snowden, his words might have gotten more traction. But in the aftermath of the debacle involving the former NSA contractor, who revealed the depths of spying undertaken by the U.S. government through a series of leaked documents provided to *The Guardian* newspaper and other outlets in 2013, the words fell flat.[45] Even conservative U.S. Supreme Court Chief Justice John Roberts thought the government's contention that the data contained in a mobile smart phone were no different than the contents of a wallet failed to pass the sniff test.[46]

Writing for the court, Roberts said, "That is like saying a ride on horseback is materially indistinguishable from a flight to the moon. Both are ways of getting from point A to point B, but little else justifies lumping them together. Modern cell phones, as a category, implicate privacy concerns far beyond those implicated by the search of a cigarette pack, a wallet, or a purse."[47]

"Before cell phones," Roberts also concluded, "a search of a person was limited by physical realities and tended as a general matter to constitute only a narrow intrusion on privacy.... Today, by contrast, it is no exaggeration to say that many of the more than 90 percent of Americans who own a cell phone keep on their person a digital record of nearly every aspect of their lives—from the mundane to the intimate."[48]

The Court's decision, as well of that of Apple, Google, and others to increase privacy protections for consumers, highlights what *The*

Wall Street Journal called "the continuing challenge for law enforcement in responding to new technologies."

In an article from September 2014, the newspaper summed:

"Other innovations, such as texting, instant messaging and video-game chats, created hurdles to monitoring communication, though law-enforcement agencies in almost every instance eventually found ways to overcome them. But this time, two of the best-known U.S. companies are advertising that their phone systems may be able to beat a court order, and putting the technology in the hands of tens of millions of people."[49]

In an interview with *The Wall Street Journal*, Brian Pascal, a fellow at Stanford University who has worked on privacy issues at Palantir Technologies Inc. and IBM, said, "All of a sudden, a for-profit company has decided, 'We're going to step in and be the first line of defense for customers against their own government.'"[50]

It was a remarkable observation considering the number of technologies being developed for the Internet of Everything that will make it easier than ever for the government to intrude into the lives of everyday citizens. This includes spy technologies such as the "dirtboxes" that the Department of Justice has mounted on the bottom of small airplanes to track the smart devices of suspected criminals (not to mention anyone else who happened to be in their vicinity) and consumer technologies such as WiFi-enabled cars that can be hacked using basic computer skills.[51]

Speaking at a technology conference in 2012, then CIA Director David Petraeus said smart, connected devices provide members of the clandestine tradecraft an unprecedented and "transformational" opportunity to keep tabs on individuals.

"Items of interest will be located, identified, monitored, and remotely controlled through technologies such as radio-frequency identification, sensor networks, tiny embedded servers, and energy harvesters—all connected to the next-generation internet using abundant, low-cost, and high-power computing," Petraeus said.[52]

What technologies will allow this? Everything from individual cloud storage accounts used for archiving photos to connected appliances designed for personal convenience, wrote *Wired* magazine in

2012. "With the rise of the 'smart home,' you'd be sending tagged, geolocated data that a spy agency can intercept in real time when you use the lighting app on your phone to adjust your living room's ambiance," the magazine reported.[53]

Clearly the potential for abuse is there. This is especially true in the aftermath of new revelations that the U.S. Department of Justice and Drug Enforcement Agency was tracking international phone calls for "nearly a decade before the Sept. 11 terrorist attacks," according to *USA Today* and other media outlets.[54] In an attempt to better protect its citizenry, various authorities have gone to extreme measures to monitor communications and track individuals' activities. Some of these measures have, obviously, completely trampled on personal privacy either guaranteed outright by law or implied by decades of government restraint.

In response to these developments, private groups and business interests have proposed that governments and other controlling authorities adopt reasonable guidelines that would serve as "rules of the road" for preserving privacy in the IoE-enabled era. AOL, Apple, Dropbox, Evernote, Facebook, Google, LinkedIn, Microsoft, Twitter, and Yahoo have banded together under the aegis of the "Reform Government Surveillance" coalition, with "the goals of ensuring that government law enforcement and intelligence efforts are rule-bound, narrowly tailored, transparent, and subject to oversight." The principles they espouse include limiting governments' authority to collect users' information, oversight and accountability, transparency about government demands, respecting the free flow of information, and avoiding conflicts among governments.[55]

Similarly, Cisco has assembled a list of principles that it wants governments around the world to adopt. Specifically, they call upon governments to not interfere with the lawful delivery of products in the form in which they have been manufactured, not seek the inclusion of undocumented backdoors into IT technologies delivered to the commercial marketplace, not interfere with the private sector's development or use of encryption technologies to protect the privacy and security of customers, and not demand the release of source code, which could facilitate the development of offensive capabilities. Cisco has also asked governments not to develop guidelines that require companies to collect and retain records of customer communications or transactions and not to create conflicts of laws by demanding access to data across national borders instead of leveraging bilateral or Mutual Legal Assistance Treaty (MLAT) procedures.

The latter is particularly contentious given the effort of several national governments to create laws relating to data sovereignty and data residency. Developed at least in part in response to the U.S. government's data-collection efforts, foreign governments from Brazil to Russia to China have passed laws and the EU Member States are requiring similar measures that restrict flows of data outside their territory, require local storage, or assert jurisdiction over data in ways that conflict with other territories.

Intel's David Hoffman sees three distinct approaches that countries are adopting toward data localization: asking for data to be stored locally in-country and in a format that can be accessed locally (the Russia/India approach), asking that data not go somewhere else where someone else (for example, the NSA) can access it (the Germany/Brazil approach), and using privacy and security concerns as a smokescreen to protect local industry competitively (the China approach).[56]

While often drafted to protect the privacy of individual citizens, these laws can disrupt the opportunity of people to make use of innovative cloud services and might make it impossible for them to use credit cards outside their home country or travel on an electronic ticket issued by an air carrier based outside their homeland.

Although such laws aren't a reasonable fix, they are one indication of how concerned individuals and governments alike are when it comes to government surveillance. That goes for citizens of Europe, Asia, South America, the United States, and everywhere in between.

Another indication? An April 2015 video featuring an interview between TV host and comedian John Oliver and NSA whistleblower Edward Snowden. In the week after the interview aired on HBO, it was viewed nearly 5 million times on the Internet. As of this writing, it has been viewed more than 9 million times.[57]

Bowed but Not Broken: The Evolution of Privacy

The monetization of you. The right to be forgotten. The contents of your head.

Or, as we mentioned earlier, privacy versus profit, privacy versus free speech, and privacy versus security.

More than mere abstract concepts, these privacy issues loom large in a world where everything is connected.

As more people connect to the Internet of Everything in different ways, their rights to privacy will be further tested by for-profit organizations or individuals hoping to make money with personal data.

Privacy will also be tested by the well-meaning interests of the legal, media, and non-profit worlds—they want to serve the greater community good by promoting free speech at every turn, sometimes at the expense of individual liberty.

Then there are the very guardians whose mission it is to ensure our security: the men and women who work for various security branches of our governments. As they expand their use of the IoE, they, too, will threaten privacy as we know it.

In response, powerful forces are converging to preserve what's become of privacy and redefine it for a new generation. This includes no less than U.S. Supreme Court Justice Sonya Sotomayor, who helped the court come to grips with the new way to apply the right to privacy in an opinion issued in 2012. Writing in support of the majority decision to require law enforcement to secure a warrant before tracking a suspect's vehicle with a GPS device, Justice Sotomayor noted that "it may be necessary to reconsider the premise that an individual has no reasonable expectation of privacy in information voluntarily disclosed to third parties."[58]

In the digital age, she wrote, "people reveal a great deal of information about themselves to third parties in the course of carrying out mundane tasks. People disclose the phone numbers that they dial or text to their cellular providers; the URLs that they visit and the e-mail addresses with which they correspond to their Internet service providers; and the books, groceries, and medications they purchase to online retailers."[59]

While people have shown a willingness to trade some secrecy for convenience, she added, they expect their right to privacy to be preserved. This includes who has access to their data and how that data is put to use. They want trust and transparency, in other words. When they don't get it, they expect accountability still.

To legal scholar and Microsoft General Counsel Brad Smith, this is the new understanding of privacy. Speaking at a gathering at the Brookings Institute in 2014,[60] he said the meaning of privacy evolves as new technologies and ideas come forward. But its value doesn't wane.

For example, your digital footprint can be mined to infer a lot about you. And it may exist for a long time in a manner that cannot be changed by you. Does that mean that your digital footprint becomes as immutable as, say, your race? And how can that be used or abused?[61]

As consumers and watchdogs get a better handle on the scope of the challenges to privacy that digitization creates, they have been better able to articulate their expectations and demands to private technology companies and the government itself. These efforts have helped shore up privacy since the Snowden revelations and other technology-related developments.

Take consumer behavior.

Today, more consumers than ever are weighing in on how companies use their private information. As a result of the immediate, global, and public discourse that consumers can create with social media, the pressure on profit-minded interests to make their actions more transparent has never been greater.

In addition to consumers, many legislators have stepped up efforts to shore up privacy laws. Today about 100 countries have privacy laws on their books protecting individual citizens. A generation ago, the number was far smaller.[62] And more laws are being proposed every year. In California alone, more than 30 new privacy bills were introduced during the state's legislative session in 2013. While not every bill passed, important laws protecting student privacy, consumer data integrity, and "revenge porn" victims were signed into law by Governor Jerry Brown in October 2014. A year later, additional laws strengthening privacy and consumer protection were signed by the Governor.[63]

If you value privacy, these and other developments—including the Supreme Court's decision to require law enforcement to get permission or a warrant before searching your phone—should give you hope. When taken as a whole, it is clear that the convergence of evolving public attitudes, governmental reaction, and corporate accountability is having a positive effect.

While some worry that the threats to privacy posed by digitization and the IoE are unprecedented, Smith and others point out that privacy has been imperiled before.[64]

Consider that when United States' founding father John Adams was president, concerns over possible spy activity in the newly minted country led to the passage of the Alien and Sedition Act of 1798, which curtailed individual freedoms. Sixty-four years later, during the Civil War, President Abraham Lincoln suspended the Writ of *Habeas Corpus*, which is the right of any imprisoned person to ask to be brought before a court. Lincoln decided to compromise individual liberty in the name of public safety. So did President Franklin Roosevelt when he ordered the internment of Japanese-American citizens in 1942 in response to the attacks on Pearl Harbor, which pushed the U.S. into World War II.

After each of these instances, public outcry, governmental action, and industry response stepped up to restore the freedoms that were taken away or compromised.

As Microsoft's Smith posed to his audience at the Brookings Institute in 2014, "There have been...multiple times in the nation's history when steps were taken in a moment of crisis to protect the public safety. But ultimately when the moment has passed, the question has always arisen: Where should the pendulum rest once that moment has come to an end?"[65]

For nearly 250 years, the values enshrined in the Bill of Rights have withstood the assault of war, the challenge of shifting public attitudes, and the mind-boggling pace of innovation.

Though it will undoubtedly evolve and be tested or abused from time to time, I believe privacy will survive and thrive in the digital era.

7

Security
Before, During, and After an Attack[*]

Ten percent off housewares, clothing, personal care items, and more.

In the chaotic, uncertain days after discovering that it had just suffered one of the largest commercial data breaches in U.S. corporate history—one that put millions of customers' credit card and personal information at risk—officials at retail giant Target made this offer in an attempt to restore customer faith and inspire investor confidence in the beleaguered Minneapolis-based retailer.[1]

By almost any measure, the limited-time offer came up short.

Instead of rallying around the company, which boasts 1,800 stores nationwide,[2] outsiders treated it warily in December 2013, which was not surprising considering the company had what amounted to a 21st-century version of a feared contagion: malware. Malware is computer code written with the specific intent to cause harm. Instead of people, it infects computers, networks, smart devices, and, in the case of Target, digital cash registers. When customers used their credit cards at infected Target stores, malware was able to capture their digital information and crack open a digital back door at Target headquarters so that cyber criminals could abscond with it.

When it was all said and done, the malware that was inserted into Target's digital systems by cyber thieves cost the company millions of

---

[*] For their guidance with this chapter, I am grateful to Chris Young, President of Intel Security; Amit Yoran, President of RSA; John Stewart, Chief Security Officer of Cisco; and Michael Siegel, Principal Research Scientist and Associate Director of MIT's Interdisciplinary Consortium for Improving Critical Infrastructure Cybersecurity, known as MIT-(IC)[3].

dollars and incalculable goodwill with consumers. It also cost then CEO Greg Steinhafel, as well as several of Target's senior managers, their jobs.

So how did the nation's fifth largest retail giant—behind Walmart, Kroger, The Home Depot, and Costco—wind up as the poster child for corporate cybercrime?[3] The answer might surprise you. The back door that hackers used to infiltrate one of the most sophisticated companies in all of retailing was left open by an unlikely source: a third-party contractor that provided maintenance services on Target's heating, ventilation, and air-conditioning (HVAC) systems. That's right: the demise of one of the highest-flying CEOs in all of American retailing can be traced to a single piece of electronic spam that an employee of an outside HVAC service and supply company clicked on.

Here's how.

As part of its contract with Target, Fazio Mechanical Services of Sharpsburg, Pa., was granted access to Target's corporate network so that it could electronically bid for work, submit contracts, and remotely manage projects. After one of its employees clicked on an email solicitation infested with a software virus in early summer 2013, the employee's computer became infected with malware. That malware began to spread throughout the offices of Fazio, providing hackers access to the contents of its employees' hard drives and the company's data servers. When one of the hackers noticed the access code to the Target corporate network, the hacker used it to log on and spread his malware to Target.[4]

Soon, criminals found themselves behind the retailer's locked doors and electronic firewalls, free to rummage through its vast troves of electronic files and promulgate their malware to as many devices as possible. This included the point-of-sale (POS) devices used in more than 1,800 Target stores in the U.S. After "casing the joint" from within for several months, the criminals appropriated customer credit card numbers and personal identification credentials, including email addresses and PINs.[5]

Once they had that info and began putting it to use in late November 2013, banks across the U.S. began seeing an alarming number of suspicious credit card transactions. The common denominator behind each card in question: every one had been used at a Target store within a few days of one another. In cybersecurity circles, that's the functional equivalent of a smoking gun.[6]

As for Target's top man, Steinhafel said he did not learn of the break-in until Sunday, Dec. 15. He told CNBC that he was having coffee with his wife in their suburban Minneapolis kitchen when his phone rang with the bad news.[7]

The following day, Target began notifying payment processors and card networks of a potential problem. But it kept word of the security breach from consumers. On Dec. 17, computer expert, popular security blogger, and author Brian Krebs got wind of the story and reached out to Target for comment. As he told NPR interviewer and host Terry Gross afterward, Target officials rebuffed his inquiries by telling him to "talk to the hand."[8]

Not one to be thrown off the scent so easily, Krebs continued investigating the story and published a blog on Dec. 18, "Sources: Target Investigating Data Breach," that broke the story wide open.[9] Within hours, news media from all over the world were jumping on the news. The following morning, Target released a statement confirming that it was "aware of unauthorized access to payment card data that may have impacted certain guests making credit and debit card purchases in its U.S. stores."[10] Not until the third paragraph did Target reveal that "approximately 40 million credit and debit card accounts may have been impacted between Nov. 27 and Dec. 15, 2013."[11]

While Wall Street preoccupied itself with the company's sales results from Black Friday, the cybersecurity community was growing very uneasy. Forty million records compromised? That was a big deal to security experts. In what turned out to be an almost foreboding understatement, Krebs signed off his explosive post on the 18th with the following: "This is likely to be a fast-moving story. Stay tuned for updates as they become available."[12]

They came fast and furious.

Within days, Target disclosed that the number of consumers impacted was not 40 million but 70 million, instead.[13]

In mid-January 2014, Steinhafel went on CNBC to apologize to consumers and vow to put things right. How he would do that was not exactly clear.[14]

The following month, Target CFO John Mulligan testified to the Senate Committee on the Judiciary about the data breach.[15] A few weeks later, he was back in Washington testifying before the Senate Committee On Commerce, Science, and Transportation.[16]

Over the winter, Target began revealing the toll associated with the massive breach. When it reported year-end 2013 earnings, for example, Target said it incurred $61 million in unexpected costs relating to the cyber break-in.[17] Target also said that customer wariness over the company's credit card systems contributed to a 46 percent decline in 2013 fourth quarter income. (The total sum would eventually reach more than $160 million by early 2015.)[18]

After Target's finances started going south, so did the careers of some of its top executives. Executive Vice President and Chief Information Officer Beth Jacob was the first to go.[19] Then in May, Steinhafel was fired.[20]

As with so many other fiascoes, a post mortem of the events surrounding the attack on Target revealed that the entire episode could have been avoided without human intervention if only its information technology technicians had properly configured their IT systems and devices. Even after the attack had begun, Target could have prevented a major catastrophe if company officials had heeded warnings sent to their mobile devices and email boxes, concluded a U.S. Senate Commerce, Science and Transportation Committee report on the episode. In its "A 'Kill Chain' Analysis of the 2013 Target Data Breach," Senate staffers noted that Target "failed to respond to multiple automated warnings from the company's anti-intrusion software."[21]

Afterward, Target tried to make amends by offering customers a year's worth of free credit-report monitoring.[22] But that only drew scorn from experts. The offer, which has become the default *modus operandi* of hacked organizations, according to Krebs, requires wary consumers to turn over *more* of their personal information to third-party companies that are in the business of selling consumer profiles for a profit. One of them, Experian-owned Court Ventures, has unwittingly sold information to criminals. They and the others, meanwhile, are targeted every day by some of the most sophisticated cyber thieves on earth. The fact that Target thought that a free, one-year agreement with these companies would appeal to consumers who had just been compromised is laughable, Krebs adds. In an editorial that appeared in *The Guardian*, he summed up what many in the security community felt about the entire incident.

"It's now clear that Target and other major retailers have been spending money in the wrong places—and that they've left a gaping hole in the Internet for hackers to keep stealing yours," wrote Krebs. "By the time the industry grasps that a bottomless budget for security software, hardware and services means little if you don't have the empowered geeks to help recognize a breach early on, it may already be too late."[23]

He's right, of course. Target should have mobilized greater resources to help impacted customers and remediate its defenses. But all of this speaks to a broader problem: Internet security in the modern age has to move beyond the conventional thinking that protects perimeters with guns, guards, and gates. Today, the new paradigm must prioritize data and systems that are located everywhere and create ways to protect them with insights and innovation. This is especially critical as the Internet of Everything (IoE) takes shape. Thanks to the ubiquity of the IoE, there will be no clear-cut boundary as to what is and what is not behind a firewall, for example. Again, take Target.

As mentioned, the back door to Target was unwittingly left open by an HVAC contractor that had access to Target's corporate network. While the company did not remotely manage Target's HVAC's systems over the Internet, that capability is real. As more organizations leverage the ability to remotely monitor things that were once offline and considered "dumb," at least digitally, hackers will have many more entry points from where they can launch their mayhem.

This is already raising significant alarm among healthcare professionals who worry about the vulnerability of insulin pumps, defibrillators, and other medical devices that are connected to the Internet, and consumer watchdogs who have chronicled hacks on everything from automobiles to baby monitors to lightbulbs to, yes, thermostats—the kind that HVAC professionals remotely monitor every day.

Why is security so hard?

Chris Young, president of Intel Security, points to a few things. "In most organizations, most things can be measured and hence managed. But with security you don't have that," he says. "There is not a good standard lexicon, nor a good standard methodology through which a CEO can really understand how vulnerable they are. In many instances, a CEO doesn't even know what questions to ask the Chief Security Officer. The CEO's biggest concern is 'what do I not know?'"[24]

To Young and other security experts, there are three forces at work in security today: the first is that the attack landscape is changing, with attackers getting more sophisticated. The second is that there is more surface area to attack. And finally, the complexity and fragmentation that comes from running a mix of new and legacy systems across an organization creates an enormous burden.

"We're not going to solve this problem with the next appliance or the next software application," adds Young. "This is a highly complex problem where you've got a massively diverse attacker community that's out there with very different motives and approaches. You've got a hugely decreasing cost of an attack because the tools and the capabilities are becoming cheaper and easier to use. What is more, the sophistication levels are going up, while the consequences are still relatively low. So to assume that you're just going to be able to just throw technology at the problem to solve it with some silver bullet is not going to happen."

Amit Yoran, the President of RSA, offers a sobering assessment. "Every modern nation state, and every organized crime element operate intelligence collection and monetization schemes online. They enjoy limitless bounty and perfect impunity."[25]

If you're beginning to have second thoughts about the viability of the IoE, or the entire drive toward complete digitization, don't. For starters, there is no stopping its roll out, especially given benefits such as compelling operational efficiency, revenue potential, reduced environmental footprint, and convenience. But more importantly, there is a way to properly secure the modern technology landscape—not with a silver bullet that Young mentioned, but with strategic thinking and determined actions. This idea doesn't revolve around any one technology per se or any particular philosophy. Instead, it tackles the problem of Internet security by focusing on the attack continuum. This means taking the right steps *before* an attack occurs, the proper ones *during* an episode, and the smart ones *after*. Cisco refers to it as the "Before-During-After" framework. Young, meanwhile, refers to it as the "Protect-Detect-Correct" approach, which is a modified version of a strategy developed by the U.S. Commerce Department's National Institute of Standards and Technology (NIST).

No matter what you call it, the underlying theme here is that there are certain actions and ideas that consumers and organizations can leverage to increase their security in each phase. While they each have the same ultimate objective, which is to increase security, these actions and associated ideas have distinct characteristics and considerations. In the sections that follow, I'll go through them one by one. Let's start with the right steps *before* disaster strikes.

Before the Dam Breaks: Building Trust Instead of Borders

If you're into home automation, one of the most desirable capabilities is the ability to control any appliance in your home from a single device. Want to turn on a light? Change the channel on a TV? Lower the blinds? With the right equipment and proper settings, you can.

If you want to see this capability for yourself, you can attend a home automation trade event, visit a local home automation showroom, or check into one of a growing number of luxury hotels where the technology is on display. The glamorous St. Regis Shenzhen is one such place. Situated in the heart of the Luohu District Financial Center, the hotel's 297 guest rooms and suites are equipped with what the St. Regis calls "signature St. Regis amenities and floor-to-ceiling windows with sumptuous bespoke décor and state-of-the-art technology."[26] This includes an iPad 2 remote that can control virtually everything in a guest room. Think lights, blinds, entertainment systems, and more.[27] While dazzling, the technology was, until recently, burdened with one spectacular flaw: it had no security, says San Francisco security consultant Jesus Molina.

A former researcher for Fujitsu, Molina has served as a chair at the Trusted Computing Group, as a National Sciences Foundation (NSF) grant reviewer, and as a guest editor at the IEEE *Security & Privacy* journal.[28] Among other things, he's known for his work in offensive security research around smart meters and other technologies. He is a frequent speaker and commentator in the security field and is taken seriously just about everywhere he goes.

When he visited the St. Regis Hotel in Shenzhen in 2013, Molina was struck by the in-room iPad 2. After playing with the device and marveling at its capabilities to work as a remote, he began to wonder if he could instead control the room with his laptop. After some effort, he found he could turn on a light in his room. Then he wondered if he could control other things in his room. After some experimentation, he found he could control not only the things in his room, but in every single other room in the hotel. He could change the channel on every TV, raise or lower all of the blinds, or crank the music whenever he wanted.[29]

And he could do so without being detected by anyone or anything.

How? By simply exploiting three different and, in retrospect, questionable technology decisions made by the hotel's administrators. First was their decision to deploy unsecured iPads that any guest could use or tamper with. Second was their decision to connect the iPads to the same network that guests used when connecting their personal devices to the Internet. And third was the administrators' failure to put sufficient safeguards in place to protect the integrity of their network.

Without getting too technical, the hotel used a common protocol to connect the iPads to the in-room entertainment system, the lighting system, and the blinds. It did this so that all of the devices could essentially talk to each other and be understood. This is quite common when integrating technologies that rely on different standards as manufacturers of various devices connect their goods to the IoE.

In the case of the St. Regis Shenzhen, the hotel chose the most commonly used home automation protocol used in China, KNX. KNX was developed for wired devices in the 1990s. Because wired devices connected to one another over short distances are difficult to hack, the original developers of KNX didn't put much security into it. When KNX was later modified to connect wireless devices to one another, it became a liability ripe for exploitation, explains Molina.

With some basic programming, the hotel was able to use KNX to establish a reliable connection between the in-room devices and the iPads. When it did, it was able to dazzle guests and enthusiasts alike. But in its haste to deploy the technology, the hotel failed to secure these connections, leaving its devices vulnerable to electronic manipulation.

Which is what Molina did.

With a modest amount of effort and some simple guesswork, he was able to make a map of the hotel's IP addresses. From there, he could control almost anything in the room that was connected to the network. In a YouTube video of his speech at the DEF CON 22 security conference in 2014, he explained how.[30]

Molina was so stunned by his ability to access devices throughout the hotel that he decided to go straight to hotel management and tell them about his experiences. In what he later described as one of the most "awkward" conversations of his life, he spoke to the Chief Information Officer (CIO) of Starwood, which manages the St. Regis Shenzhen, and the company's attorney.[31]

Clearly interested in what he had to say, Molina was asked by the hotel chain's head of information what was the worst that could happen to its facilities and guests given its current set up. Molina knew a real hacker could do unbelievable mayhem. But he framed his answer in terms that a consumer-oriented, service-minded company would understand clearly: Would a guest likely stay in your hotel if he or she knew that someone else could control the major appliances in their room, including ones that might one day have a camera?

The hotel executives thought long and hard about his answer. Then they did something smart: They asked Molina for his advice, which he gladly shared. First, he told them, update security policies whenever new technologies are introduced. Second, make sure that any open protocols used to connect disparate devices have adequate security, and, finally, create securable barriers between networks used by guests and hotel administrators.

Take control of devices, harden vulnerabilities, and enforce security policies, he essentially advises.

"The good thing is that this is a story with a happy ending," says Molina. "They disabled the system right away, and they have changed their policies for all of their hotels, which includes the Sheratons, St. Regis, etc., because of this."[32]

While the hotel chain listened, others have simply shrugged when he's spoken out on corporate and personal security. "Why should I care if someone can turn my light on?" some ask him. Molina insists there's a bigger issue afoot than mere inconvenience: peace of mind. If others can control the devices around us at their will, they could eventually control us, he says.

Fortunately, there are basic steps that organizations and individuals can take *before* an attack occurs. This is the period to install proper firewalls, set up virtual private networks (VPNs), and embrace unified threat management tools (UTMs) and other advanced security tools. It's also the time for developing policies and procedures for monitoring threats, especially those that target older technologies that have been modified to work in the interconnected digital world, and for performing the associated analytics and enlisting proper security services that might be needed. It is the time to have a clear "fail-safe" mode of operation that defines what has to stay running. It's also the time to create "Red Teams" of internal "hackers" whose job is to spot weaknesses or exploit deficiencies before an intruder does. Some tech companies have gone so far as to pay outsiders money for finding vulnerabilities in their commercial products. Microsoft, for example, has offered up to $15,000 to anyone who can find a critical flaw in its new Spartan browser, which goes with Microsoft's newest operating system, Windows 10.[33]

The key, of course, is to anticipate all of the inter-dependencies and dynamic vulnerabilities that exist throughout a modern digital environment. This includes technologies at all levels of the classic technology stack—from chips to motherboards, storage systems, operating systems, networking protocols, applications, and more. While traditional hacks have targeted the lower end of the stack, where damage can be done more broadly, newer attacks have focused on technologies higher up the stack, including end points and email systems, which present new vulnerability challenges to security professionals.

One good place to start with your "before" preparation is with the security reports produced by "security equipment and software manufacturers, security service companies, Internet service providers, and other security associations," says Scott Hogg, Chief Technology Officer at Global Technology Resources, Inc. (GTRI), a Denver-based technology consultancy. Writing for *Network World* in 2015, Hogg recommended security professionals make a commitment to pore over the Verizon Data Breach Investigations Report, the Cisco Systems Annual Security Report, the Microsoft Security Intelligence Report, and the annual Ponemon Institute report, among others.[34]

"Parallels can be drawn between IT security and using dental floss," Hogg wrote. "We know that using dental floss can add years to your life expectancy but it requires discipline and a small time commitment every day. Similarly, IT security requires a relatively small capital investment and a relatively small investment in time to configure granular policies and be vigilant."[35]

While this advice sounds simple, it isn't always easy to implement.

For starters, customers need to know what they are defending against, which is difficult given the number and diversity of the attacks that occur on a daily basis. Security software specialist Kaspersky Labs identifies 325,000 new malicious files online every day.[36] That's nearly 120 million per year. For an idea of what that looks like visually, the company developed an interactive map of the earth that shows where and when attacks are occurring day and night. The map, which is available online at http://cybermap.kaspersky.com, is a blur of changing colors and frenetic activity. If you've ever seen a dynamic map of global airline flight schedules, you get the idea.

For all its visual impact, however, there is one important thing to note about cyber attacks, concludes Verizon's 2014 Data Breach Investigations Report. "The universe of threats may seem limitless, but 92 percent of the 100,000 incidents we've analyzed from the last 10 years can be described by just nine basic patterns," researchers note.[37]

The nine categories include cyber espionage, denial-of-service (DOS) attacks, Web application attacks, payment card skimmers, malware, insider misuse, and so on. While the nature of these attacks vary, organizations can blunt the impact of many of these intrusions before they occur with proper planning and up-to-date technology.

RSA's president, Amit Yoran, says that it is important to "have some cadre of people who really know their stuff, are passionate about security, have a hunting mindset, and an inquisitive personality. That is because this is an asymmetric battle—the Department of Defense may claim that they have 50,000 cyber warriors—what matters most is who are the key ones. You have to scale up, not scale out."[38]

Another way to drive security discipline is to align incentives and leverage enforceable legal frameworks. Alex 'Sandy' Pentland, a professor at MIT and the creator of the famed MIT Media Lab, points out that the reason the SWIFT banking network, which transacts $3 trillion of currency every day, has not been breached despite having thousands of participating banks in scores of countries around the world is partly because they have enforceable contracts, with clear costs of non-compliance, that the participating institutions understand. Coupled with appropriate technology, this system of common contracts and clear incentives/penalties has so far proven effective in ensuring security.[39]

But even the best of intentions won't guarantee absolute protection. As John Stewart, Cisco's Chief Security Officer, says, "I don't think anyone feels comfortable—myself included—that anyone has this totally under control."[40] This is because one or more attacks will likely defeat your defenses. The key is knowing when they happen. Unfortunately, many intrusions go undetected until it's too late.

This is why it is so important to have a plan for what to do *during* a cyberattack, which could be sooner rather than later.

Under Fire: Springing to Action During an Attack

In early January 2015, finance giant Morgan Stanley did what every brokerage firm dreads: it contacted clients to inform them that their account names and numbers had been compromised. (It had to because New York, along with 46 other states plus the District of Columbia, Guam, Puerto Rico, and the Virgin Islands, has legislation that requires private or government entities to notify individuals of security breaches of information involving personally identifiable information, according to the National Conference of State Legislatures.)[41]

A rogue Morgan Stanley employee looking to make some money by selling client information was found to be behind the theft. The individual allegedly stole information on roughly 350,000 of the company's wealth management clients and posted data on approximately 900 of them in an attempt to attract cyber criminals who troll the Internet for this type of information, said *The Wall Street Journal*.[42]

In a statement, Morgan Stanley said the employee was terminated and that law enforcement and regulatory authorities were advised of the incident. To the best of its reckoning, none of Morgan Stanley's clients lost any money and no account passwords or social security numbers were believed to have been stolen.[43]

But still, you might wonder, how could a blue-chip financial giant whose very livelihood depends on customer privacy and organizational security sustain such a blow without realizing it before it was too late?

Experts say the question isn't "how" but "when." Sooner or later, they agree, every major employer in the U.S.—and plenty of smaller ones, too—will be the victim of a cybercrime. It could be an inside job (employee mischief is one of the most common security threats facing organizations today, according to Verizon's 2014 Data Breach Investigations Report), an outside hack from a rogue, criminal outfit, or even a concerted effort to purloin trade secrets coordinated by a state-sponsored espionage team.

In the past when they detected an assault, IT managers have typically reacted by cancelling staff vacations, calling in outside experts, quarantining certain areas of the network, and even temporarily shutting down their systems. All of these actions are perfectly rational responses to a cyberassault. But they have one shortcoming: They only work if you are aware you are under attack.

What if you are under attack and don't know it? It happens a lot more than you think. Take Sony Entertainment. No one is likely to forget the damage that it sustained after it was hacked before the release of its controversial film *The Interview*, which tells a fictional story involving the assassination of North Korean leader Kim Jong-Un. The intrusion led to the release of private corporate documents as well as the personal information (including medical records) of thousands of Sony employees, their spouses, and their children.[44] In one email exchange, Sony executives exchanged racially insensitive jokes about President Obama, according to *The Hollywood Reporter*.[45] In another, a Sony executive called actor Kevin Hart a "whore" for asking for more money to promote a movie via social media.[46]

In the aftermath of the debacle, there were heated debates within the security community about whether the cyberattack was done by angry North Koreans or a disgruntled company insider. Lost amid the dispute was one noteworthy point: While the attack was occurring, Sony was completely unaware of it.

By any measure, Sony failed miserably in the *during* phase. It is hardly alone. In a chilling interview on global cybersecurity with *60 Minutes* that aired in October 2014, FBI Director James Comey said that there were two kinds of big companies in the U.S.: "those who've been hacked by the Chinese, and those who don't know they've been hacked by the Chinese."[47]

Those that don't know that they have been hacked are especially vulnerable to damage because, unlike a "smash and grab job," criminals can take their time to inflict maximum harm. They can peruse network connections, analyze proprietary data, and even infiltrate business applications. They can also install malware that adds itself to as many devices as possible, key-stroke readers that remotely copy every password that users create, and even computer worms that can manipulate software code that controls everything from traffic signals to industrial machines to power grids.

This is true regardless of whether an attack is originated by a Chinese hacker, a West African scammer, or a neighborhood kid down the block.

So how does a company protect itself *during* an attack? The key is to think about the problem in a new way. Instead of viewing attacks as one-time episodes, business and community leaders should think of them the way that hospital administrators do about emergencies. While every case in the Emergency Room is distinct, traumas are constant. Managing the crisis continuum, thus, is a never-ending pursuit.

Once organizations embrace the idea that they are constantly under attack, they are more likely to do the things required to detect, block, and defend attacks that come their way. Companies that assume they are under attack at all times are much more likely to monitor their email and web traffic continuously, for example. They are also more likely to take alerts—the kind that Target officials ignored—more seriously. And they are more likely to avail themselves of innovations designed to blunt ongoing threats.

Take Cisco. Based in San Jose in the heart of Silicon Valley, Cisco is the world's largest developer of Internet technology. If you make a phone call from work, send an email from home, or tweet about a traffic snarl from your car, chances are high that your interaction will touch some piece of Cisco gear or software along its digital journey.

Today, Cisco employs 70,000 people and engages another 50,000 outside contractors. With a global footprint in more than 130 countries, the company also relies on an additional 85,000 business partners and hundreds of suppliers and manufacturers on a daily basis. Because of the complexity of its operations and the virtual nature of its workforce, protecting intellectual property is a significant challenge for the company. This is especially true when you consider that cyber criminals will pay millions of dollars for a single blueprint of one of Cisco's advanced product designs.

The job of protecting Cisco's intellectual property from hackers falls to Steve Martino, Cisco's Vice President of Security. Like a lot of professionals, Martino understands that it is impossible to prevent every attack beforehand. So in addition to meticulous preparation *before* an attack or theft, he devotes a great deal of time looking for suspicious activity that might be occurring right under Cisco's nose. *During* is just as critical to organizational security as *before*, in other words.

"If you think about some of the big breaches that have hit the news, they didn't happen in two weeks. The damage done at Target took months. Our goal is to detect crimes in 24 hours and contain them within 36 hours so you don't have those kind of events," says Martino. Ninety percent of the time, he says, Cisco hits its objective. To reduce the other 10 percent, Martino has worked with Cisco engineers to develop better Advanced Threat Detection (ATD) tools and processes. Unfortunately, the better the visibility into the network threats that its tools provide, the more threats they detect.

"Everyone knows when an organization is getting hit with a denial of service (DoS), which is when spammers overwhelm a server with so much incoming traffic that it effectively blocks out all legitimate activity. But discrete, external events are only one form of attacks that companies must look out for," says Martino.

Two more insidious attacks that organizations must guard against at all times are ongoing, internal threats such as illegal file transfers and ongoing malware attacks that have proven extremely difficult to identify due to their increased sophistication.

One of the tools Cisco's uses to protect its intellectual property is its Intelligent Context Aware Monitoring (iCAM) technology. iCAM is a tool that helps Cisco detect abnormal behavior on its network. With iCAM in place, Cisco is able to identify data traffic patterns and then correlate them to user, device, and data profiles. If the software senses rogue or abnormal activity, it can send out alerts to network administrators and to managers in easily understandable language; they can then take steps to block individuals from doing additional harm to the company.

Today, iCAM oversees some 40 billion Cisco files that are stored on the company's network. Each day, it tracks more than 3 billion events collected from more than 14,000 servers globally. In addition, the system tracks data generated by more than 130,000 users and 200,000 devices. It also monitors 200 Cisco product profiles and 500 policy rules from multiple data sources.[48]

Since its implementation in 2011, iCAM has identified more than 240 confirmed incidents, saving the company an estimated $70 million in damages. This includes the time that a college intern tried transferring more than 4,000 source code files to his laptop the day before he left the company.

To combat advanced malware attacks, Cisco relies on ATD technology that studies viruses and looks for patterns among more than 25 million interactions and machine connections daily. When it identifies an anomaly, it alerts Cisco managers who can intercede.

With iCAM and ATD technology, Cisco is able to analyze both individual behaviors and organizational patterns. This helps it defend its systems, devices, applications, and data during the most aggressive attacks known.

But even Cisco knows that no single technology or policy can provide comprehensive protection for all conditions.

"What happens when that 5 percent slips through?" Martino wrote in a blog for Cisco in 2013. "A mitigation plan is critical. You need data collection processes, analytics and a dedicated team to spot these incidents before serious damage occurs. You also need processes to minimize damage and react to your business partners and customers with a precise and timely reaction to minimize any impact."[49]

This is especially true for the Internet of Everything, where threats will be targeted at devices that have historically been beyond the reach of hackers and cyber criminals. This includes power grids, building systems, automobiles, municipal works, medical devices, and more.

In the era of the Internet of Everything, new paradigms for reacting to cyberattacks will emerge. In the traditional world of information and communications technology, for example, protecting intellectual property and institutional assets was the single highest security priority. But in the world of the IoE, continuous availability will become an equally important priority, especially when it comes to physical safety. If you discovered that your PC or smart phone became infected with a virus, for example, you might want to shut it off immediately to contain the damage. But doing the same thing to an Internet-enabled vehicle on the open road might not be only inconvenient to its passenger, but potentially dangerous as well. The same is true for an attack on an insulin pump or traffic signal.

Another consideration? What to do about devices created with different design philosophies in mind. In the electronic world, smart digital devices were designed to be upgraded or retired after a mere few years. Not so in the industrial world, where power meters, railway switches, and assembly line robots were expected to be deployed for many years without enhancement. How does this model work in the era of the IoE, where new malware attacks are launched every day?

It doesn't, obviously—especially when you accept that *"during"* never ends.

After the Crisis: Picking Up the Pieces

As vital as it is to prepare accordingly *before* an attack and act appropriately *during* one, it is perhaps most important to act responsibly *after* disaster strikes. Why? Because brilliant plans created before an attack and admirable steps taken during one will count for nothing if an organization fumbles the aftermath.

Unfortunately, many organizations do not get this. This includes Target, obviously, but plenty of others with a footprint in the digital world. Take eBay, which boasts more than 150 million active users.[50] eBay, of course, is the world's largest online auction house, where virtually anything from a new car to used pair of socks can be bought. Since its founding in 1995, more than 200 million people have used the service. In 2013 alone, eBay handled more than 50 million transactions between customers who used the service on their PCs, smart phones, and other devices.[51]

For each of its customers, eBay has in its possession user account names, email addresses, mailing addresses, phone numbers, dates of birth and, in millions of instances, credit card numbers. As you can imagine, the company has spent millions of dollars on information security. It has also trained its employees on security prevention and defense. But after it was hacked in the winter of 2014 by an unauthorized person or persons who used an internal eBay corporate account to infiltrate the company network and then abscond with 233 million records, it was evident that eBay had no idea how to handle the *aftermath* of an attack.[52]

Rather than alert users directly that their personal information had been stolen, eBay posted an innocuous note on its Web site that suggested customers change their passwords. Mind you, the information was not posted on the main auction site that every user lands on when they go to ebay.com; it was posted on a corporate site, ebayinc.

com, where the company puts legal and financial data for investors, journalists, and other professionals.

Inexplicably, eBay failed to directly notify users of its PayPal payment subsidiary, which is with whom many eBay users invest their financial trust. On the PayPal site, it posted a notice that users should consider changing their passwords but it gave little explanation. As *Wired Magazine* noted, eBay "offered no further information in the post's body, only the words 'place holder text.'"[53]

When media started calling, eBay removed the message. After realizing the disaster on its hands, the auction house finally posted a notice of the theft of consumer records on its main site. But again it withheld critical information, including whether or not financial information was stolen. Odder still, eBay waited several days before emailing customers directly, something it does routinely for other communication.

With pressure bearing down, eBay officials posted an explanation on their main corporate blog. Because some of it was written in stilted language and in third-person voice, it was difficult to discern whether the post was intended to help customers or protect the company itself.

"After conducting extensive tests on its networks, the company said it has no evidence of the compromise resulting in unauthorized activity for eBay users, and no evidence of any unauthorized access to financial or credit card information, which is stored separately in encrypted formats. However, changing passwords is a best practice and will help enhance security for eBay users," the blog read.[54]

The company went on to say that its network was compromised "between late February and early March." Afterward, eBay customers' names, encrypted passwords, email addresses, physical addresses, phone numbers, and dates of birth were captured. eBay conceded that it took more than two months to detect that it had been hacked and then took two nervous weeks before alerting consumers.

Despite this, the company insisted that "information security and customer data protection are of paramount importance to eBay Inc.," and that it takes "seriously our commitment to maintaining a safe, secure and trusted global marketplace."[55]

The feeble response left users fuming and the collective cyber-security community scratching its head. Why did eBay wait so long to inform consumers? In an interview with the Reuters news service, Devin Wenig, eBay's global marketplaces chief, didn't win anyone over with his response: "For a very long period of time we did not believe that there was any eBay customer data compromised."[56]

Despite its vow to look at its procedures, harden its operational environment, and add levels of security, eBay was hit again by hackers just a few months later in September 2014. Then, thieves posing as eBay users created scores of bogus auctions on the site. Many included a link that read "contact me first before buying" that lured users to click. When they did, eBay users were surreptitiously taken to another site where their payment information was collected. The thieves never sent the merchandise they promised and essentially ran off with users' money.[57]

Since the hacks, several states, including Connecticut, Florida, and Illinois, according to *Forbes*, have mounted investigations into eBay's security procedures, while New York Attorney General Eric Schneiderman has called for eBay to provide free credit monitoring for anyone impacted by the attack.[58]

The attacks could not have come at a worse time for the company, as it is splitting off its PayPal subsidiary in an attempt to unlock its hidden value by taking it public. The success or failure of such a venture will depend, at least in part, on consumer trust in the company. Right now, that has been tested, which is a shame because eBay was, after all, a victim of a crime.

"This is one of the worst responses I've seen in the past ten years from a company that's experienced a breach," said Dave Kennedy, the CEO of TrustedSec, a security consultancy in an article that appeared on the Web site of *Wired Magazine*, which said eBay's response "represents a more special form of a train wreck."[59]

What should eBay have done instead? According to experts, it should have pursued a proper plan for getting a complete scope of the damage, containing the event to limit its impact, and taking remedial steps to bring operations back up as securely as possible. This is easier said than done because it is hard to know definitively that you are back to a known good state. RSA's Yoran says, "The single greatest mistake made by security teams today is under-scoping security incidents and rushing to clear up compromised systems without really understanding the scope of compromise and possibly the broader campaign."[60]

To do this right, an organization must have plans in place to identify a broad range of attacks, including where threats originate. Today, this can be almost anywhere, including a network itself, an endpoint that might not be a traditional IP-enabled device, a mobile smart phone used throughout the world, or even a piece of software that exists only in "virtual" terms.

After an attack occurs, smart organizations work quickly to determine the scope of the damage incurred. This might require surreptitiously monitoring hackers in a controlled environment and following their movements to determine where they might have uploaded malware and which files they accessed. This, of course, cannot be done in an atmosphere in which management's focused is diffused. Judging by its actions, Target's management, for example, was clearly as focused on sales and public relations as much as consumer security. The mismatch of priorities cost it dearly.

The same is true of other organizations in which management has tried to keep word of a cyberattack private—so much so that they opted against hiring outside experts. This is a huge mistake because outsiders often have the unbiased eyes required for spotting architectural vulnerabilities borne of poor purchase decisions or sloppy procedures. They also have experience with eradicating malware and identifying compromised pieces of equipment. This includes scouring data for lingering infections, recommending new gear or software for bolstering defenses, and even helping to communicate effectively with outside constituents (such as investors and the press). This can help scope, contain, and remediate the situation effectively.

In the new world of the IoE, establishing a secure environment for your company, employees, customers, and more isn't about avoiding a single threat, locking down one device or network, or containing one intrusion. Instead, it's about something altogether different: changing your mindset.[61]

Threats are continuous, amorphous, and unpredictable. Sooner or later, they will visit you. Some will do you harm. How much harm depends not on who attacks you, but how well you have prepared.

When It All Goes Crazy: Calming Reassurance for a Jumpy World

"You've just won $1 million dollars"

"Find out who is searching for you"

"Your account is about to be closed"

Sound familiar? It does if you use email to any extent.

Every day, tens of millions of cyberattacks are launched at individuals and organizations alike through messaging services. It's one of the most common ways cyberattacks penetrate digital defenses. Like a classic con, these phishing come-ons prey upon our frailties and vulnerabilities. If not for our greed, vanity, and fear, cybersecurity would be a whole lot easier.

But we are human. So we click on things we shouldn't, search for things we ought not to, and ignore common sense for the sake of expediency.

If the preceding pages have convinced you of anything, it's that we must change with the world around us. Greater conveniences demand greater protections. Brian Krebs, the researcher and author who broke the Target story, recommends that consumers follow a few basic rules.

If you weren't in search of software while browsing the Internet, don't download something unfamiliar when prompted, he says. Also, he and others recommend, keep your systems current and your software updated. The same with your passwords. Take them seriously and change them often. Finally, when you're skeptical of unsolicited information sent to you, don't click on it. Instead, go directly to the source where a solicitation or request claims to be from—your bank or phone company, for example. If no one there is looking for you, throw away any suggestion to the contrary.

These handy tips are surprisingly beneficial. But they are not enough.

Nor are the similarly helpful guidelines that the National Institute of Standards and Technology (NIST) developed at the behest of the White House in 2014[62] or the well-meaning advice from security authorities and consultants around the world. Despite their best efforts and finest thinking, they can only do so much.

Why? That human thing we all share in common.

So long as we are curious, callous, or careless, we will create vulnerabilities for ourselves and the things that we connect to the Internet of Everything. One day, an oversight or slip-up will come back to haunt us.

If you don't believe so, then remember the lesson of the Sony electronic break-in, which was perpetrated by an outside intruder who wanted his or her trespass to be known. Experts say this happens in less than 1 percent of all attacks, which are perpetrated by individuals who prefer to leave no footprints inside the organizations they penetrate.

If that makes you wonder about the place in which you work, you are right to be concerned.

But instead of panic or fear, we can respond with confidence, the kind that comes from knowing what to do before, during, and after a malicious attack.

8

Governance
*New Game in Town, Clear Rules Needed**

The 301 square miles that comprise New York City include some of the most expensive real estate properties in the world. Recently, a private apartment in New York with views of Central Park sold for more than $70 million. While a record, deals for $15 million apartments are made every week with little notice or surprise.

The city is not only expensive for residents who devote, on average, nearly 60 percent of their income to housing, but also to visitors.[1] In 2014, 56.4 million tourists visited New York, according to the Office of the Mayor and NYC & Company, Inc., a city repository of statistics on tourism.[2] Tourists generated an astounding $61.3 billion in economic activity.[3] A lot of that spending is devoted to hotel spending. On average, visitors spend nearly $300 per night for hotel rooms.[4] The amount is the highest average in the nation, according to Statista.[5]

Given the price of hotel rooms—and a citywide occupancy rate that is now approaching 90 percent[6]—it's no wonder that tech innovator Airbnb has become popular among the city's residents and visitors alike.

If you're not familiar, Airbnb is one of a growing number of companies that participates in the "sharing economy," which connects consumers who have demands to individuals and/or organizations that have the supply. In the instance of Airbnb, the commodity exchanged

---

* For their guidance with this chapter, I am grateful to Michael Timmeny, Senior Vice President of Government and Community Relations at Cisco; Travis LeBlanc, Bureau Chief of the Enforcement Division of the Federal Communications Commission (FCC); and Dr. Robert Pepper, Vice President of Public Policy at Cisco.

is lodging. This includes everything from a deluxe apartment to a spare bedroom to an empty spot on a couch.[7]

On any given day, there are more than 1.5 million listings on Airbnb, which has accommodated more than 40 million guests since its founding in 2008. The service is available in more than 34,000 cities in more than 190 countries worldwide.[8]

Airbnb is loved by its fans, who spent an estimated $250 million with the company in 2013, according to *The Wall Street Journal*. Its supporters include millions of homeowners who never entertained the idea of renting space in their homes before and consumers looking to stretch their travel dollars to their furthest. "Whether an apartment for a night, a castle for a week, or a villa for a month, Airbnb connects people to unique travel experiences, at any price point," the company says in its literature.[9]

Inc. Magazine was so enamored with Airbnb that it named it "The Company of the Year" in 2015. In an article describing its rise to prominence in the world of travel, it encapsulated what sets Airbnb apart from other tech innovators with clever ideas: "What makes this company so noteworthy this year is that it has moved beyond building a disruptive business to battling entrenched interests," it wrote in December 2014.

Battling entrenched interests, it turns out, has become a significant challenge for the company in many places around the world. Detractors are particularly galled by the company's disregard for regulations covering rental properties. Unlike hotels, which have to follow strict guidelines covering everything from room size, sanitation, parking, security, and visitor safety, Airbnb "Hosts" don't follow many of the traditional municipal codes covering the hospitality industry.

In New York, for example, Hosts ignore the city's minimum stay requirement of 30 days, which prevents owners of traditional, multi-tenant apartment buildings from transforming their properties into makeshift hotels. Hosts also ignore rules governing how many people can stay in any one room or even what constitutes a rental unit. The aforementioned spot on the couch? You can rent one of those for roughly $80 per night in New York and San Francisco using Airbnb.

As you might imagine, the existing free-for-all isn't sitting well with landlords, who have strict policies against nightly rentals in their buildings, and local governmental authorities, who have been flooded by complaints against Airbnb users. While most Airbnb users are gracious guests, some have used the service to promote prostitution, gambling, and illicit drug use. In some instances, Airbnb Hosts have been as surprised as their neighbors as to what Airbnb customers have done inside private residences.

When he returned to his apartment in the Manhattan neighborhood of Chelsea in 2014, Airbnb Host and comedian Ari Teman ran into his building's management, which was in the process of breaking up a wild orgy that was underway in his bedroom. "The worst part of the Internet right there was in my apartment," he told *The New York Post*.[10]

Fed up with complaints, New York State Senator Liz Krueger, a Democrat who represents much of New York City, has mounted a campaign to get Airbnb and companies like it to adhere to local regulations. In 2010, she championed the "Illegal Hotel Law," which added teeth to rules that address short-term rentals in the city.[11]

Krueger has been so focused on stopping Airbnb in its tracks that she has developed a nickname in the media for her quest: "Airbnb Doubter-in-Chief."[12] Of the company, she said to "Freakonomics" co-author Stephen Dubner in a podcast from September 2014, "Some people seem to think that if you're a business model that's on the Internet it's like magic and hocus pocus. It's just business. And there's a reason for government to regulate business, whether it has a physical site somewhere or whether it's in the cloud."[13]

Love her or loathe her, Krueger has a point: We need governance in our lives to protect us from ourselves and those who would do us harm. I'm not talking about overly burdensome rules, such as the ones that require hair-braiders in certain states to obtain cosmetology licenses even though the classes required to get a cosmetology license offer no hair-braiding instruction.[14] Instead, I'm talking about the commonsense governance that helps keep markets moving and protects the unsuspecting from physical damage, monetary exploitation, and more.

When you think about macro economies, you realize that there are many constituents that need these kinds of protections. Consumers, for example, depend on standards and rely on protections to keep them safe. Businesses, meanwhile, count on policies and regulations to provide fair competition and a rule of law. And governments rely on regulations to ensure fair trade, equitable taxation, and policy enforcement.

Traditionally, these constituents have been protected by a mix of government and commercial mechanisms. They will in the era of the Internet of Everything (IoE), too. Much of what the Internet of Everything means—digital cities, digital factories, digital enterprises, and so on—is already governed by the current policies (on privacy, on security, on consumer protection, and on anti-trust). However, regulators will need to address some new challenges due to the distinct opportunities and challenges that new innovation creates. As the market matures, it will become increasingly clear who or what is responsible for ensuring quality commercial services, competitive market prices, appropriate market safeguards, sensible consumer protections, and a level playing field for all.

In the main, I believe that market forces in the era of the digitally enabled economy of the future will prove themselves capable of creating world-class services and competitive prices. But market forces alone won't protect consumers from harm or markets from damage akin to the sub-prime mortgage crisis. And when it comes to creating a level playing field for all, we will likely need more forward-looking policies to promote the best interest of businesses.

In many ways, the controversy that Airbnb has created in the world of hospitality is emblematic of the broader conundrum that many industries face: what to do about the transformative and sometimes disruptive impact that results from putting information, people, and things onto the Internet together.

In this chapter, I look at governance challenges from three perspectives: protecting the vital interests of consumers, supporting the important agendas of business, and preserving the legitimate role of governments—the rules of play in the digital era, in other words.

Let's begin with consumers and something we can all relate to—how to get around in a safe, easy, and affordable manner.

From De Jure to De Facto: Protecting Vital Consumer Interests

"They should not be here illegally."[15]

Undocumented immigrants? Not this time. Instead, the preceding condemnation was expressed about the technologically savvy men and women who drive for Uber.

Founded in 2009, Uber is the most widely used ridesharing service.[16] Its digital technology leverages up-to-date market information (the demand created by users' online requests for service) to connect people (including available drivers) who can be monitored with things (such as the GPS capabilities of drivers' smart phones, which provide waiting users visual feedback of when their rides will arrive).

Unlike traditional transportation providers, Uber doesn't own a fleet of vehicles or employ a legion of drivers. At least, not yet. In June 2015, the California Labor Commissioner's Office ruled that an Uber driver in the state should be classified as an employee, not an independent contractor, which would theoretically qualify the driver for healthcare and other benefits.

Uber is appealing this because it doesn't even consider itself to be in the transportation business. Its executives like to say Uber is a technology company with a platform that allows independent contractors to connect with everyday consumers.

With Uber, passengers summon drivers to a destination of their choice and then pick within the app from a passel of drivers willing to give them a ride. At the end of each ride, passengers and drivers alike can rate their rides. The information is made readily available to everyone who uses the app.

In addition to greater convenience, Uber brings something else to transportation that it hasn't had before: complete transparency and optimum efficiency. Take the former. With Uber, passengers not only have the name, make of car, and license plate information of their drivers at their fingertips, they also have the drivers' ratings. Knowing this, the overwhelming majority of Uber drivers make it a point to keep their vehicles clean and their driving safe. (Given that most drivers pilot their own vehicles, they are less inclined to run over potholes or gun it through intersections.) As for better efficiency, Uber better matches supply and demand than traditional taxi companies, which means drivers spend less time waiting around for fares, and passengers spend less time trying to flag down rides.

If all this sounds mundane to you, then consider Uber's global impact on the taxi and limousine business worldwide. Today, Uber is used by an estimated 8 million people worldwide to get to work, to get home from a dinner out, or to pick up the kids from school.[17] As of January 2015, Uber had more than 162,000 active drivers in the U.S. alone signed up and approved to cater to consumers' needs.[18] This is fast approaching the total number of taxi and limo drivers nationwide. And Uber is adding 40,000 new drivers every month. Each day, Uber drivers complete 1 million trips in nearly 300 cities worldwide.[19]

While it's tempting to dismiss Uber as just another application in the iTunes app store, the innovation is so much more. Uber isn't just challenging the taxi and limousine industry, which is estimated to be worth roughly $100 billion worldwide;[20] it's transforming the transportation industry, which is a $2 trillion industry. Here's why.

Uber is an end-to-end process that leverages assets owned by others to produce value that is shared by workers and consumers alike. Digital technology enables this, and because the process is *digital*, it is inherently cheap, broadly available, and disarmingly simple to use. Thanks to this ingenuity, Uber can scale its service to virtually anyone who has a connection to the Internet.

In fact, the technology company is credited for persuading tens of thousands of Millennials to reconsider or postpone car ownership,[21] helping to revive entire urban centers such as downtown Los Angeles,[22] and compelling the leaders in car manufacturing to reconsider the way they design, build, and even sell their products. After announcing that it was considering launching a ridesharing service to compete against Uber in January 2015, Ford CEO Mark Fields said he was trying to prepare the car maker to compete in a world of autonomous vehicles and cost-effective ridesharing services.

"We are driving innovation in every part of our business to be both a product and mobility company—and, ultimately, to change the way the world moves just as our founder Henry Ford did 111 years ago," said Fields.[23]

Little wonder it is so disruptive. Today, Uber faces stiff opposition in places where it challenges the status quo, such as Paris, Las Vegas, and elsewhere. But make no mistake; the company is leveraging digital innovation not just to transform a market segment (taxi and limousines, in this instance) but an entire global industry. In doing so, it is influencing a significant number of lives everywhere it goes.

To its loyal fans, Uber is a godsend that has transformed urban life by providing a reliable, comfortable, and affordable means of transportation that is vastly superior to what municipalities or traditional transportation companies provide. To its detractors, Uber is a menace that is putting consumers at risk, professional drivers out of business, and regulators into a tizzy by ignoring guidelines designed to protect consumers and provide a level playing field for all transportation providers.

So which sentiment is correct? Both, actually.

Take the above sentiment "they should not be here illegally." It was said in frustration to a reporter from *KTNV* television by a Las Vegas taxi driver in November 2014.[24] That night, the driver and dozens of others staged a protest against Uber by driving down the center lane of Las Vegas Boulevard, the heart of what is otherwise known as "The Strip." The driver expressed a belief that is held by many taxi drivers around the world: Uber is nothing more than a taxi and limousine company that should adhere to the same regulations that other transportation companies do. This includes limits on the number of cars or "medallions" in service at any one time, regulated fares, background checks for drivers, safety inspections on vehicles, proof of insurance, licensing fees, and more. Uber insists that many of these regulations don't apply to it, and thus Uber disregards some rules that have regulated traditional transportation providers for decades.

Instead of relying on municipal regulations to protect consumers, Uber insists that its commercial policies are strong enough to protect consumers. This includes background checks on drivers, safety inspections on cars, and so on. While it is undeniable that these have worked successfully for the most part, the safeguards have not prevented some bad outcomes.

For starters, Uber has failed to weed out some unfit drivers. Some have been accused of crimes against passengers, including one of sexual assault in Boston and another of a brutal rape in India.[25] Generalizing from individual incidents like this, however, does not present the full picture. Moreover, taxicabs have assaults too. For example, as *The Atlantic* reported in March 2015, "Taxi drivers have been in the headlines just like Uber has. In the past year, there have been assaults against taxi passengers reported in Seattle, Washington, D.C., Portland, Fort Lauderdale, and elsewhere. In 2012, a rash of incidents in Washington—seven assaults over the course of a few weeks—prompted the District's taxicab commissioner to issue a warning to female passengers."[26] The magazine concluded that "there's little to suggest that the newest form of ridesharing is significantly riskier than the old one."[27]

Uber has also imposed "surge" charges in times of high demand or inclement weather. In December 2014, for example, Uber drivers in Sydney, Australia, were criticized for gouging passengers *during* a downtown hostage crisis, though the company apologized afterward and offered free rides and refunds.[28]

In addition to some of its drivers, some Uber executives have demonstrated poor behavior of their own, especially when it comes to consumer privacy. At least one company insider has been disciplined for using a previously unknown "God View" dashboard to track the whereabouts of a journalist.[29]

Despite its missteps, Uber has moved forward with few apologies. After one of its executives suggested hiring investigators to dig up dirt on journalists who chronicle its shortcomings, company CEO Travis Kalanick tweeted his regrets on behalf of the company.[30] But because he sidestepped a direct apology and did not fire the executive in question, he was accused of more brash behavior.

Not that it has hurt its net worth. Since 2010, Uber has attracted investment from a Who's Who of Silicon Valley venture capital firms and global wealth management funds—including Benchmark Capital, Google Ventures, the Qatar Investment Authority, and more—who think the company can leverage digitization to transform transportation and a whole lot more. Their support has given Uber an estimated net worth of $50 billion as of this writing.[31] That's more than what corporate stalwarts FedEx, United Airlines, Charles Schwab, and Macy's are worth.

While some municipalities around the world are pushing back against Uber—Las Vegas banned the service from operating within its city limits in late November 2014 and New York Mayor Bill de Blasio threatened to limit its footprint in the city until a last-minute settlement was reached—others are welcoming it as much as consumers.[32] Mexico City officials have praised Uber (though drivers of the city's 140,000 cabs have responded with protests and fists).[33] So have civic leaders in underserved markets such as Cedar Rapids, Iowa. There, Mayor Tom Corbett told *The Cedar Rapids Gazette*, "Uber and companies like Uber have really transformed the way the whole cab industry is operating. Their embracement of technology and the features have really made their service more attractive than the cab service."[34]

So let's examine the alternative view of Uber, which has millions of fans, including drivers, riders, and community leaders. As previously mentioned, community leaders in Southern California are crediting Uber, Lyft, Sidecar, and other ridesharing companies for helping to spur an urban revival in downtown Los Angeles, which hasn't enjoyed a vibrant night scene for decades due to parking problems, unpredictable taxi service, and strict policing of impaired driving. In November 2014, Uber user and television writer Ryan O'Connell told *The Los Angeles Times* that, after moving to LA from New York, "It became very clear to me that I could use Uber and have the kind of life I wanted."[35]

Then there are the men and women who drive for Uber. Take Salt Lake City driver Oleyo Osuru. A native of war-torn Sudan, he came to the U.S. in 2009 to make a better life for himself and his family. For five years, he scratched out a living in Salt Lake City's western suburbs driving a cab for one of the oldest cab companies in Utah. But life was tough. The salary he made enabled his family to live modestly, but always close to the edge of society's margins.

When Uber came to town—first without the official blessing of Salt Lake City regulatory authorities—Osuru watched his fellow drivers one-by-one quit the cab company, which consumed more than half of their wages. They then signed up for Uber. When Osuru would see them at the airport waiting for passengers, he would inquire how the new job was working for them. Always the answer was the same: much better, thank you.

When Uber received the green light from local Salt Lake City governing authorities to operate legally, Osuru quit, along with four fellow drivers, and signed up with Uber the next day. Soon, he made enough money to buy a bigger and newer car (a Dodge Grand Caravan) that he now ferries passengers around in. Then he made an even bigger leap that not only impacted his professional life, but his personal life, too: he bought a house.

"As a taxi driver I was always living paycheck-to-paycheck and only able to afford to rent," he says. "Though I was living here in America, I really didn't feel like a part of it. But after working for Uber, I was able to earn more and keep more—so much that I was able to buy our first house. It's not a big house, but it makes me feel like I am now a part of the American Dream."[36]

If you're still unsure how we should balance innovation with governance, then consider the effect of existing regulations that govern the taxi industry. Ever taken a cab from JFK International into New York City? If you have, you couldn't help but notice that the experience is regulated mediocrity. For starters, you have little choice of vehicle; you take the next car in line at the airport. You also have to put up with regulations that mandate that an impenetrable Plexiglas barrier separate passenger from driver in the name of safety. (In addition to being obnoxious, the screen limits passenger leg room to a mere few inches.) Then there are fees added to your fare, which are also regulated. These can include a charge for airport pickup, additional passengers, or tolls incurred at different points of entry into the city. Or *not*, due to confusing inconsistencies.

Upon arriving at your destination, you wonder what part of your experience was improved or protected by municipal regulations. The skill and knowledge of your driver? The condition and age of your vehicle? The amount you were charged? None seem devoted to protecting vital consumer interests.

Uber comes along and says to consumers like O'Connell, in effect, "we can do it better and give you the life you want." And, in many ways, it has. Consider vehicle maintenance.

Uber cars are overwhelmingly modern, clean, and well maintained—not because of some municipal rule, but because drivers' reputations depend on them. Like eBay, Uber relies on a user-generated ratings system. After a transaction, both the driver and the passenger have an opportunity to rate their experience. A bad rating from a passenger, which would persuade Uber users to choose another driver with a higher rating, is all the motivation drivers need to keep their vehicles operating in top working order and equipped with special amenities, such as a variety of smart phone charging cords for riders' convenience.

In essence, the Uber rating system has supplanted *de jure* government regulations with *de facto* consumer conventions. But just as municipal regulations have come up short when it comes to protecting vital consumer interests, so, too, have industry conventions.

So what's a consumer to think? My view is neither totally free market nor entirely big brother. Instead, I believe the world is better off with a blended framework of governance, which is a mix of law, policy, industry standards, and even consumer evaluations.

Consider: For all their faults, Uber and other ridesharing companies have proven that the personal transportation market was underserved and, moreover, artificially constrained by the issuance of taxi medallions by local municipalities. This practice has better served the needs of local taxi companies than it has served the public at large. It's also perverted the benefits that competitive free markets produce—for example, competitive prices, superior service, and so on.

To state it another way, the harm that comes from too much governance is far greater than the harm that might come from short-term perturbations caused by disruptive innovation.

Ridesharing, of course, turns the status quo on its head. Since its arrival in places like New York, Chicago, and Los Angeles, demand has spiraled and economic activity has increased. Moreover, the abundance of supply has led some to rethink how they get around. It's not inconceivable to think that future generations will come to think of ridesharing the way that previous ones thought of car ownership. This could lead to a reduction in single-use vehicle trips, which contribute greatly to traffic congestion, pollution, parking woes, and more.

Furthermore, ridesharing has proven that the market is a better regulator of everyday pricing, vehicle cleanliness, driver knowledge, and more.

That said, *de facto* regulations are far from perfect. They have failed to adequately protect consumers from price gouging, insurance lawsuits, driver assaults, and universal access.

This is why I believe a mix of *de jure* regulations and *de facto* practices, rooted in a sensible governance framework that rewards innovation while protecting consumers, is what we need in the digital era. To provide consumers with more creative consumer services, we must give market innovators room to maneuver. That said, we need sensible governance to ensure that customers can count on basic security and fair prices. If there's a snowstorm in Boston, for example, Uber drivers should not be able to charge exorbitant fees for a simple ride. But Uber should be able to encourage more drivers to hit the streets with some surge charges to make it worth their while. Wouldn't a reasonable "surge charge cap" work better for all?

Our point is that current efforts to pit government authorities against free-market interests is counterproductive for all. A better way? Leverage the best from each and ensure that one doesn't overwhelm the other. If policy makers decide that some regulations are needed, then they need to be targeted and proportional. If Uber drivers need to be insured, which is something most people would agree that they do, then the governance structure should prioritize legal protection for passengers instead of creating barriers to entry for new market entrants.

In practice, this might mean ending the medallion monopolies that have been in place for decades, while at the same time insisting rideshare companies provide the same level of insurance coverage that taxi and limousine companies provide.

If done right, we can create policies for the digital economy that promote the digital services consumers want and the protections they need. This goes for ridesharing and beyond. Consider the new wearable devices that attach to the Internet. Their ability to monitor health conditions and physical activity will lead to the creation of a bevy of new and beneficial applications for consumers. Because some will capture data that heretofore was measurable only with medical devices, they will require some oversight to ensure that HIPPA regulations are carefully followed. Some of this will have to come from government, obviously, but some—such as policies and standards—will have to be provided by industry due to the advanced nature of the new connected digital applications we are talking about.

The point is that we don't need a new adversarial system; quite the opposite, actually. We need a system that promotes innovation while protecting consumer interests.

From consumers, let's shift attention to commercial enterprises and the new governance questions that digital technology raises in the areas of intellectual property, industry standards, and more.

No Time for Trolls: Advancing Important Business Agendas

If you are into yoga, you probably know that there are few poses as difficult as the Full Locust or Peacock—unless, of course, you're talking about the YogaGlo Patent Twist.[37] Now that was some *contortion*.

If you're not familiar with YogaGlo, it is a company based in Santa Monica, Calif. As you might imagine, its focus is yoga—not just any yoga, but classes streamed online to scores of customers nationwide. Just a mere few years ago, the company had a stellar reputation among its client base. But things got twisted after the company filed for a patent in 2010. In its application, YogaGlo claimed that it had developed a unique—and proprietary—filming technique. In particular, the company claimed, the camera angles and audience position determined by the company amounted to a breakthrough in the world of online exercise class streaming. In late 2013, the U.S. Patent and Trademark Office (USPTO) agreed, awarding the company a patent, No. 8,605,152.[38]

Shortly afterward, the company began sending letters to other yogis, some of whom were YogaGlo customers, informing them of its patent and its rights to defend it. It included "an application" that fellow yoga providers could complete, allowing them to go about their business so long as they paid YogaGlo a royalty. In legal circles, this is known as a "shakedown."

When the yoga world got wind of YogaGlo's tactics, the response was neither kind nor soothing. When he heard that YogaGlo was awarded a patent for its filming technique, "Tom," a YogaGlo customer and NBC cameraman, wrote the following in response to a YogaGlo blog defending the company's actions:

"I've worked as a professional videographer for NBC news for years. I'm also trained as a yoga teacher and a member of Yogaglo. I feel like my experience as a yogi and cameraman gives me some perspective to say that your patent is insane. I've filmed thousands of stories and all cameramen go to the spot that makes the most sense to tell the story or capture the event. This is what photographers and videographers do. I've filmed yoga classes long before yogaglo existed in the exact manner you are claiming for yourself. I didn't choose this angle because I was a genius cameraman. It was the obvious place to put the camera."

In addition to Tom, scores of customers cancelled their subscriptions, telling the company, in effect, where it could put its patent. After months of bad press and industry outcry, YogaGlo backpedalled in October 2014. It said it would narrow its attempts to defend the "look and feel" of its classes. A few days later, it updated its Web site to say that it would forfeit its patent and not seek another.[39]

While yogis rejoiced, others were in no mood to celebrate, given the enormity of the problem. This includes the Electronic Frontier Foundation, a non-profit organization devoted to promoting civil rights in the digital realm. Earlier, it gave YogaGlo one of its dubious "Stupidest Patents of the Month" awards. After the company forfeited its patent, the EFF praised YogaGlo for coming to its senses but said the saga offered a cautionary lesson about the new wave of innovation being developed around the Internet of Everything, which offers tantalizing intellectual property opportunities.

In a blog from October 2014, the EFF said, "Even though the patent owner, YogaGlo, Inc., has already given up, we think the story of this patent is still worth telling. We think it reveals a lot about how our patent system is desperately broken. This story is one of a grave series of omissions and errors that resulted in a patent that should never have been granted in the first place, and a patent applicant incentivized to do everything in its power to keep filing for more."[40]

Unfortunately, the same could be said for literally thousands of patents issued today. Instead of advancing important business agendas, the existing governance framework for intellectual property is too often setting them back. Today, patents are used more as swords than shields, say legal experts, resulting in a zero-sum game in which one company armed with a broad patent portfolio attacks another in a preemptive attempt to avoid becoming the target of a suit. Within the last few years, numerous companies that do nothing but amass large patent portfolios and then sue those they deem to have violated those patents have sprouted like weeds in an abandoned lot. Patent "trolls" like these and others are imposing what amounts to an enormous and burdensome toll on American businesses.

Writing in the *Cornell Law Review*, legal scholars James Bessen and Michael Meurer, authors of "The Direct Costs from NPE Disputes," said that non-practicing entities (NPEs) and their patent assertions cost American businesses about $29 billion a year. Much of the burden, they noted, falls on small and medium-sized companies.

"The rapid growth and high cost of NPE litigation documented here should set off an alarm, warning policy makers that the patent system still needs significant reform to make it a truly effective system for promoting innovation," wrote Bessen and Meurer. Among other things, the two men have called for the government to increase enforcement of what is known as the "claim-definiteness standard" and embrace recent Supreme Court decisions that limit the "patentability of business methods and other abstract processes that are difficult to propertize." Moreover, they call for greater transparency in the entire patent system and "greater use of fee shifting to favor defendants in cases brought by trolls."[41]

In the main, I agree.

The new digital economy is going to be a watershed of new innovation. In addition to new devices, there will also be new pairings of ideas, techniques, and things. As digital assets, such as intellectual property, become an increasingly larger portion of all assets, the need to protect these assets will become more pronounced, especially through sensible patent and IP regimes. Also, the need to have a governance environment where IP can be generated easily—for example, a level playing field—will increase. These are the needs of the hour in the digital era.

As an example, Federal patent reform legislation is needed "to curb excessive patent litigation and improve patent quality." Cisco, for one, supports efforts to pass common-sense patent reform legislation and is working with industry groups and legislators to address these issues.

"Patent reform legislation to repair the broken U.S. patent system will foster more innovation, increase investment in research and jobs, and lead to greater shareholder value and enhanced U.S. competitiveness in the global marketplace," says Mark Chandler, chief legal counsel for Cisco.[42]

Among the priorities Cisco is calling for are increased efforts to improve the quality of patents, more timely patent review, more proportionate damages, more justified punitive damages, and a prohibition of "forum shopping" (in which would-be plaintiffs file their cases in the most "patent litigation friendly courts" possible).

This is especially true of trolls that not only go after big corporations with deep pockets and legions of lawyers, but also smaller and more vulnerable firms as well. In one case, Cisco, NetGear, and Motorola joined forces to block a patent troll that sent out 14,000 letters to small businesses seeking upward of $4 billion for using commercial products that it said violated its patents. After spending $13 million to defend its customers, Cisco was able to reduce the award to a mere $2.7 million, protecting millions of consumers from what it said was "the overblown and specious claims of a very aggressive patent assertion entity that wielded a questionable claim."[43]

"It's imperative that we return to a patent system that incents and rewards innovation and discourages the speculators and opportunists who are using litigation leverage and bad patents to extract money from the productive elements of the economy," says Chandler. In particular, he and other legal professionals are appalled at private interests that attempt to take advantage of under-funding at the USPTO, which has created an environment in which over-taxed patent examiners cannot easily find examples of what is known in the legal world as "prior art" that would prevent the issuing of questionable patents.

"When our patent examiners can say, 'We know what we know,' we'll be one more step toward a patent system that meets the Founders' goal of truly 'promoting progress in science and useful arts,'" says Chandler.

While I am not in favor of heavy-handed government intervention, I believe that patent reform is an area where government has a legitimate role to play when it comes to intellectual property protection. Rather than working against one another, businesses and policy makers must work together to create a framework that is fair, predictable, and consistent.

The same is true when it comes to standards development, tax policy, primary scientific research, licensing, open access to data, and so on. In each of these instances, the role of government is to ensure that markets function efficiently and properly and that businesses can prosper legitimately. It is, however, not to pick winners and losers (which is tempting any time new innovation upends the status quo) or to promote special interests with unworkable laws (such as data sovereignty) that cannot be enforced or even adhered to in an era where disruptive innovations are coming to fore almost weekly. In most instances, existing laws and regulations can adequately protect consumers and provide for a level playing field for business interests. But in certain areas, such as privacy and security, as we discussed in previous chapters, we will need better governance to fully protect consumer and business interests.

Because of the disruptive nature of technology development, key industrial sectors such as healthcare, transportation, communications, manufacturing, finance, and beyond are undergoing significant change. Naturally, powerful forces looking to protect existing interests are massing against up-and-coming challengers looking to exploit opportunities created by significant market transitions.

We will need cooperation among consumers, businesses, and regulatory authorities to ensure that the legitimate interests of businesses are advanced while safeguarding consumers' interests. In the new digital age, this is more difficult than in the physical world. In addition to a level playing field and traditional intellectual property protections, we need a framework that specifically protects and promotes *digital* innovations. Corporate America will accelerate its investment into digital technology only if the right incentives exist, the right protections are provided, and the right market opportunities can be monetized.

In the next section, we look at how government discharges its responsibilities to protect consumers and advance businesses while ensuring its own efficient functioning. It is a tricky balancing act worthy of the fittest yogi.

From Adversaries to Allies: Preserving the Legitimate Role of Governments

If you've ever walked through California's Yosemite Valley on a morning following an evening snowfall, you know in an instant that the memory will stay with you forever. The sound of the crisp snow under foot. The smell of the fresh mountain air. The brilliant blue of the dazzling, almost sparkling sky. These sensations will literally take your breath away. If you stand motionless in the Mariposa Grove, the forest where towering sequoia trees have stood for more than 3,000 years, you might experience a quiet that you have never encountered before in your lifetime.

It's magical.

If you should ever be so lucky to enjoy the experience, be sure to silently thank the 38th U.S. Congress and President Abraham Lincoln for the opportunity. It was they who, acting at the behest of well-meaning Californian business and community leaders, set aside the land for preservation and public use. This had never been done before at such scale in the U.S. and laid the groundwork for what was to eventually become the National Park Service, which today oversees some of the nation's most beloved treasures. The Park Service's list of holdings includes Yosemite National Park, Arches National Park in Utah, Yellowstone in Wyoming, Acadia in Maine, and the Great Smoky Mountains in North Carolina and Tennessee.

While it's almost impossible to imagine it now, in almost every instance, creating a new national park meant overcoming opposition from entrenched individual citizens and powerful business interests. Fortunately for generations to follow, the Federal government recognized that it alone had the unique power and authority to set aside these lands for all in perpetuity. And that role—the stewardship of shared public assets—is just as important in the digital world as it is in the physical one.

Why? Because no one person or entity actually owns the Internet, which, as you probably know, was cobbled together by a relatively small number of scientists, academics, government officials, and dedicated enthusiasts. Working together in a loose, often ad-hoc manner, they established technical standards, ownership rights, naming conventions, and more without firing a single shot, filing a single lawsuit, or unleashing a torrent of computer viruses to establish their superiority.

Although their methods have changed over the decades, their overriding objective remains as true as it was in the early days of the Internet, when the Internet was comprised only of three research labs in California connected to one in Utah. This objective is to keep the Internet as free, accessible, and beneficial as it can be.

For some perspective on how this ideal is possible in the modern world, I spoke with Dr. Robert Pepper, who serves as Cisco's vice president of Global Technology Policy. A former policy and planning chief with the FCC for 16 years, he has a sensible, albeit progressive, view of consumer and commercial interests.

"Governments and regulators need to be very humble, especially when it comes to technology," he said in a presentation delivered in London for the Turing Lecture Series in February 2015.[44] Among other things, he advocates for what he calls a multi-stakeholder approach to governing shared technological assets such as broadband access.

"If you ask people who owns and controls the Internet, you'll get a variety of different answers. But only 15 percent of the people know the truth, which is no one," Pepper says. "Since its earliest days, the Internet has always been managed by a bottom's up approach. There was a time when everyone on the Internet knew each other. Some of us remember the actual people who came up with the naming conventions and address systems. Now it's impossible to know everyone and everything online. But in many ways, the governing structure remains the same."

Instead of trying to seize control of the Internet, private-sector companies, regulators, academic researchers, and consumer advocates alike worked collaboratively and transparently to achieve what he and others call "rough consensus" to govern the global communications treasure.

Rough consensus, Pepper explained, is the idea that after debate, thoughtful people come together and agree upon a set of guidelines, principles, and policies that protect and advance the interests of the greatest many possible. Afterward, they implement these ideas knowing that they aren't perfect or even permanent. Once these ideas are implemented, interested parties can operate with the understanding that the sidelines and goalposts might move from time to time, but they will be in place long enough for capital investments to be made and big bets to be played out.

In an era of decentralized, distributed computing—in which every device will have some sort of connection to the Internet—this approach will surely be tested like never before for a multitude of reasons. For starters, there is simply so much money at stake that it will be difficult to keep commercial interests from trying to claim a bigger share. It will also be very difficult to prevent sovereign governments from abusing their authority, given how easy it is to collect and analyze citizen's data.

In the U.S. and in many other parts of the world, a grand battle over how to regulate and govern the Internet is playing out right now. It pits competing interests against one another and typifies what can happen when rivals choose to fight instead of collaborate. The issue, of course, is Net Neutrality, which is a policy framework that various stakeholders in the U.S., Europe, and elsewhere developed to prevent major telecom carriers from blocking or deteriorating traffic over the Internet and to ensure non-discriminatory access to the Internet. But the Net Neutrality policies that are being adopted go beyond preventing bad behavior and severely limit the capacity of telecom carriers to develop new business models over the Internet. As you might imagine, it's a highly controversial debate.

To U.S. Senator Ted Cruz (R-Texas), Net Neutrality is "Obamacare for the Internet"—a needless, short-sighted, and burdensome guideline that will only harm business.[45] To author and Columbia

University law professor Tim Wu, who coined the term "Net Neutrality," the idea embodies "a universal and ancient principle, preventing nondiscrimination in public infrastructure."[46]

Like the Affordable Care Act, or "Obamacare," Net Neutrality became a contentious issue within Washington and elsewhere that divided not only Republicans and Democrats, but also business interests and consumer advocates. Many Republicans, for example, decried the concept and labeled it "anti-business" and "interventionist." Democrats and consumer groups, meanwhile, called it nothing less than a fundamental human right. Speaking for millions of consumers everywhere, HBO TV host and comedian John Oliver said, "I would rather listen to a pair of Dockers [pants] tell me about the weird dream it had" than ponder Net Neutrality. But, he told viewers of his HBO show, "Last Week with John Oliver," in 2014, that the issue was "hugely important."[47]

In late February 2015, the Federal Communications Commission (FCC) voted to adopt rules that support many of the principles enshrined in Net Neutrality.[48] These include bans on paid prioritization or "fast lanes" advocated by those who wanted to charge extra fees to content producers. It also included prohibitions on blocking or throttling lawful content in an attempt to push consumers toward more expensive pay plans. If adopted, the new rules will also apply to the wireless spectrum, which is the newest frontier of broadband expansion.[49]

Not surprisingly, opponents of Net Neutrality vowed to fight the FCC's ruling. But the real question for business practitioners is this: did the system work to produce the best outcome for the greatest good possible?

Consider the fact that in many places in the U.S., there is insufficient competition on the broadband that is available to consumers. Where this is prevalent, prices are high and customer service is, not surprisingly, rather poor.

By contrast, you'd be hard-pressed to find anyone who can honestly say they have paid the full fare for the broadband and Internet services they take for granted—including the cell towers that provide 3G or 4G wireless connectivity and the free Wi-Fi broadband service at Panera Bread, where you can browse your free email and read free newspapers while watching Netflix in the background.

A better question to consider is this: how do we preserve the system that has brought so much value to so many while creating an environment that encourages innovators to challenge the status quo and provide a basic level of service for all?

The beauty of the Internet as an innovation platform is that it has evolved without major government regulation; there has to be a very good reason (for example, market failure) for governments to get involved. When market failure occurs, it is easy to over step with a heavy hand and potentially freeze investment.

Generally broadband is available to almost everyone who wants it. For example, the spectrum has not only been made available, it has been made available with the flexibility to repurpose it innovatively—and that's very different from the heavy-handed regulation that controls exit, entry, pricing, and so on. This is not to say that it's as fast or as cheap as it should be—far from it—but to simply point out that the existing governing structure has led to prosperity, innovation, and opportunity for millions.

All of this is true in many places around the world.

Contrary to those who believe government has no role in regulating how technology markets operate, I believe it does have some role. I'm not advocating a large role, but a role nonetheless. One that ensures competition without picking favorites; that protects consumers without stifling innovation; and that enforces the rule of law without overstepping its mandate.

Today, many in the business world are opposed to government regulation and intervention of any kind. They denounce it in almost pious tones, until, of course, they *need* it.

Conversely, consumers want protections of almost every imaginable kind, until they get in the way of cool, new services that might trample the rights of others, including commercial enterprises. When this occurs, consumers want to dispense with the very protections that serve them.

Instead of battling one another, consumers and businesses would do best to compromise around sensible policies developed by multiple stakeholders. This goes for Net Neutrality as well as a host of other issues, including broadband spectrum allocation, standards development, fair market access, data collection, the rule of law, and more.

Where the Rubber Hits the Road: Policy That Drives Innovation, Regulation That Ensures Safety

Protecting consumers. Promoting business. Preserving shared assets.

These are but a few of the real-world issues that the new digital economy will make more complex. As it evolves, everything from consumer privacy to anti-competitive behavior to worker safety to fair market access and more might need a fresh, new look.

Though still in its infancy, the new digital economy is already revealing certain things to us. For starters, the companies propelling it have proven themselves to be remarkable equilibrators of supply and demand. They have also proven to be clever innovators and robust competitors despite their relatively small size and inexperience.

But they have also shown that they can create challenges. They can upend mature markets, marginalize consumers, and sometimes unfairly drive out competition.

There will be times when it will be necessary to adjust governance to avoid asymmetries that can unduly impact market incumbents or new entrants. If a regulation unwittingly creates market scarcity or dominance and then a disruptor enters the market and makes it more efficient, a proper response might be to lower the regulation on the incumbent rather than raise the regulation on the new entrant. In other instances, the opposite might be the better approach. The key is creating a flexible, workable framework that can be adjusted on an as-needed basis.

New digital services and providers might need some new regulation. But where and how much? Take ridesharing.

Love them or hate them, you cannot deny that companies like Uber have shaken up the world of personal transportation despite some challenges. They have proven that market-driven mechanisms such as driver and passenger rating systems produce a better consumer experience—superior in terms of vehicle cleanliness, driver enthusiasm, and competitive pricing.

To regulate these entities, however, we need to develop policies that meld the best *de jure* protections and *de facto* conveniences. This will only be possible if we get all market constituencies working together. This includes consumers, businesses, and governments. As with a three-legged stool, no one leg can stand taller than the rest without compromising stability.

If we think of governance as something more than a necessary evil left to government bureaucrats, we can advance the protections that consumers need, promote the agendas that businesses thrive on, and preserve the assets that we all depend on.

If we do, we can take full advantage of the benefits that the digital revolution offers, both in terms of technological innovation and social advancement. It'll take some clever thinking to pull off, but we should be more than up to the task.

It's time for good governance to shine.

9

Financial Performance
Making Money the Old-Fashioned Way°

The Lake Shore Limited. The California Zephyr. The Cannonball Express.

If you're a fan of train travel in the U.S., you recognize these names instantly. They are some of the most iconic trains in American history. These and others have been featured in novels, cast as lead characters in numerous films, and immortalized in song. In the folk hit "City of New Orleans" from 1972, Arlo Guthrie sings romantically about trains passing in the night and traveling 500 miles in a single day.

You can still ride the City of New Orleans from the Windy City to the Mississippi Delta. For all the history and romance that trains conjure, however, they've lost their starring role in the consciousness of the American people. Little wonder, thus, that there is no simple way to travel coast to coast in the U.S.; you have to change trains in Chicago or New Orleans to complete the trip.[1] Unless you live in the crowded Northeast corridor, trains really don't make much sense as a form of passenger transport.

But they cannot be beat for moving freight.

While known as the land with an "endless ribbon of highway," the U.S. is becoming a railway powerhouse. With each passing year, trains move more of the goods and raw materials that America depends on. Take crude oil. In 2008, U.S. Class I railroads transported just 9,500

° For their guidance with this chapter, I am grateful to Kelly Kramer, Chief Financial Officer at Cisco; Saori Casey, Head of Corporate Finance at Apple; and Doug Davis, General Manager of the Internet of Things Group at Intel.

carloads of crude oil, according to the Association of American Railroads. By 2012, the number increased to more than 233,000. The following year, the number of carloads shipped by rail topped 407,000.[2] And that's just a drop in the barrel compared to the percent of other commodities railroads handle. Today, 70 percent of the coal used to power homes and businesses in the U.S. is shipped via rail,[3] and so is 70 percent of the ethanol used for fuel.[4]

One reason for the growth in the railroad industry is efficiency. A single rail car, for example, can carry enough corn to feed 2,300 chickens for an entire year or enough coal to power 62 homes for 12 months.[5] Another key factor is fuel efficiency. The 500 miles that Guthrie sang the City of New Orleans could put behind it in a single day? That's almost as far as many modern trains can move a ton of freight on a single gallon of fuel.[6]

To achieve this kind of fuel efficiency, railroads have embraced a variety of conservation practices over the past decade, according to *Progressive Railroading*. This includes acquiring more fuel-efficient locomotives, installing Auto Engine Start Stop (AESS) devices, and better lubricating rails to reduce friction. But these measures, the publication noted in 2010, represent the "low-hanging fruit" of energy efficiency in railway transport.[7] To achieve additional gains in fuel economy, rail companies have turned to more advanced forms of automation—digitization especially.

"Trains are no longer the lumbering hunks of metal of the 20th century," writes *Forbes* staff writer Dan Alexander. "Today's locomotives are computers on wheels, and they're beginning to take business from fuel-guzzling semi-trucks."[8]

To maintain their edge over trucks, railroad companies have installed radios and sensors on individual cars and alongside train tracks. They have also installed computer-assisted braking and throttling systems and they have invested millions of dollars into business analytics. These investments are helping rail companies cut back on the more than 3.7 billion gallons of fuel they use annually in the U.S.[9] In particular, the technology is revealing to rail companies where efficiencies slip away. Take hills and curves.

A properly trained engineer and brakeman can usually pilot a train efficiently over flat, straight terrain. Things get a little more difficult when an engineer comes to a series of hills and curves. That's when the space or "play" between individual rail cars can expand or contract to create friction along the length of a train. When this occurs, efficiency drops, especially on very long trains, which can be a mile or more in length.

One company helping railways better understand this phenomenon is New York Air Brake (NYAB), a 125-year old engineering and consulting company that develops integrated train control systems. NYAB's Train Dynamic Systems (TDS) division, which is based in Irving, Texas, has built a hardware and software system that helps railway customers address this very problem. With sensors, software, and radio devices, the TDS Locomotive Engineer Assist/Display & Event Recorder (LEADER) technology helps companies in North America, South America, and Australia increase efficiency and improve schedule compliance by pinpointing where and how trains lose efficiency.

As good as the system was, however, it was not as flexible as some customers wanted. Data collected by the sensors, radio systems, and other sources was often unstructured and thus required significant manipulation before it could be analyzed. Even after it was put into a standard format, the data wouldn't give up insights until teams of people working long hours on spreadsheets pored over it.

Believing there was a better way to extract knowledge from the information it had at its disposal, TDS decided to invest in new analytical technology, according to a company case study.[10] After some review, it settled on a software platform developed by a promising company based in San Francisco called Splunk. Founded in 2002, Splunk made a name for itself by helping customers diagnose problems with their IT infrastructures. The company's big breakthrough was a tool comparable to Google Search that helped customers examine the log files that errors and system crashes left behind after failures. Within a few years, the company realized that it was adept at helping customers mine new insights with previously unusable data. So it built several tools to that effect.

With Splunk Enterprise software, TDS is now able to create dashboards for railroad customers that help them better understand how small adjustments to speed, braking, driver training, and more can overcome the strain that terrain, track conditions, weather, and even scheduling put on fuel economy. "The dashboards report on fuel efficiency, impacts on time-to-destination, in-train force reduction, driver compliance and other factors, then correlate that to overall savings and other business objectives," says Splunk.[11]

TDS has been so impressed with Splunk that the company is working to integrate its software with its LEADER technology to extend its capabilities. "The TDS engineering team is already using Splunk software to incorporate new types of sensors being deployed on locomotives and train cars," says Splunk. In addition, TDS plans to use Splunk analytics and dashboards to gain new insight from data generated during train simulator runs.

Armed with the technology and insights, rail customers believe they will be able to run trains in the most efficient manner possible. The benefits companies will derive from achieving "golden runs" are many.

Obviously, reducing fuel consumption will help improve bottom lines. But there is more. Easing up on brakes and reducing gaps between cars on turns and over hills will also help railway companies reduce wear and tear on rolling stock, which will cut down on the number of cars that are out of commission for repairs and thus improve asset utilization. In addition, smoother train rides will help minimize de-couplings and other malfunctions that lead to derailments and other safety issues. This, in turn, will help rail companies both reduce their risk and generate higher revenues by having more cars running.

While you might not do business in the manner that railways do or even operate in industries that rely on them, you no doubt have similar objectives as the men and women who "work on the rails," so to speak. Increase revenue? Reduce costs? Improve asset utilization? These are outcomes every business wants.

In this chapter, I'll examine several ways that companies in different industries pursue these objectives by leveraging sensors, big data, mobility, social media, and ubiquitous connectivity to drive financial performance.

Let's start with a familiar place: your own home.

Increasing Revenue

"Where there's mystery there is margin."

Heard that adage before? It was a staple in travel, car sales, and computer reselling for years—that is, until Travelocity, Edmunds. com, and CNET came along. They pulled back the curtain on some of the machinations that went on behind the scenes in these respective industries—forever changing the way business is done. Instead of booking your next trip through a neighborhood travel agent, you're more likely to use an online travel Web site. Today, online travel agents (OTAs) account for nearly half of all airline, hotel, and car rental bookings, which translates into hundreds of billions of dollars of re-directed revenue per year.[12]

The "mystery-margin" adage still holds true in a few industries where sellers and suppliers continue to drive the bulk of industry revenue, thanks to their access to knowledge and product inventory that customers do not have. How hospitals calculate bills for patients, for example, is not only baffling to patients but a mystery to many industry insiders as well.

But in market after market, disruptive innovators are asking "why?" What if the same level of information transparency that democratized the travel industry was available to customers in other fields? Wouldn't this lead to a reallocation of industry revenue in a significant way?

These are questions I want to discuss in this section.

In just about any industry you can name, some company is leveraging digital technology to change the status quo. In some instances, newcomers going after greenfield opportunities are setting the terms of how business is done. In others, it is established organizations that are leading the way in digital transformation.

Let's start with the former and look at how innovative newcomers, both large and small, are leveraging new digital technologies to reduce the gaps that exist between those with something to sell and those with money to buy. In doing so, they are making life more convenient for consumers and more difficult for those with outmoded business models.

Need to make out a simple will today? You don't need a lawyer if you have access to Legal Zoom, which can help you create one from the privacy of your home. Nor do you need a doctor to help diagnose simple maladies, thanks to WebMD and other tools, or an insurance agent to find you a good deal on car insurance, thanks to Esurance, Progressive, and other Web services.

When it comes to decorating a new home, you have plenty of new options. Today, there are several innovators that are upending the decades-old model of furniture distribution and sales. Special show-rooms open only to the trade? Exclusive distribution deals for licensed decorators only? These and other perks created a lot of mystery in the industry—and a lot of margin for a select class of practitioners. But the rise of newcomers proves there was plenty of profitable growth trapped within tradition.

Take Houzz, for example. It and other décor companies are demystifying the market for millions of consumers. Like a lot of new companies, Houzz was molded from frustration. It was formed in 2009 after the husband and wife team of Alon Cohen and Adi Tatarko tried remodeling their Palo Alto, California, home. They got so fed up with the "whodunit" mysteries embedded into the home decorating economy that they decided to start their own décor business.[13]

For the uninitiated, Houzz is a design and décor destination Web site and mobile app with more than 25 million members. Most members are everyday consumers looking for inspiration; they pay nothing to belong. The rest of the Houzz ecosystem is comprised of architects, designers, and home contractors who pay an annual subscription fee for access to Houzz members and Houzz-developed tools to help them engage with potential clients. In addition to this revenue, Houzz sells ads to its site and collects 15 percent on every "curtain rod or hanging lamp" sold on the Houzz site, writes Yoree Koh in *The Wall Street Journal*.[14]

"For professionals, it's become a way to get their work in front of potential clients. For home remodelers, it's a place to gather ideas, connect with experts and most recently, buy the products they see in the photo galleries," Koh writes.[15]

More than simply connecting buyers and sellers, Houzz has made the home decorating business a more transparent industry. Instead of the mystery surrounding the discounts on products that traditional decorators receive from manufacturers and distributors, Houzz gives consumers better insight on what sells and for how much. It also gives consumers significantly greater choice when it comes to choosing a design professional. Instead of visiting local showrooms and consulting with a small team of professionals, consumers can browse thousands of designer profiles online and see in full high-definition video examples of their work.

More than design aficionados are getting excited about the business. Since it launched in 2009, Houzz has attracted more than $215 million in investment from Kleiner Perkins Caufield & Byers, Comcast Ventures, Sequoia Capital, T. Rowe Price, and others. As of October 2014, the company was valued at a whopping $2.3 billion, which is roughly three times the market value of Ethan Allen, one of the largest furniture retailers in the U.S.[16]

With sales growing and overseas markets coming online (the company aims to be in 15 markets outside of the U.S. by the end of 2015, according to Koh), you can bet that the company's value will continue to rise. Not surprisingly, Houzz has attracted a bevy of direct competitors hoping to replicate if not localize its business model. This includes One Kings Lane and Porch.com. Not all of these companies will likely survive. But their combined disruptive businesses are generating a lot of revenue and transforming not just furniture sales, but other industries far and wide.

Uber, for example, is expected to generate more than $10 billion in annual revenue in the transportation industry and is growing at more than 300 percent annually.[17] Airbnb, meanwhile, is expected to generate more than $500 million in hospitality sales in 2015.[18] In addition to Houzz, these new companies have proven that they are more than a fad. They are the transformative force that is setting the new standard in terms of monetization, customer experience, and more.

That said, digital transformation doesn't require a new company, just fresh new thinking. From a furniture and decorating upstart, let's look at how one company leveraged digital assets that it had at its disposal for years to transform its business.

The company is The Weather Company (né Channel), which pursued new digital revenue ever since it realized that it could be more than a scrappy cable TV company watched primarily by weather enthusiasts and senior citizens with time to kill. After organizing its assets and putting its data to work, The Weather Company blossomed into a diversified media company that helped more than 30,000 organizations around the world leverage information on how to set prices, stock shelves, and adjust staffing levels, just to name a few things.

"By analyzing the behavior patterns of its digital and mobile users in 3 million locations worldwide—along with the unique climate data in each locale—the Weather Company has become an advertising powerhouse, letting shampoo brands, for example, target users in a humid climate with a new antifrizz product," writes *Fast Company*. Digital advertising and business-to-business services became such revenue drivers that they eventually grew to generate more revenue than the company's television business, which hit some rough spots as cable providers cut back on programming to save money.[19]

To achieve this momentum, The Weather Company identified several industries—including media, aviation, logistics, energy, and consumers—to serve with special products built just from data. Take aviation. The company developed a product called Total Turbulence that collects turbulence data from sensors mounted on planes. It then runs this data through a patented algorithm called the Turbulence Auto-PIREP System (TAPS), which yields insights that can help airline companies improve decision making in the air and on the ground. Among the air carriers that have used the system is Delta Air Lines, which provides its pilots with "turbulence graphics" reports every time they fly. They are included with the traditional weather package that the air carrier's pilots download to their iPads before taking off.

Just a few years ago, pilots received texts with weather updates on turbulence; now they get detailed graphics—soon in real time. "By combining real-time weather and sensor data with sophisticated modeling, the company built a solution to help reduce turbulence on flights by up to 70 percent," writes Allison Caley in a blog for The Digital Initiative at the Harvard Business School.[20]

After building a successful franchise around data, David Kenny, CEO of The Weather Company, turned in 2015 to IBM to see what the computer giant's cognitive Watson computing platform could do with the 4 gigabytes of data that The Weather Company collects from around the world every second. IBM was so enamored with the potential to put weather data to work that it decided in October 2015 to buy the digital assets from The Weather Company, which include the Weather.com and Weather Underground news sites and a mountain of weather data and collecting technology, outright.[21]

"Why would Big Blue, purveyor of mainframe computers and business software, acquire a company that brought us Hurricane Sandy coverage?" *Fortune* posed after the deal. "Data."[22]

"On an annual basis, about half-a-trillion dollars worth of business is affected by the weather," says Bob Picciano, senior vice president of IBM Analytics.[23] For Big Blue, the assets amassed by The Weather Company offered a unique opportunity to get in on the ground floor of a potentially very lucrative business.

More than an isolated example, the Weather Company is one of many established companies that has benefitted handsomely from exploration into new opportunities with digital technology. Burberry and John Deere are other examples. These companies understand that digital tools provide an opportunity to generate significant new revenue. They also recognize that unless they act, the same tools can be exploited by competitors to redirect revenue away from them.

Whether you work for a native digital organization or an industry standby, the opportunities to drive profitable growth both inside and outside your organization are many. But they will require moving past challenges and launching into markets aggressively. If you move too cautiously, expect someone else to occupy a position that could have been yours.

From increasing revenue, let's turn our attention to another financial priority: reducing costs.

Reducing Costs

In the time it takes to read this sentence, some criminal somewhere in the world has penetrated the cyber defenses of an unsuspecting organization. Imagine the company were yours. What would you do?

You'd call in outside experts, update management, and tell your team to prepare for long hours until the crisis passes. Then you'd do your level best to assess the damage.

One of the companies you'd likely call is my own. Cisco, after all, is one of the largest suppliers of security technology around the world. Our stuff, experts will attest, is world class. But how we demonstrate that prowess? Well, sometimes that leaves a little to be desired.

In past years, the wait time for a buyer to get a demonstration of a hot-selling piece of Cisco equipment was four weeks. This was true whether you had a security emergency on your hands or merely went to a trade event or opened your door to reseller sales partners and said, "yes, show me more." Even customers with major security breaches had to wait as long as four weeks before Cisco could arrange for them to kick the tires on our latest pieces of gear.

Ridiculous, right? Yes, but true just the same.

The reason for the long wait wasn't for want of effort; it was due to complexity. High-end networking gear is difficult to assemble and ship to a customer's location. It's also very expensive and time consuming to configure due to the literally millions of configurations that different customers might require. This is doubly true when it comes to a product that is in high demand. When a product is in short supply, Cisco doesn't typically have a lot of extra pieces of equipment available to show customers. And the ones that it does have, everyone seems to want at the same time.

To make sure it didn't send out something in short supply to just any tire-kicker, Cisco salespeople spent an extraordinary amount of time pre-qualifying customers before providing them with demonstration goods. A salesperson and sales engineer would often work together to come up with resources to fund an on-site demonstration, find the equipment (which could easily cost tens of thousands of dollars), configure it to a customer's specifications, and then deliver it to an account.

All this effort added greatly to the company's costs. Some $600 million annually, in fact.

What is more, Cisco was never sure when it would get its demo gear back or in what condition it would be returned. Customers, after all, liked to see how our gear performed in real production environments, where they often beat the heck out of it while testing it with different inputs under a variety of conditions.

Ideally, getting demo gear to a company in need, especially a company that's been hacked, should be straightforward. But for years at Cisco, is was not. For years, the company tried several ways to speed the delivery of demo goods to customers. But these methods always involved attacking the problem from an atom-based perspective. Then in 2013, Cisco addressed the problem head on with a new digital solution. The solution is what we call "dCloud."

Although technically a destination Web site that lives in the Internet cloud, dCloud is a complete product demonstration platform that features all of Cisco's core technology products, including collaboration, video, network infrastructure, and more. The platform is available to virtually any Cisco salesperson or qualified business partner. From the site, a salesperson can access not only the technology but also sales pitches, scripts, and instructions on how to provide the most engaging sales presentation possible. dCloud provides a rich, immersive experience that can be customized, too. From the platform, salespeople can configure Cisco technology to replicate customers' exact configurations so they can see how new technology can enhance their existing environments and provide them with new technological capabilities.

dCloud has had a transformative impact on Cisco's financial results. While sales teams have leveraged it to close deal after deal, from a cost perspective, it is even more impressive. Thanks to dCloud, Cisco spends less than half the $600 million on product demonstrations that it did before. The average cost to demonstrate a piece of gear has dropped from roughly $2,000 to just $100, according to company figures.

Similarly, asset utilization, as measured by the amount of time saved by our sales engineers, has improved dramatically as well. Demos that once took four weeks to set up now take as little as 15 minutes. According to internal calculations, an average sales engineer spends 20 fewer hours on each demo than before. In the three months ending in April 2015, the time saved translated into 812,747 hours. To achieve that kind of impact, Cisco would have to add roughly 1,500 people to its payroll.

And what happened to the number of demos while all these cost savings were being realized? They have more than doubled to nearly 200,000 annually.[24]

The benefits don't stop there. Because of the increased capacity, Cisco has been able to dramatically increase the number of demos it conducts with its business partners, which has led to a rise in their sales and loyalty. What is more, the dCloud technology has opened the door to new revenue possibilities at the company. As of this writing, a team of engineers and sales specialists were looking at ways to use dCloud as a training platform. Put another way, the platform that we built to save us money could actually provide us new revenue streams that we never imagined previously.

Not bad for a single cost savings measure.

But it's hardly isolated.

When I was writing this book, GE began running a provocative television commercial that depicted two nearly identical fuel gauges from two different airplanes. The voiceover asked viewers if they could see any difference. Most, obviously, could not. But the voice went on to say that one of the gauges depicted was from an airline that achieved a 1 percent fuel efficiency edge over the other. Spread over an entire airline, the difference amounted to extraordinary cost savings.

"To an airline, a 1 percent difference could save enough fuel to power hundreds of flights around the world," the ad suggests. It then closes with the following: "GE Software. Get Connected. Get Insights. Get Optimized."[25]

My interest piqued, I did a little digging. The company that GE described in its TV ad? It was AirAsia, which flies nearly 1,000 flights per day. On average, 80 percent of the seats on each of its flights are occupied, which translates into a good utilization rate among air carriers.

If you know anything about air travel, you know the biggest variable cost in commercial aviation is fuel. At AirAsia, for example, fuel accounts for half of the air carrier's costs. Each year, the company burns 12 million barrels of fuel. That's three tons of fuel per hour.

It's a lot, in other words.

No matter what companies like AirAsia do to improve their bottom lines, almost nothing matters more than achieving better fuel economy. To address this issue, AirAsia turned to GE, which has developed a data capture and analytics platform called Predix to help air carriers better understand where cost savings can be achieved. With GE's help, AirAsia set out to become nothing less than the world's most efficient airline, at least as far as fuel consumption was concerned.

GE outfitted AirAsia planes and pieces of equipment with sensors. It then ran all of the data captured by these devices through GE's Asset Performance Solutions technology. The data revealed a number of places and ways that AirAsia could reduce fuel.[26]

Take its activity on the ground. GE told the air carrier that if it were to power down one of its engines during taxiing before a flight, the company could save 60 kilograms of fuel per flight. Spread across the entire airline, the amount is equal to 500 barrels of oil per day.[27] Modest? Yes. But compounded over time, the amount saved adds up to real money.

GE then helped AirAsia determine the best settings for its flaps and how to reduce idle reverse fuel consumption during taxiing, a savings of 17 kilograms of fuel per flight. It even helped AirAsia improve the way its planes drove around on the ground at airports, for an additional savings of 21 kilograms per flight.

And this was just the beginning.

With GE, AirAsia determined the most fuel-efficient way to fly its planes. This included developing an optimal climb profile, which saved 21 kilograms of fuel per flight. GE also helped the air carrier analyze its data to determine an optimal descent profile, which shaved nearly 15 miles from each flight.

When AirAsia added up all the little ways that GE helped it save fuel, the savings totaled 250 kilograms of fuel for an average one-hour flight, or 1 percent of fuel consumption.[28] That's millions of dollars annually.

Saving on fuel, as GE did for AirAsia, or saving on demos, as Cisco did for itself and its partners, are just two examples that we have discussed for reducing costs. Many more examples exist where digital technology is helping companies save large sums of money. Similar opportunities might exist in your own organization, too.

From costs savings and increasing revenue, let's turn to another financial imperative: asset utilization.

Improving Asset Utilization

Imagine you found that perfect cottage you've always dreamed of along the water's edge. It's high on a bluff with a gorgeous view. In addition to the location, the size is right; there's enough room for you and a special someone and perhaps a weekend guest or two. Although the kitchen could use some new appliances, the basement is dry and the landscaping well maintained.

It's a lovely place, in other words, and the price is within your budget. Now all you need is a reasonable mortgage and a comfortable chair or two for the little porch that wraps around the side of the house.

You look online and you see plenty of options—for mortgages, that is. But you have a lot of questions. The answers you need, alas, are either buried too deeply in the documents you see on the Web or appear in such small type that you feel intimidated to read on.

You need to speak with an expert, you conclude. What better place to start than your friendly branch bank, which happens to have an on-site mortgage expert? Without hesitation, you book an appointment for your next lunch hour and plan to arrive early so you can get the answers you need. Unfortunately, the agent with whom you made the appointment is swarmed on the day you arrive. He waves apologetically but cannot shake the other customers who surround his desk like pigeons looking for crumbs. You wait as long as you can for the lending agent, but after 45 minutes you must return to your office.

As you drive back to work, you wonder if someone else—perhaps one of the others commanding your lending agent's time—will buy the cottage by the water instead. Irrational? Sure. But that's how you feel. This was a dream home, after all, and with each stoplight you encounter, the fantasy of sipping iced tea in your new Adirondack chair fades. What adds insult to injury is the distinct memory of the agent the last time you were inside your branch. There he was on a Friday at 3 p.m. checking his email and rearranging items on his desk.

If only there were a better way, you think.

At many branches of the Bank of America (BofA) nationwide, there is. Instead of just one lending agent, the bank's branch offices have thousands of professionals available to customers. How is that possible? Videoconferencing technology. In recent years, BofA has seen a sharp decline in the number of customers who visit its branches to make deposits or withdraw cash. More and more of its customers prefer to handle these tasks online from their computers or, increasingly, from their mobile devices. According to *USA Today*, "Bank of America has 50,000 customers a week downloading its mobile app. And the bank is seeing 250 million to 300 million customer log-ins to online banking each month."[29]

That said, 1 million customers per day visit the bank's more than 5,000 banking centers, according to *Computer Weekly*. "Behavior is changing, but the banking center is not going anywhere any time soon," Tyler Johnson, senior vice-president of ATM/kiosk strategy and innovation at BofA, tells the publication. "Around 85 percent of our products are still sold within the four walls of the banking center."[30]

These, of course, are more sophisticated investments and loans that require more customer care than a basic deposit or withdrawal. Many require some consultation with a financial advisor, small-business banker, or mortgage loan officer. To make better use of the space within its branches, BofA has begun remodeling them. It has outfitted them with more digital technology and reduced the square footage devoted to teller counters and other underutilized bank operations. Today, many BofA branches have private suites available for meetings with financial specialists and rooms with videoconferencing capabilities so customers can meet with specialists remotely when a branch agent isn't available onsite.

"The new Bank of America is focused on buffing up digital services while transforming its branches to be places customers can come to for advice and expertise, since they've almost stopped coming there for everything else," reports *USA Today*.[31]

The advantages to remote specialists are many. For one thing, there are significantly more agents available to customers than in traditional bank settings. And the agents offer a broader set of capabilities. If a customer walks into a BofA branch looking for someone who speaks Swedish and has knowledge of rolling over investments into a Roth IRA, BofA can accommodate the customer, thanks to the Cisco TelePresence systems now in use in almost 100 branches and soon being expanded to 500 branches nationwide. Thanks to these capabilities, business that would have slipped through the bank's fingers now shows up on its income statement. In addition to driving more business, the bank is able to increase the utilization of its branches and the financial experts who, when previously based in branch offices, spent only a portion of their time leveraging their extensive expertise and experience. Now they put their skills to use pleasing customers face-to-face more frequently.

"We want to make interactions more human," Johnson told *Computer Weekly* in 2014. He said the systems "offer more human interaction and more flexible access" than sterile telephone consultations with specialists that the bank previously offered.

In ways great and small, more organizations around the globe are putting digital technologies to use to increase the utilization of their assets. The BofA example demonstrates how human assets can be better utilized. Nationwide in UK is doing the same and its mortgage advisors are seeing three times as many customers in a day, with customers actually more satisfied when using remote advisors than when using in-branch advisors.[32] But let's segue to assets that most practitioners struggle with every day, *physical* ones. Hospitals, for example, are putting sensors on crash carts and other pieces of life-saving equipment that tend to get lost in plain sight in busy medical centers. Others are putting them on devices that operate far from view, often in nooks and crannies that are hard to find and even get to. Take the Éléonore gold mine in Canada, which has an acute need to better manage its physical assets.

A Goldcorp facility, the Éléonore mine is located on the edge of the Opinaca Reservoir in the James Bay region of western Québec, Canada. The land is Indian territory (Cree, in this case) and is rich with wildlife, timber and, come winter, ice. Beneath the rugged beauty of the land are large gold deposits encased in quartz-tourmaline-arsenopyrite rock. To get to the gold, the mining company has to dig deep and wide.[33]

Following a four-year ramp-up period, the mine began commercial operations on April 1, 2015. To extract enough gold to make the mine viable, miners will eventually have to dig through 7,000 tons of rock per day. If all goes according to plan, their efforts will produce as much as 330,000 ounces of gold annually.[34]

To dig through that much earth daily, the mine requires an enormous amount of equipment. As the tunnels beneath the earth grow in size and length, tracking of all the mechanical assets underground becomes an ever-greater challenge. To aid in this effort, Goldcorp teamed with Cisco, which recommended that the mining company install a "Cisco Connected Mining solution" underground.

Built to withstand harsh conditions, the solution provides unified, secure connectivity to any device and location. That might not sound like much, but it means the world when you're trying to locate a particular drill or earth mover or cart or jack hammer that is located several hundred feet underground in a mine shaft that might be half a mile long in total darkness. More than mere networking connectivity, the Connected Mining solution provides benefits contributed by several companies. For example, a "smart" ventilation system inside the mine helps conserve energy and improve airflow. Automated fans respond to signals emitted from the AeroScout Industrial's RF tags worn by all underground employees and installed on all major pieces of underground equipment.

"With the combined solution, Goldcorp can track real-time locations of both employees and machinery, and measure air quality for optimum working conditions. As miners and vehicles pass into various areas of the mine, the system powers on the fans only as needed, even adjusting the fan speed based on the carbon emissions expected from the specific vehicle type. This solution allows the company to optimize ventilation and also reduce its energy costs," says Cisco.[35]

Instead of running fans continuously, which burns out their motors, the company is better able to manage its ventilation units and run them only when needed. In a traditional mine of this size outfitted with conventional ventilation systems, for example, a mine operator would typically pump 1.2 million cubic feet per minute (CFM) of air into the shafts. But with the new smart technology, the Éléonore mine can run efficiently on just 650,000 CFM at a time, according to Goldcorp.

This translates into better asset utilization and huge costs savings, not to mention improved safety.

It's an outcome that is hard to beat.

Conclusion

No matter which type of business you're in, digitization can certainly help you improve your business results. As we have covered, it can help stimulate new revenue that would otherwise never be realized. It can help organizations reduce their costs. And it can help them improve asset utilization.

From any perspective, that's good business. Actually, make that *great* business.

Any time you leverage digital technology to make an improvement in one part of your business, you tend to achieve improvements in another. When you do, the financial benefits begin to compound, providing an organization with a virtuous multiplier effect that yields and yields and yields.

Remember when I said GE helped AirAsia save 1 percent on fuel costs annually? Well, guess which Asia-based air carrier boasts an industry-leading 25-minute on-the-ground turnaround per plane? That's right: it's AirAsia, whose planes require less refueling than they would otherwise if they weren't used so efficiently. And thanks to the company's work with GE, the air carrier boasts one of highest asset-utilization rates in the business.

Not only are its planes in the air more than most, its engines—thanks, in part, to all the on-ground powering down that it does—are among the best performing in the industry from a utilization perspective as well.

GE, of course, is a big believer in "asset-performance management," which is the discipline to leverage technology to drive more efficiency within asset-intensive companies. What's new in asset-performance management, says John Magee, chief marketing officer at GE Software, is how new digital innovations such as connectivity, data integration, mobility, and analytics are changing the entire business science. They are transforming the ways organizations are approaching their problems, Magee says.

"What asset performance management can do is deliver the insights, the data, and visibility so you can make all of your [facilities] operate as effectively as your very best," he says in a GE promotional video.[36]

Like others, GE is keen on helping companies build out the "Industrial Internet," which will very soon connect all of the objects, processes, and people not currently "online" through a system of machines, sensors, control systems, data sources, and devices.

As the Internet of Everything matures, companies of all kinds will be able to leverage asset-performance management tools to reduce their operational risks, improve efficiencies, and avoid unplanned downtime, which, whether you drill for oil offshore, manufacture advanced communications gear, or fly consumers around Asia, translates into significant benefits. For AirAsia—and GE itself.

Which brings me to an important point. If you leverage digital technology, you, too, can grow your revenue, reduce your costs, and improve your asset utilization. If you ignore it, however, you can be as sure as the sun will rise that someone else will gain the advantage.

Innovative companies like GE that thrive in good times and in bad understand the full significance of existential challenges such as the one digitization presents. The industrial powerhouse, of course, has been challenged by technological innovation before. In fact, it has a deep history that dates to the late 19th century, when inventor Thomas Edison teamed with famed financier J.P. Morgan and Anthony Drexel to consolidate Edison's many burgeoning electrical ventures.

Since then, of course, GE has entered and exited dozens of markets as GE has evolved over time. As of this writing, it is once again exiting a business (commercial finance) that once made it a pile of money but no longer serves its broader strategy, which is to thrive in good times and in bad.[37]

While that's the goal of many industrial giants, few achieve it. How many industrial companies do you think have survived since the dawn of the 20th century? Too many to ponder? How about I make it easier and frame the question the way that Mark Perry, a scholar at the American Enterprise Institute and economics professor at the University of Michigan, did in a 2014 study. At the time, he set out to determine how many companies from the Fortune 500 list of 1955 are still around. He found that only 12.2 percent of the Fortune 500 companies from 1955 were still on the list six decades later. The rest? Either bankrupt, merged, or still around but not large enough to make the list.[38]

As to why most have disappeared, Perry is unflinching in his assessment of how poorly most companies have reacted in times of "creative destruction"—the kind of period we are in today. Despite the upheaval it creates, new destruction—the kind that digitization creates, anyway—is ultimately a good thing.

Perry notes, "[I]t's probably safe to say that almost all of today's Fortune 500 companies will be replaced by new companies in new industries over the next 59 years, and for that we should be thankful. The constant turnover in the Fortune 500 is a positive sign of the dynamism and innovation that characterizes a vibrant consumer-oriented market economy, and that dynamic turnover is speeding up in today's hyper-competitive global economy. Steven Denning pointed out a few years [sic] in *Forbes* that fifty years ago, the life expectancy of a firm in the Fortune 500 was around 75 years. Today, it's less than 15 years and declining all the time."[39]

The point here is this: if you're not leveraging digitization to overhaul your business, you can safely assume that someone else is using digitization to challenge it. While it might have been fashionable once to question whether information and communications technology (ICT) was capable of producing the returns necessary to justify its purchase, today it is clear: sensors, collaboration software, business analytics tools, social media, and more can transform a business for the better. They can help it rise to meet any challenge and take advantage of any opportunity.

And that's what will drive financial performance in the coming years.

10

Customer Experience
*Happier Than Ever**

While every parcel matters to shipping giant FedEx, some shipments receive a bit more time and care than others. Take the bundle of crates shipped via FedEx from the Museum of the Rockies in Bozeman, Montana, to the Smithsonian Institution's National Museum of Natural History in Washington, D.C., in April 2014.

Their travel time point-to-point? Somewhere between 65 million and 67 million years, scientists say.

The bulk of this time, obviously, the contents—a nearly intact, seven-ton skeleton of an adult *Tyrannosaurus rex* dinosaur—were buried in the Rocky Mountain countryside near what is now the Fort Peck Reservoir in Montana. After being discovered there in 1988 by a rancher named Kathy Wankel, the remains found their way to the Museum of the Rockies in Bozeman, Montana, shortly thereafter.[1] In 2014, the priceless specimen, which is one of the most intact T-Rex dinosaurs ever discovered, was packed up and sent to the Smithsonian as part of a 50-year loan arrangement.[2]

While it might sound unusual to turn to FedEx to transport priceless cargo, it happens all the time. Unbeknownst to many, FedEx has a special division that deals with one-of-a-kind shipments. Over the years, FedEx Custom Critical Solutions has transported medical supplies such as human organs for transplant, antiquities such as the

---

* For their guidance with this chapter, I am grateful to Professor Peter Fader of the Wharton School at the University of Pennsylvania and Co-Director of the Wharton Customer Analytics Initiative; Ed Jimenez, Director of the Customer Experience Practice at Cisco; and Carlos Dominguez, President of Sprinklr, a leader in customer engagement through social media management.

historical artifacts of Russian Empress Catherine the Great, and even two giant panda bears between zoos in the U.S. and China.[3] The company's Custom Critical White Glove Services team boasts specially equipped vehicles and specially trained drivers "for the safe transport of your most sensitive shipments."[4]

When the time came to ship the Wankel T-Rex from Montana to the nation's capital, FedEx Custom Critical "worked closely with museum personnel from both the Museum of the Rockies in Bozeman, Montana, and the Smithsonian to strategically place the bones on pallets and develop a safe and secure packing method prior to embarking on the four-day trip," reported *Supply Chain Digital* in April 2014.[5]

The "safe and secure" method relied heavily on FedEx's ShipmentWatch capabilities, which leverage the company's proprietary "SenseAware" technology. SenseAware is an "advanced multi-sensor device [that] travels with the shipments to provide near real-time access to its current location and environmental conditions including temperature, humidity, exposure to light, barometric pressure and shock," says FedEx.[6]

Because SenseAware sensors continuously transmit their location and status, FedEx can track the whereabouts and condition of sensitive shipments throughout their journeys. And so can customers, thanks to the company's SenseAware tracking app. FedEx developed the app to soothe anxious shippers with priceless and often irreplaceable cargo. This includes parcels that literally have "out of this world" destinations from customers who work in the space industry.

"FedEx handles the terrestrial movements so we can focus on the celestial movements," says Dr. Benjamin Malphrus, chair of the Department of Earth and Space Sciences at the Space Science Center at Morehead State University in Huntington, West Virginia. Like other space pioneers, Malphrus relies on FedEx Space Solutions to ship sensitive cargo between laboratories, launch sites, and beyond.[7]

Going the extra mile for such exacting customers, of course, is nothing new for FedEx. The company that pioneered overnight shipping with the FedEx Letter in 1981 has regularly added conveniences and capabilities for customers since its founding more than 40 years ago. In 1986, it implemented a barcode tracking system that revolutionized logistics. In 1996, it became the first company to "allow customers to process package shipments on the Internet."[8] And in 2009, it introduced a mobile app for the iPhone and iPod Touch.[9]

Since then, the company has introduced additional digital innovations, including Internet of Everything-enabled technologies such as the SenseAware sensor technology. In 2013, it rolled out a warehouse application called Equipment Detection, Event Notification (EDEN) that leverages big data and sensor technology to optimize freight handling inside its massive distribution centers, according to *Information Week*.[10]

When combined, these digital innovations enable FedEx to offer a customer experience that is tough to beat in the highly competitive shipping industry. This translates into a significant competitive advantage for the company worldwide.

When you break down what FedEx does so well, you realize that the company is leveraging digital innovations to *engage* you in a deeper way, *satisfy* you to a degree that you didn't anticipate, and then *personalize* the experience just for you.

The company's Web sites and mobile aps, for example, make it easy to engage it in an efficient way. Completing a shipment form is no longer the task it used to be. And once you've completed your shipping and billing information, FedEx stays connected with you. It can send you alerts on when your shipment was picked up and when it was delivered should you desire. (Of course, it will also provide you a link so that you can track your package along its destination.) And if anything should get delayed, misplaced, and so on, the company will stay in touch with you by whatever means you desire—from social media to text alerts to online chats to telephone consultations—until you are satisfied.

This is what deep, connected engagement means today.

Similarly, FedEx exerts significant effort trying to create experiences that are deeply satisfying as well. If you think that's something only Disney or Apple care about, guess again. With new digitally enhanced innovations, FedEx can create experiences that are as wonderfully pleasing as any travel, entertainment, or consumer goods company. Its investments into ShipmentWatch technologies, for example, provide you with an unexpected boost of assurance that the company will handle your precious cargo with utmost care. Likewise, knowing that their most precious cargo can be transported via specially-equipped Custom Critical White Glove Services trucks with specially trained drivers gives consumers the confidence that they are managing their inventory, cherished possessions, or rare antiquities in the most responsible manner possible.

When you have the weight of a one-of-a-kind T-Rex on your shoulders, that's a big relief.

Then there's the level of personalization that FedEx provides. With FedEx's online and mobile applications, customers can access their shipping histories, spending habits, and mailing lists from virtually any device. With FedEx tools, consumers can now nickname their shipments, create personal watch lists, and filter settings to display only the shipment details that matter to them.[11] And they can do it 24 hours a day and in more than 220 countries and territories.[12]

FedEx, of course, is not alone in leveraging digital IoE technology to enhance customer experiences. Today, leaders in retail, entertainment, healthcare, manufacturing, and other industries are leveraging smart, connected innovations to do the same.

Why now? Again, the reason comes down to a confluence of new technologies that, when combined, create new opportunities for individuals and institutions alike. These innovations include ubiquitous mobile smart devices that provide remote access to information, applications, and more. They also include cloud computing systems, which effectively put the power and reliability of an industrial data center in the hands of any person regardless of whether they work in a classroom, office, or remote setting and regardless of their device. And it includes sensors and other devices that collect data in real time from things never before connected to an intelligent network. With this data, trained informaticists can analyze unstructured, real-time data and mine it for insights that are actionable in literally millions of new, portable applications that run on the most basic of devices.

Engage. Satisfy. Personalize.

These are the ways in which you create great customer experiences. And digitization helps immensely with each. Here's how.

Engaging Deep

Leaving a dog out in the rain? That's not a good way to win friends and influence enemies—especially when you do it in front of the entire Internet. But that's exactly what United Airlines did in late December 2014.

On a blustery, rainy day in Houston, with temperatures close to freezing, United ramp agents left a dog outside for an hour while they loaded cargo onto a plane. When United passenger Barbara Gattetly spotted the pooch in a crate on the tarmac, she snapped a photo with her smart phone and tweeted the following: "Evil United Airlines leaves dog on rainy cold runway for more than a half hour despite alerts to staff :-((((boo," according to the *New York Daily News*.[13]

Unfortunately for United, her tweet was picked up by scores of followers who then retweeted it to their followers. United responded with a tweet of its own that tried to put the matter to rest. But in the tweet, the company suggested that concerned citizens contact a third-party company that handles animal transport on behalf of the airline. Then things went viral. Shortly thereafter, television pundit Keith Olbermann saw the tweet and retweeted the following to his followers—all 549,000 of them: "Now, how an airline - @United - should NOT treat dogs or the bipeds who love them."[14] And then a few hours later, Australian pop singer Sia, who is followed by 2.1 million followers, chimed in with this: "I will never fly @United again. Thanks @theregoesbabs for exposing their shitty treatment of our beloved pets."[15]

From a public relations perspective, United stepped into a mess.

Afterward, the air carrier issued a statement defending its actions. It claimed the dog was protected under a wing the entire time and that it was left outside so that it would be the last thing loaded to ensure that it would be the first item to be taken off the plane after it landed at its next destination. But the media and "Twittersphere" were not buying the message.

The following day, London's *Daily Mail* newspaper ran a story with the headline, "United Airlines faces angry backlash after pet dog was left on tarmac in the pouring rain 'for more than half hour despite alerts to staff.'"[16]

What makes the story all the more unfortunate for United is that the company had made a concerted effort to turn around its industry-worst customer satisfaction (as reported by the 2014 American Customer Satisfaction Index), in part, with its aggressive use of social media.[17] In fact, the air carrier was a finalist for a 2014 Shorty Award, which is an honor given by Sawhorse Media to the "best of social media, recognizing the people and organizations producing real-time short form content across Twitter, Facebook, Tumblr, YouTube, Instagram, Vine, and the rest of the social Web." United was chosen for its use of Twitter to improve customer service.[18]

The episode with the dog notwithstanding, United had achieved a 99.5 percent response rate to complaints and inquiries sent to @United, which is pretty remarkable when you consider that roughly 70 percent of customer-service complaints made on Twitter go unanswered, according to a report published in *Knowledge@Wharton* that cites numbers from evolve24, a market research company based in Fenton, Missouri.[19]

United's goal is to respond to customer queries within 30 minutes no matter their area of concern. Ticketing? Baggage claim? Upgrades? Connections or even weather? United's social media team is eager to lend a hand. When necessary, team members will bring representatives from flight scheduling and airport customer service into conversations to help address customer concerns.[20]

"At its heart, this is a comeback story," said The Shorty Awards organizers. "Airlines and other brands in the travel industry have historically been leaders in social media, particularly customer service. But for many years, United was not one of them." After putting a team in place and dedicating resources, "Positive sentiment on tweets mentioning @united have increased more than threefold...."[21]

Like many, United learned the hard way that social media is a two-way street. It's a terrific tool for communicating with followers. But it can be turned against you if you do something embarrassing or off-putting. One airline that recognizes this is JetBlue, which, not coincidentally, is the industry leader in customer satisfaction among air carriers, according to the annual American Customer Satisfaction Index. In fact, the company has been the undisputed industry leader for the past three years, according to the Michigan-based index.[22]

Reasonable baggage policies and comfortable seats are a big reason why. But so is the company's dedication to creating customer experiences with social media that engage at a much deeper level.

Take JetBlue's response to the disastrous start of March 30, 2015. In the wee hours of the morning as passengers were getting out of bed to prepare for their early morning flights, a computer glitch shut down JetBlue's computerized check-in and reservations systems. The malfunction "left JetBlue passengers in Boston and across the country unable to obtain boarding passes or check baggage early Monday, creating long lines and delays as the airline manually checked-in passengers until the issue was resolved," reported *The Boston Globe*.[23]

At 6:03 a.m., JetBlue sent out a tweet from its global @JetBlue account alerting passengers, the media, and anyone else who followed it. The company said it had experienced a system outage and was working to get things up and running as quickly as possible. Twelve minutes later it responded to a customer who wondered if JetBlue was slowly trying to kill her with long waits at JFK International in New York. The airline apologized and reiterated that it was working as fast as possible to restore service.

At 7:05 a.m., the company tweeted that its system was back up and running, and by 7:22 a.m. the mass of people who had crowded inside the JetBlue terminal in Boston's Logan Airport while waiting for ticketing agents to hand-write boarding passes were off to their gates and ready to fly.[24]

Throughout the morning, JetBlue's team of @JetBlue social media specialists responded to customer complaints and questions with the gentle care and loving touch of a mother, which isn't a surprise since most of the team members based in Salt Lake City are indeed work-at-home mothers.

"Sure, a lot of airlines do this now. What makes JetBlue stand out from its competitors?" posed Rachel Sprung, a writer for the Web site *Social Media Examiner*.[25] "JetBlue is known to be extremely responsive to customers mentioning their brand. Whether they send a public @reply or a private [direct message] to answer a question, they are quick to interact."

In contrast to many others, JetBlue is proactive in its use of social media. It is also very fast and timely in its engagement. In a graduate case study for the Stanford School of Business in 2010, authors Jennifer Aaker, David Hoyt, Sara Leslie, and David Rogier explain that rather than use Twitter, Facebook, and other social media streams as a substitute for traditional customer service options, JetBlue recognized that it could leverage them to make all of its existing customer services better. They wrote, "The JetBlue Twitter team was able to serve as the 'canary in a coal mine' by instantly addressing customer service issues and resolving them. As [JetBlue corporate communications specialist Morgan] Johnston explained, 'Generally, the customer service model is one of recovery. It's not until a week later that you get an angry e-mail from a customer that you try to work to recover them. If you're watching what's going on in a real time medium, you have the opportunity to step in and effect change while they're having issues, while they're sitting at a gate. That is powerful for us.'"[26]

Powerful to customers, too. Many simply aren't accustomed to this level of engagement—at least not yet, anyway. Take Hyatt Regency guest Sean Morrison. One January afternoon in 2014, he sat poolside at the Hyatt Regency Scottsdale Resort and Spa at Gainey Ranch outside of Phoenix. On a whim, he sent a tweet out to his friends and followers: "Lunch poolside? Well, if I gotta. (@Hyatt Regency Scottsdale)." He attached a photo of his luxurious surroundings with his tweet.

Within minutes, the social media team at @HyattConcierge saw his note and sent back the following: "I hope you are enjoying your stay at the Hyatt Regency Scottsdale. If you need anything feel free to tweet me. –JS"

Feeling adventurous, he replied, "I definitely will! Great to see [my Tweet] closely monitored. How about a mojito? :-)"

Minutes later, a complimentary drink in a tall cup arrived at his table. Morrison snapped a picture of it, capturing the beads of moisture clinging to the side of the cup and the mint leaves and lime wedge inside. Then he sent out one more tweet: "@HyattConcierge the power of social media - behold! Thanks! #customercompany #win pic.twitter.com/RRQsXXpsjl."[27]

Since 2009, the lodging giant has used its Twitter account to exceed the expectations of key customers. The account is monitored 24 hours a day by a staff of hotel veterans located in Omaha, Nebraska; Mainz,

Germany, and Melbourne, Australia. Each is hand-picked and specially trained to respond to guest requests and anticipate them as well. The team responds to more than 8,000 tweets per month and hears back from guests 50 percent of the time in one form or another.[28]

When it comes to creating experiences that engage customers at a deeper level than others, JetBlue and Hyatt are difficult to beat. So is camera giant GoPro, which did something that even Cisco could not achieve—prevail with video recorders.

At the very moment when Cisco, Kodak,[29] and others concluded that affordable stand-alone video cameras were going the way of the dodo because mobile phone makers were building video-recording capabilities directly into their smart phones, GoPro's sales began to take off. A mere six months after Cisco exited the handheld consumer video recorder market, for example, GoPro unveiled the Hero2, an HD-capable device that featured an 11-megapixel camera and improved low-light video capture in a rugged, dependable package. With the Hero2, consumers shot millions of hours of video from literally all around the world. This includes the slopes of tall mountains, curls of big ocean waves, and floors of deep canyon passages. With their shock-proof, water-resistant cases, Hero cameras became a favorite of adventure seekers everywhere. The cameras were mounted to race cars, ski poles, hang gliders, zip lines, hockey helmets, and more.

Since then, the company's imprint on Internet culture has been indelible. Name a sport, activity, or event and you can bet there is a GoPro video of it online today. The world-record leap from a hot air balloon in 2012 by Austrian daredevil Felix Baumgartner? It was captured by a GoPro camera. Several of them actually.[30] In 2014 alone, consumers uploaded 3.9 years worth of content to YouTube with "GoPro" in the title; this was 40 percent more than the 2.8 years of content consumers posted in 2013, according to GoPro.[31] With its cameras in demand around the world, GoPro's revenue has swelled several times over. In 2014, full-year sales totaled $1.4 billion, 42 percent more than what the company achieved in 2013.

So how did GoPro prevail at the same time that others surrendered? Or JetBlue soar when United stumbled? Or Hyatt dazzle amid an environment when one bad viral review can thrash a brand?

The answer is this: the companies that are providing superior customer engagement with digital technologies are not only learning how to use the technology but also committing themselves to understanding how its use changes the rules of business.

JetBlue, for example, understands not only how to use social media properly, it understands that the technology compels organizations to act more proactively than before. Contrast its proactive use of social media to alert customers that its systems were down to United's reactive use of the technology to defend its actions after leaving a dog out in the elements. Both companies used the technology in delicate situations, but the outcomes turned out to be very different.

Which brings us to Hyatt. Hyatt understands that social media has reduced its ability to control its brand. No matter how much it spends on advertising, for example, it understands that reviews on Internet travel sites such as TripAdvisor or Expedia, or rants and complaints posted to Facebook and Twitter, have immense influence on consumer spending.

Rather than resist, it looks for opportunities to engage deeply when the moment presents itself, as it did when Sean Morrison tweeted, "@HyattConcierge the power of social media - behold!"

Then there's GoPro. Although fiercely proud of its cameras, the company recognized that they were only part of the overall customer experience that it offered. The video channels, social media services, and events that it supported were equally important to its success because they created *experiences*. While other camera makers focused on features and specs, GoPro put equal energy into creating engaging experiences that celebrated the human spirit to a degree that others simply did not understand.

What distinguishes JetBlue, Hyatt, GoPro and others is how they leverage digital technology to *engage* customers to create great customer experiences.

While beneficial, superior engagement alone doesn't always transform experiences into long-standing relationships with customers. For this, you must go one step further: you must *satisfy* customers, sometimes beyond their expectations. Once again, digitization is helping company after company do exactly that.

Satisfying Beyond Expectation

You know those irreverent photos that college seniors take on commencement day as they celebrate their graduation? Sure you do. In some, the kids have affixed cut-out letters to their mortarboards that spell out funny expressions. "Thnx Mom" some say. "Got Wrk?" others ask.

In a lot of the pages in albums and photos on Instagram, you also see graduates wearing sunglasses. But you've probably never seen a picture of an entire graduating class wearing cool shades—the dean included. Yet that's what the graduating class of The Wharton School of the University of Pennsylvania wore when two alumni, Neil Blumenthal and Dave Gilboa (both from the class of 2010), delivered the commencement address at the school in May 2015. The two are the co-founders and co-CEOs of Warby Parker, an upstart eyewear company that has become a sensation in the world of retailing by exceeding their customers' expectations.

When Blumenthal and Gilboa spoke in Philadelphia, the founders gave the entire graduating class of seniors, as well as members of the faculty, nifty Warby Parker sunglasses as a way of saying congratulations and good luck. (If you haven't seen, Google the photo; it's priceless.)[32]

But so is the way that Blumenthal and Gilboa have upended the world of eyewear, which is a business dominated by a handful of global giants—one in particular, Luxottica. If you're not familiar with Luxottica, note that it is a $9 billion Italian eyewear giant behind nearly every major fashion brand, manufacturing plant, retail store, and even vision-insurance payer that you can think of.

If you've ever wondered why eyewear, especially fancy designer eyewear, is so pricey, the answer has a lot to do with the near monopoly Luxottica has on nearly every facet of the business—from design to production to distribution to retail sales to insurance. By all accounts, Luxottica should have literally crushed Warby Parker like a schoolyard bully stepping on the spectacles of a smaller classmate. But it could not match the nimbleness of the upstart—at least not yet.

In 2010, Blumenthal and Gilboa recognized that the global, $90 billion-plus market for eyewear was ripe for disruption.[33] Figuring they could design and manufacturer glasses themselves—in New York City, no less—for far less than what Luxottica charged, the duo from Wharton sprang into action. Emerging digitization technology, which allowed them to take on a market force that was much larger than they were, helped propel them at every step.

Writing in 2015 for *Fast Company*, which named Warby Parker the #1 Most Innovative Company in the World, Max Chafkin explains, "By designing and manufacturing their own frames and selling directly to consumers over the Internet, they're able to charge as little as $95 per frame, a fraction of what a similarly nice pair of glasses would cost at a typical optical shop."[34]

The company also promotes them aggressively through the use of social media. In addition, Warby Parker provides customers with a "Home Try On" service that lets customers select five pairs of glasses over the Internet and then try them at their home for five days free of charge. If they cannot settle on a frame, they can mail all five back and request another set.[35] (A colleague of mine went through 15 pair of glasses before he found a model he liked.)

Warby Parker can do this because its back-end systems are tightly integrated with shipping companies and its supply chain via the Internet. The company has thought of almost every aspect of making the experience positive—from selecting to reviewing to returning, if necessary. And yes, just in case a customer desires to return something, each shipment comes complete with a pre-printed return shipping label and pouch for returning frames. It literally is fool-and-idiot proof, which takes the hassle—if not anxiety—out of eyewear shopping.

"People have no clue how to buy eyeglasses," says Barbara Kahn, director of the Jay H. Baker Retailing Center at Wharton, in a 2013 report on Warby Parker published by *Knowledge@Wharton*. "It's a completely overwhelming chore. You go into a store where there are thousands of pairs, and you don't know how they're going to look and which frames are right for you. The salesperson 'helps' you by narrowing [your selections] down to five pairs. So how do you do this without the salesperson's expertise? Warby Parker figured it out with an offer to let customers choose five pairs of glasses for five days. You can try them on in front of your mirror, show your friends, post it to Facebook and get other people's opinions."[36]

Though clearly a product of the Internet age, the founders consider Warby Parker to be more than a mere e-commerce or technology-lifestyle brand. Since its rise to fame, the company has opened select retail stores in New York, Los Angeles, Chicago, and elsewhere.[37] It has also begun eying an expansion into other market categories, though eyewear is its sole business as of this writing.

Since its success, the company has inspired a lot of other entrepreneurs to leverage digital technologies and open businesses that aim to be the "Warby Parker" of their market niche. Razor supplier Harry's, for example, is trying to do to Schick and Gillette in razorblades what Warby Parker is doing to Luxottica in frames. Similarly, Bikyni, which launched in 2015, is trying to upend the market for swimwear with an Internet business for women to mix and match swimsuit tops and bottoms to find the right suit in the right size that suits their body style, lifestyle, and fashion sense. And it's doing so for a simple price of $95.[38]

In each case—Warby Parker, Harry's, and Bikyni—upstart companies are leveraging digital technology to create experiences that satisfy customers uniquely and upend the entrenched business models of competitors by way of extension. The same technology is also helping large, established organizations satisfy customers in new ways. Take Luxottica, the company most directly impacted by Warby Parker. Not one to rest on its laurels, Luxottica has looked long and hard at what its smaller rival has been able to accomplish with digital technology and has committed itself to topping it. Among other things, Luxottica has teamed with AirWatch EMM to create "virtual try-on" kiosks inside its retail stores that allow customers to try on dozens of combinations of frames and lenses. Luxottica has also developed a myLook app for its Lens Crafters stores that customers can use to capture images of themselves wearing different styles, and they can compare and share these images with their friends.[39]

In 2014, Luxottica made a bold move to acquire glasses.com, an online eyewear retailer known for having one of the more engaging "virtual try-on" technologies in the business.[40] When a customer goes to Luxottica's Ray-Ban branded Web site, for example, he or she can now use the Virtual Mirror capability acquired from glasses.com to try on many different styles in near 3-D quality from the privacy of their home.[41]

Another corporate giant using digital technology in an innovative way to improve customer experiences is Starbucks, which is using technology to address the one thing that sours its customers' experiences most—waiting in line for a cup of coffee.

If you're like most people, you generally don't stick around if you're not among the first few people in line at a Starbucks restaurant. Starbucks knows this. It even has a term for the number of people who decide to leave one of its stores after peering their heads in and deciding they don't have the time to stick around. It's called the "balk rate."

The longer the line at a typical Starbucks, the higher the balk rate. In an article for *The Suburban Times*, a community Web site based in Lakewood, Washington, reporter Joe Boyle wrote about the balks he witnessed firsthand at a neighborhood shop that routinely has lines out the door. In a blog entry entitled, "Westside Story—Starbucks Customers Walk Out," Boyle wrote, "Sunday morning around 10:00 am, I stopped in at Starbucks for a cup of beverage, some fun talk with friends and to do some writing on my laptop...While standing in line, 4 customers became frustrated and left the store without making their intended purchase."[42]

While four "balks" in 30 minutes might not sound like much, it adds up to hundreds of millions of dollars a year in lost revenue to a company with more than 21,000 stores in 65 countries.[43] If Starbucks were to reduce its balk rate by just one customer per store per day, it would increase its revenue by more than $30 million annually, according to company figures.

Over the years, the company has tried various methods for reducing the balk rate. But the work hasn't been easy. Starbucks offers 80,000 different drink combinations and recognizes that a big reason why customers flock to it is the care and effort that the company puts into every individual drink.[44] Reducing or eliminating the time customers have to wait for hand-crafted beverages could improve one aspect of the overall customer experience, but at what cost if it destroyed coffee quality or selection? executives wonder.

Knowing they could only do so much to reduce the time it took to make a quality, hand-crafted beverage, Starbucks thought leaders began experimenting with several different IoE-enabled technologies several years ago. Their first breakthrough: the myStarbucks and Starbucks Card Mobile apps for smart devices, which debuted in 2009.[45] The apps allowed customers to load money directly into their electronic Starbucks accounts and pay for items from their phones at Starbucks' stores that were equipped with special barcode readers.

Since their introduction, Starbucks' technology team has added several enhancements. In particular, Starbucks upgraded its apps so that customers could use them to find a nearby Starbucks store using the GPS capabilities built into their phones, place orders from within the app, pay for the orders directly, and then pick up their orders without ever standing in line. Walk-in, walk-out just like the people who "balk"—only this time with a beverage in hand.

And Starbucks keeps improving the customer experience. Rachael Antalek, Vice President of Concept Innovation at Starbucks, told me that recently when she was driving to work one day she ordered her coffee from the Starbucks app, and a message showed up on her smart phone screen asking to confirm if she really wanted to order the coffee right now—because it takes 3–5 minutes to make it, but she was 15 minutes away (based on her GPS location).[46] Pretty cool.

With the latest version of the app, you can earn Starbucks "Stars" credits and redeem rewards and more, according to the company. "...You can Shake to Pay for a speedy purchase, digitally tip your barista and download our free [iTunes musical] Pick of the Week," the company wrote in a corporate blog.[47]

Consumer response to Starbucks' efforts to increase convenience with IoE technology has been positive. "As a college student, I often have to run from building to building between lectures, and it is great to be able to order and swing by and grab my drink without affecting my schedule," said one app reviewer on Starbucks' corporate Web site. "I love the mobile order function!" wrote another. "Easy to use, haven't had a glitch yet. Drink order is ready when I walk in the door. Nice when I am in a rush."[48]

One reviewer on Apple's App store went so far as to write that the app made her "addicted to Starbucks." "I once was just a casual

Starbucks drinker. Once a month, sometimes 3 when I felt daring, but it all changed when the Starbucks app attacked...then I fell into a routine of getting Starbucks 5 times a week," said the reviewer, who gave the app a five-star rating. "I love you Starbucks app."

Since their debut, Starbucks apps have been downloaded several million times. And today, Starbucks apps account for an estimated 15 percent of all Starbucks purchases, according to the company.

As much as they love the current app, users want Starbucks to enhance it so that it is easier to use when ordering multiple drinks at once. They'd also like an easier way to designate which Starbucks shop is their favorite, where inside individual stores they should pick up their pre-orders (it varies from store-to-store today), and how they can add specialized instructions for custom orders. In addition, they want stores to be able to communicate with them if an order will take longer than usual or cannot be made due to a shortage of ingredients or some other difficulty. Mostly, they simply want Starbucks to keep beverages warm while they search for a place to park.

Starbucks is working on several of these ideas and more. If customers are open to the idea, Starbucks could use the GPS positioning capabilities on their phones to help coordinate the preparation of beverages with the arrival time of their customers. Starbucks could also send loyal customers promotional offers and other enticements any time they walk by a store. In addition, Starbucks has also looked at ways to send customers discounted gift cards if they enter an over-crowded store and leave quickly without making a purchase. Doing so could go a long way to helping to reduce the dreaded "balk rate" within its coffee shops.

Starbucks isn't the only company leveraging technology to improve customers' overall experience. Burger chain Five Guys, for example, has developed an app that customers can use to order food from their phones. They can designate the time they want to pick up their orders and then swing by a Five Guys restaurant without standing in line to pay.

Talk about convenience.

Professor Peter Fader, Director of the Customer Analytics Initiative at the Wharton School of the University of Pennsylvania, offers a word of caution, though. "While digital technology offers ways to satisfy, even delight customers uniquely, we must be careful to not use such tactics blindly, i.e., without any knowledge of (1) the value of the customer, (2) the changes to the customer's value as a result, and (3) the overall cost/benefit of these tactics,"[49] he says. In other words, don't forget the economic and business context. Interestingly, digital technology actually helps answer these questions as customers increasingly reveal more about themselves, and businesses analyze that information.

So what can we take away from these examples?

For starters, we can see that digital technologies can be applied to satisfy, even delight, customers to a degree not possible before the rise of social media, smart mobile devices, and predictive analytic software applications, just to name a few ideas. Tiny Warby Parker, for example, is upending a $95 billion industry with its ability to leverage digitization to make customers happy with better pricing, convenience, and innovation. And Starbucks? It's grown into a $16.5 billion giant in the food and beverage retail business by doing innovative things, technology among them. The company is so digitally focused, in fact, that it was one of the first to name a senior executive to the position of "Chief Digital Officer."[50] Digitization helps the company overcome customers' No. 1 complaint: wait time. It helps it bond more deeply with customers to better understand and even anticipate their needs and desires.

To grow even bigger, Starbucks, along with other companies, is going one step beyond engaging and satisfying customers. It is using digital technology to *personalize* the offers it extends to them.

Here's how.

Personalizing at Every Turn

An ATM for clothes.

That's what New York-based startup Bombfell set out to be for men of a certain age and sartorial disposition. Founded in 2011 by two former Harvard University roommates (yes, the parallels to Warby Parker are indeed there), the company sells clothes to men over the Internet. Initially, it focused on men who just wanted a simple way to buy denim. But since then it has added fresh brands that are shaking up the menswear industry. Think Uniqlo, Standard Issue NYC, Big Star, and others.

Today, Bombfell is more than a mere e-commerce company that spits out denim on demand like an ATM dispenses cash; it's also a personal advisor as well. Bombfell leverages digital technology not just to simplify transactions, but to enhance them with intelligence—both of the technological variety and human kind.

When customers sign up with Bombfell, they typically complete user profiles that ask for their fashion likes and dislikes, sizes, and other information, including budgetary constraints. Bombfell then pours this information into its computer algorithms, which have been designed to match customers' data profiles against its inventory of goods. At intervals and quantities chosen by customers, Bombfell will send members a parcel of clothes approved by its stylists that customers can review for as long as they like. The items customers want, they keep. The ones they don't, they return free of charge.

Like other shop-by-mail destination Web sites, including Trunk-Club, Stitch Fix, and others, Bombfell excels at making shopping not only convenient, but personal.

"We use technology to make personal styling orders of magnitude more efficient," the company says. "Our stylists are supported by an algorithm that surfaces the best matches for a user based on fit and style. The stylist then has the final word in making a selection, taking into account special requests and other factors like skin tone."[51]

Skin tone? You cannot get much more personal than that. Or more impactful, when it comes to customer experiences.

Using digital technology to engage customers is a first step to making experiences better. Leveraging it to delight them takes commerce to another level. But using it to personalize experiences? That's the Holy Grail for many organizations looking to provide unique experiences to customers in a replicable, consistent way. Mass customization is possible; Bombfell and others are proving it.

For more on those who excel at personalizing experiences, look no further than those who deliver a digital product like information, video, and music. When it comes to providing a personal experience, Spotify is hard to beat.

If you're not familiar, Spotify is a music-streaming service similar to Pandora, Beats Music, and iTunes Radio. The company boasts 75 million users. Like these services, it serves up music over the Internet. Users can use a limited version of the service for free (so long as they can tolerate advertisements and limited device playback options) and can listen to music by a certain artist, genre, or album to their heart's content. A premium service, which costs $10 per month, provides greater flexibility and convenience. It's used by more than 20 million customers per month—a base so large that even Apple, which is accustomed to dictating terms in the music business, had to react to Spotify's ascendency with a competing service that it launched in June 2015.[52]

Once subscribed, Spotify customers can create "stations" based on their musical preferences and share favorite playlists with fellow users of the service. The more customers use Spotify and rate or reject songs, the more the service adapts to their personal tastes. After learning a consumer's personal likings, Spotify is able to leverage this information and then make reasonable calculations as to what a consumer might like next. The "predictive" nature of what Spotify and other innovators are able to provide is what sets them apart from other organizations, including financial services companies that have used real-time analytics to make on-the-spot-decisions for years. Visa's software systems, for example, are able to spot fraud instantly whenever your credit card is being used in a manner that is inconsistent with your prior shopping patterns. But that's very different from being able to predict that you'll like Jimmy Cliff's reggae classic "The Harder They Come" based on your repeated playing of the ska tune "Rankin' Full Stop" by The English Beat.

In a comparison with other leading streaming services, *Digital Trends* writer Rick Stella named Spotify the pick of the bunch in late 2014. He singled out Spotify for its ability to leverage its vast library of music and provide customers a way "to spend hours going on your own discovery tangents, all of which are completely controlled by you."

"What makes Spotify so great is its deep library of artists and albums, many of which get updated each week with new releases. If there's a new album you look forward to hearing, Spotify typically has it ready for streaming the day it's released. It brings a record store right to any smart phone or computer, and features none of the frustrating plastic wrap," Stella writes. "With Spotify's endless library of songs, it's easy to get lost in the sea of music they offer. Moreover, for just $10 a month, premium subscribers get access to uninterrupted song playback, high-quality audio recordings, mobile access, and the ability to download and listen to their playlists offline."[53]

From a technological perspective, Spotify, Pandora, and others use very complex algorithms to better understand what appeals to its customers and, conversely, what does not. To develop these, the companies spent thousands of hours decoding songs—distilling them down into their essential elements. Take Pandora. By the time that it went live in 2005, the company had tagged the attributes—including beats per minute, melody, lyrics, and so on—of hundreds of thousands of songs. Its Music Genome Project is the core personalization engine. When the service serves up a new song or artist to a listener, there's a lot of science that makes that listening experience truly unique.

When blended with social media and other apps produced by music-streaming companies, including Spotify's lyrics apps, which display the words to whatever song you're listening to, the experience can be transformative. And uniquely yours and yours alone.

By personalizing music to a greater degree, Spotify and others have yet again changed the recording industry for the second time in little more than a decade. In 2001, Apple revolutionized the music business when it launched the iTunes Music store. It liberated consumers from buying music in a physical format (such as a vinyl album or digital CD) and freed them from buying collections created by record labels. Spotify and others have taken digital personalization one step further by providing music on demand in a searchable, customizable, and convenient format that is available from virtually any digital device and playable through almost any output.

The result? The $4.5 billion recording industry is once again being turned on its head.[54]

Another industry that is undergoing a similar transition, thanks to digitalization, is video entertainment, which historically was bound by two constraints: time and access. Thanks to Netflix and others, these market restrictions are becoming a thing of the past. Netflix provides the ultimate in personal viewing experiences, serving up not only what consumers want, but when they want it, thanks to its sophisticated computer algorithms.

Recognizing that viewing tastes are uniquely individual, even among members of the same family, Netflix was one of the first to allow subscribers to create separate, personal profiles within a single account shared by different family members.

While companies with digital-based products were among the first to exploit the potential of personalization technology, others who sell hard goods and services have quickly followed. Take fashion label Burberry, which has invested millions to become one of the vanguards in digital luxury retailing. The company, which has more than 16 million followers on Facebook,[55] has an online digital flagship store that is available in more than 40 countries and in five languages. It offers click-to-chat interactivity and click-to-call customer service in 14 different dialects, according to the media site *Luxury Society*.[56]

"Personalization also plays a key role in Burberry's digital strategy, in both product and communications," *Luxury Society* reported in 2014. "Burberry Bespoke was launched in 2011 via burberry.com, whereby users can develop a unique trench coat online, by choosing style, fabric, colour, embellishments and heritage details."[57]

More recently in 2014, the company launched a unique experiment in mass customization, the My Burberry campaign, that took personalization to places it's never been before.

The campaign leverages digital technology in several ways to provide perfume customers a more personalized experience. In several cities throughout the world, Burberry has arranged with electronic billboard companies to participate in an interactive campaign that leverages smart phones and other devices.

"The British brand, which launched its interactive ad campaign at London's Piccadilly Circus, is currently gracing New York's Meatpacking District with the personalized experience," writes *Forbes*. "Once you're near the sign, simply log on to myburberry.com to submit your initials—up to three letters—and watch the countdown begin on your phone. When it's over, you'll be rewarded with the sight of your own, monogrammed bottle of My Burberry (until the next passerby comes along)."[58]

Consumers were inspired to take pictures of their personalized bottles displayed on the 60-foot screen and then post them to their Facebook, Pinterest, Twitter, Sina Weibo, Google+, Youku, QZone, or Instagram accounts. Before customers walked away, Burberry sent them an electronic map with walking directions to the nearest Burberry retail location. Once inside the store, they could recreate their monogrammed bottles on large digital screens and then have them produced right there in the stores.

Burberry also arranged for readers of *Elle* in the UK to receive copies of the publication with their initials printed directly onto a bottle that appears in a Burberry ad within the magazine. Judging by the response from social media, the simple act of personalizing a promotion appears to have been a hit with consumers. After receiving her copy of *Elle* in the mail, consumer Stacey Toth tweeted, "Clever @Burberry very very clever." Another Burberry fan tweeted, "Best ad ever? Adore this @Burberry #MyBurberry campaign with my @ELLEUK sub which has been monogrammed for me."[59]

If you think investing in personalization technology to sell expensive perfume in the UK is frivolous, then consider the effort from Burberry's perspective. The company is in the fashion business, which is an enormous and highly competitive industry. If you know the industry, you understand that the business runs on emotion—impulse, in particular—as much as anything else. Burberry gets this and naturally treats its best customers better than most. It will provide celebrities creations from its couture collection. It will invite some of its highest-spending customers to its fashion shows. And it will make sure that its big spenders are treated superbly whenever they set foot inside a Burberry's store.

This is classic customer segmentation.

Personalization is very different. It's about making *every* customer feel a little special or privileged. That jolt that Burberry customers get from seeing their names on perfume bottles up in lights? That emotion translates into real business for the company. And Burberry is keen on seizing that positive goodwill whenever it can.

That's why the company puts Q-codes in many of its advertisements. If a consumer loves the look of a particular outfit, Burberry wants to make sure that it doesn't miss the opportunity to sell that outfit in that moment. Burberry has made it possible for consumers to simply scan those Q-codes with their smart phones to find the exact item that stirs their senses and then shop for that product directly from their smart devices. Consumers can check sizes, color options, and even availability directly from their phones. Should they choose, they can buy merchandise and arrange for shipping from their smart devices as well. If an excited consumer cannot wait for delivery, Burberry will send the buyer a map to the closest retail location where he or she can pick up the item immediately.

Now, I'm not suggesting that technology alone is what made Burberry a fashion trendsetter from London to Lagos to Los Angeles. Obviously, clever designs, compelling marketing, and an efficient supply chain deserve a lot of credit, among other things. What I am saying is that all of these aspects of the company's business and more have been enhanced significantly by Burberry's use of digital technology and IoE. Thanks to these, the experiences that Burberry provides customers are more engaging, satisfying, and personal than they otherwise would be.

The results speak volumes—literally. Between 2004 and 2014, Burberry's revenue climbed from $1.1 billion to $3.5 billion.[60]

Talk about the sweet smell of success.

If you're wondering how your company can leverage data and connectedness to create more personal customer experiences, then take a cue from the companies mentioned in this chapter. In each instance—Bombfell, Spotify, Netflix, and Burberry—organizations looked carefully at the voluminous amount of information that customers knowingly share and then developed more personalized experiences using real-time data and predictive algorithms to produce new business insights. This level of personalization has historically not been possible. But now that it is, entirely new customer experiences are becoming more common. As customers experience them, entire industries—including music, movies, retail and more—are getting disrupted one by one.

Conclusion

Engage. Satisfy. Personalize.

I truly believe that new digital technologies can create unforgettable experiences—ones that truly leave customers in awe.

How? By engaging the way that JetBlue does. Delighting the way that Warby Parker does. And personalizing the way that Spotify can. This is customer experience at a whole different level than before.

In each instance, these companies demonstrate an uncanny ability to leverage technology to anticipate customer wants and needs, provide them with value they haven't even considered, and do so in a replicable and repeatable way that feels as though everything was done just for them. And in so doing, they are unleashing a wave of disruption that is changing the landscape of business.

How far can this go?

The possibilities are endless. To illustrate the point, I've highlighted a lot of examples from the consumer world. But the same outcomes can be achieved in the business and non-commercial sectors. Healthcare, for one, is ripe for digital transformation. So is education. Thanks to new devices, software applications, and business models, we will not only see healthcare delivered in a more engaging, personalized, and satisfying way, we will come to expect it. Same for education.

In the preceding chapters, I've showcased several ways care providers and educators are leveraging technology to make healthcare and learning more engaging, satisfying, and personal. What I've chronicled represents only the beginning of what is to come. Which brings me to you.

If your favorite retailer, travel brand, care provider, or educational institution can transform experiences with digital innovation, why not your own organization? If you don't believe it's possible to create experiences that are more engaging, satisfying, and personal in the field in which you work, then step back and prepare to be amazed by someone else who does.

No matter where you work or what you pursue, digital transformation is coming to your world. You can lead the change, follow along at a cautious pace, or stand back as waves of disruption wash over your industry.

There are pros and cons to each approach. But embracing digitization enthusiastically could very well spell the difference between being the innovator that gets paid to transport the Wankel T-Rex that I wrote about at the beginning of this chapter or being the dinosaur itself.

No one, especially a strong, powerful force in the market, likes the idea of being displaced by something new and different. But if history has taught us anything, it has taught us that survival isn't a matter of strength or size. It's a measure of adaptability.

If you want to prevail in the years ahead, then leverage digital innovation to create customer experiences that engage, delight, and personalize in ways never before possible.

You won't regret that you did.

11

Employee Experience
*Productive, Creative, Engaged**

If you manage people for a living, here's a statistic that will surely grab your attention: a majority of employees in the American workforce consider themselves "not engaged" with their employer. What is worse, according to a 2014 study completed by Gallup, Inc., 17.5 percent consider themselves "actively disengaged."[1]

How could this be? Globalization, technological disruption, stagnant wage growth, and reduced job security are just a few of the reasons why.

If you think this is a problem that occurs only in old-line industries and tired companies, guess again. In 2013, Yahoo! CEO Marissa Mayer created an uproar when she decided that employees of the dot com-era Internet company were not engaged sufficiently with one another and thus could no longer work from home.

"To become the absolute best place to work, communication and collaboration will be important, so we need to be working side-by-side. That is why it is critical that we are all present in our offices," wrote Jackie Reses, Yahoo's human resources chief, in a memo explaining Mayer's reasoning. "We need to be one Yahoo, and that starts with physically being together."[2]

Not long after the internal memo surfaced in February of that year, criticism for the decision began rising to the top of news sites

---

* For their guidance with this chapter, I am grateful to Prasad Setty, Vice President of HR and Head of People Analytics at Google; Lori Goler, Head of Human Resources at Facebook; and Fran Katsoudas, Chief Human Resources Officer at Cisco.

and Twitter feeds. Increasing employee collaboration doesn't mean sitting workers next to each other or corralling them in meeting rooms until they produce new insights, workforce experts noted. Instead, it means giving them the inspiration and tools to work together seamlessly and effectively no matter their geography, corporate function, duties, or even social position within an organization.

"Perplexed by Yahoo! stopping remote working," tweeted Virgin Atlantic founder Richard Branson. "Give people the freedom of where to work & they will excel."[3]

"Epic fail," said Peter Cohan, a contributor to *Forbes* and a frequent commentator on TV.[4]

While some defended Mayer's decision, scores of others piled on. Some thought the decision was anti-family and represented a setback to working moms.[5] Still more said the decision flew in the face of research from Stanford University,[6] the University of Illinois,[7] and elsewhere that showed the benefits of telecommuting on worker productivity.

Lost amid the brouhaha of the decision was Mayer's original intent—to increase workforce collaboration. On this point, she cannot be faulted. Study after study reveals that connected workers produce better outcomes. For their employers, partners, and customers alike.

So why did Mayer draw such criticism? Her implementation was flawed. Mayer foisted upon a modern workforce an old-fashioned talent strategy that is out of step with the new digital economy and the young, always connected, mobile generation that is taking over more of our workforce as the millions of Baby Boomers born in the aftermath of World War II retire at the rate of 10,000 per day in the U.S., according to the Social Security Administration.[8] By 2020, Millennials born between 1982 and 2003 will "comprise more than one of three adult Americans. By 2025, they will make up as much as 75 percent of the workforce," according to a Brookings Governance Study on "Millennials and the Future of Corporate America."[9]

In practical terms, independent and socially conscious Millennials entering the workforce today don't want to be told they cannot use their personal phones for business communication. They don't want their employers to forbid them from using social media while on the job. And they don't want to work in a rigid environment that ties them to a 9-to-5 job in a single location. They feel so strongly about these convictions that they will turn down unappealing work in favor of employment that better suits their lifestyle—even for less money. Consider an oft-cited survey of young people completed by the Intelligence Group, a Los Angeles-based market research and consultancy. It found in 2012 that 64 percent of Millennials said they would rather make $40,000 per year "at a job they love" than $100,000 a year in a "boring" one.[10]

While idealism and altruism have always measured high among the young, attitudinal differences between the young and the old have rarely been so great.

The last time there was this much upheaval in the workplace was the 1980s and 1990s. That's when corporations began offshoring manufacturing jobs to China and outsourcing call-center jobs to India. Since then, robotics and wage appreciation have reduced the gains that can be realized from shifting labor-intensive operations from high-wage economies to cheaper, less-developed environments. Today, an entirely new dynamic is driving institutional behavior. This is the need to compete more effectively in the new "digitized" economy, where technology innovation, not labor arbitrage, has become the most powerful force for driving change. This goes for both labor-intensive, blue-collar jobs *and* knowledge-intensive, white-collar occupations.

The social, technological, and economic changes of the last few years have left an indelible imprint on our world, the workplace included. Because of these changes, the nature of work is changing, especially where digital disruption is occurring. Work is moving faster. New business models are emerging. And more automation is taking root. Now, almost all jobs are being influenced by digital innovation. Data is rooting out inefficiencies and providing new insights that allow employers to rethink workforce strategies.

Employees are also rethinking careers and work. Workplace dynamics have made employment more fluid than before. People don't stay in the same jobs the way they once did. Nor do they stay within the same industry.

Workers today want flexible schedules and different opportunities at different stages of their lives. For that flexibility and opportunity, they work very hard. Remember the notions of life and work balance of a few years ago? This idea no longer applies in a mobile, digitally enhanced world where you're expected to respond to emails from your boss at a baseball game while simultaneously checking stock prices and trading instant messages with your daughter.

When you step back, you realize certain workplace realities that became a fact of life for some professionals a few years ago are now becoming the norm for most. Work is no longer a place people go so much as it is a set of things they do—continuously.

For all the upheaval, there are many ways that employers and employees alike can mitigate its negative impacts and take advantage of its positive ones. In this chapter, I look at how progressive employers are responding to improve employee engagement. Spoiler alert: many are approaching workforce modernization very differently than Mayer. While their goals might be the same—for example, recruiting the best talent possible, enabling them in the most efficient way, and then inspiring them to be their most creative—their methods are very different. And so, likely, will be their results.

According to McKinsey,[11] "Research demonstrates that companies with enlightened talent-management policies have higher returns on sales, investments, assets, and equity."

In this chapter, I examine the ways companies are leveraging digital technology to recruit the best talent, give them the tools to be productive, and foster the environment to be creative.

Building the Workforce of the Future: The Bespoke Employee

"How does a brand that's been around since 1927 continue to evolve and adapt and stay relevant?"

You innovate, says David Beebe, vice president of global creative and content marketing with Marriott Corp.[12] To demonstrate that it is more than an operator of mid-priced hotels with floral-print bedspreads and burgundy carpets, the hotel chain has let its creative juices flow.

In 2015, the company launched a movie, an online magazine, and a video production business. The company's push into creative content began in March when its newly created content studio released a 17-minute romance and action film featuring two fictional hotel employees. In a mere few weeks, "Two Bellmen" generated more than 5 million views on YouTube.[13] Shortly thereafter, the company launched its online travel magazine, *Marriott Traveler*, which includes articles and videos showcasing popular travel destinations such as New Orleans and Chicago. Some of the videos feature popular travel journalist Sonia Gil.

What's unique about Marriott's push into creative endeavors, which includes a TV series as well, is how little the brand "Marriott" turns up in the content. This is done on purpose, explains writer Tessa Wegert in a case study published by the Web site *The Content Strategist*.

"What Marriott is attempting to do goes beyond content marketing to become an entirely new marketing model. The majority of its content is designed to be not just a cost center, but a revenue center," writes Wegert. "Because it doesn't feature a strong brand tie-in, it's valuable to other distributors, and advertisers, too." Among other things, she notes, Marriott will monetize *Marriott Traveler* "by selling sponsored content and native ads to third-party advertisers."[14]

Clever, no?

It certainly is. But that's only the half of it. To make its marketing dreams come true, the hotelier got *really* creative. First, it hired some talented content specialists from Disney-ABC, *Variety*, and elsewhere. Then it tapped the collective expertise of freelance writers, videographers, spokespeople, and graphic designers everywhere. To manage this process efficiently, Marriott's content team turned to Contently, one of a growing number of online professional job sites that connect employers with contract workers who have special skills.

Contently and other sites owe their existence to the largest of all digital career sites, LinkedIn. LinkedIn is an online destination and mobile app on which professionals can post their resumes, work accomplishments, and more, and then network with other working professionals around the world. Members can view profiles, exchange

messages, and even post articles, blog posts, tweets, and other mus-
ings about the world of work.

Founded in 2002, LinkedIn boasts more than 330 million members. More than 107 million Americans alone are members—roughly
one of every three citizens. Every second, two people join the service.
And each day, the collective membership views 25 million LinkedIn
profiles.[15]

More than a social media convenience, LinkedIn has transformed
the world of work by enabling both active and passive job seekers to
showcase their skills on a platform that is now the No. 1 place employers and recruiters go to find talent. Thanks to LinkedIn, frustrated
workers no longer need to toil under inept managers; they can seek
greener pastures at the mere click of a button. And some segments
of the recruiting industry are feeling like travel agents felt after Travelocity came on the scene.

In the wake of LinkedIn, which specializes in helping professionals find permanent employment, a number of sites and apps that help
people find part-time work have grown in popularity. Contently, for
example, specializes in helping creative types who deliver content
for a living find work. Other sites, such as Work Market, focus on
information technology, the law (UpCounsel), and customer service
(Odesk), just to name a few. Quite distinct from a growing number
of low-budget, one-off job sites such as Fiverr or TaskRabbit, which
connect consumers with particular needs to people willing to move
a refrigerator or write a personalized rap song for a graduation for a
few extra dollars, Work Market, Odesk, Elance, and other sites are
designed for serious professionals.

On these sites and apps, employers can posts jobs or assignments,
vet candidates' credentials (including references), set terms, and
manage payments—and all at the press of a button. Workers looking
to augment their incomes or break into new fields, meanwhile, can
use the sites not only to search for work but also to help them with
bookkeeping, project management, time-tracking, and professional
development.[16]

While freelancing, subcontracting, and even online job boards
such as Monster.com have been around for years, the growth of new,
more focused digital services and social media sites has transformed

contract work from a "who-you-know" racket into a "what-can-you-do" marketplace. Because of its immediate, global, and expansive nature, the digital freelance marketplaces are giving rise to what has become known as the "gig" economy, which is comprised of organizations looking to supplement their workforces with part-time specialists who pay their own taxes, fund their own retirement plans and, now with the Affordable Care Act (ACA), buy their own health insurance.

In the U.S., these workers are known as "1099ers" because of the tax forms they get from employers instead of traditional W2 forms that full-time employees receive in advance of filing their taxes with the Internal Revenue Service (IRS). No one knows precisely how many people work as full-time 1099ers, but according to research published in 2015 by Ardent Partners, freelancers and independent contractors now account for about one-third of the U.S. workforce, or roughly 53 million workers. This figure is expected to rise to nearly half of the workforce in a mere few years, according to the company's "State of Contingent Workforce Management 2014-2015 Guidebook."[17]

Today, 1099ers work in virtually every sector of the economy, including financial services, healthcare, the law, and technology, just to name a few industries. They are especially active in creative fields, such as advertising, marketing, and video production. While some people work as 1099ers because they cannot find permanent work in their field of expertise, millions work as 1099ers by choice. They can choose their hours, assignments, employers, and even their work environments if they so desire.

The ability to fill a position or "gig" is transforming the labor sector in several ways. Instead of switching positions six or seven times over the course of a career, workers can now leverage these sites to work for dozens of employers over the span of their careers. If they want to make more money, workers can pile on as much work as they can handle. If they want to slow down or take a vacation, they can step back and accept fewer assignments. And they can do so without fear of reprisal or criticism.

"Workers now have real choices about how much they're going to organize their work—how much they want to work and when," says Sara Horowitz, founder and executive director of Freelancers Union. This is a far cry from years gone by when customers looking for help from third parties viewed potential partners who relied on contract workers warily. But now that so many rely on independent contractors themselves, organizations don't hesitate to do business with companies that depend on part-time workers.

While use of these workers varies from industry to industry, some companies swear by 1099ers. Take Renascence IT Consulting, Inc., of Newark, California. Since its founding in 2010, the company has provided technology services throughout the San Francisco Bay Area. From software programming to product installation to network security, Renascence is a one-stop shop for all your technology needs, says founder and CEO Kurt Lesser.[18]

As a technology service provider, Renascence takes on big integration and software development assignments from customers large and small. Most jobs are fixed in scope, meaning that Renascence's staffing needs expand and contract as projects are completed. The company has just four full-time employees but enlists a virtual army of dozens more on a moment's notice when needed. While Lesser knows most of these professionals personally, some he has never met. But he makes use of their labor just the same. And his organization is more agile and flexible than others as a result.

"By maximizing the potential of both an extended workforce and permanent employees, companies can gain critical advantages—including agility and access to valuable talent," Accenture concludes in its 2013 "The Rise of the Extended Workforce" report.[19]

And this is just the beginning.

In a guest editorial for *Forbes*, Work Market co-founder and President Jeff Wald said data-driven metrics will help in the hiring and managing of freelancers. "From crowdsourced marketplace ratings and reviews to background checks and performance metrics, companies will have access to a myriad of data about the quality and background of the workers they hire. This accumulation of data and intelligence will allow businesses to become more sophisticated about finding and managing freelancers," he wrote. "Analytics engines within [freelance management system] software will even allow businesses to optimize various aspects of their contract labor strategy and dramatically improve decision-making across the entire enterprise."[20]

If this sounds overly disruptive to you, then rest assured that the gig or freelance economy is not likely to upend full-time employment any time soon. Just as Massive, Open and Online Courses (MOOCs) aren't intended to replace the traditional, on-campus educational experience in the near term, freelance Web sites and digital job markets won't undermine the traditional, full-time work experience either. But make no mistake, they will influence it heavily.

Where contract employment will likely have the greatest impact is in areas where specific expertise is needed on a limited or as-needed basis. Take Marriott's push into creative content development. Hiring a few dozen contract professionals efficiently is a marvelous way for it to get into the content production business. But the effort is not going to change the fact that the lodging giant will still need full-time workers for their core operations.

Another way the gig economy is influencing work is the way it has reshaped how employers promote, transfer, and manage their own employees. Cisco, for example, has launched an internal "Stretch Assignment Marketplace" on which employees looking to advance their careers can apply for "stretch" assignments that last anywhere from one to six months. The assignments come from fellow workers or managers who seek part-time help on a limited basis. Typically outside their areas of expertise, these assignments provide workers an opportunity to immerse themselves in other parts of the organization and mix with business leaders they ordinarily do not come in contact with. While some assignments are modest in scope, others provide up-and-coming employees an opportunity to contribute their input to some of the company's most difficult business challenges.

In just the first few months since its inception, hundreds of employees have participated in stretch assignments advertised on the internal marketplace. And in doing so, they have gained new experiences, received recognition, and greatly contributed to key projects within the company, according to Jill Larsen, Vice President of Human Resources at Cisco.[21]

None of this would be possible without the shift in cultural attitudes within Cisco regarding part-time work nor the digital tools that make these types of flexible work arrangements possible. Along with the commercial marketplaces, they help Cisco and employers like it find the right person for the job every time.

Which is precisely the point. In our ever-more-specialized, ever-more-fluid workplace, matching the right talent to the right assignment has never been more important. With new digital technology, employers can seek talent from a much broader pool of candidates than ever before and on a much more granular level than before. And in less time. The same, of course, is true for job candidates.

At Google, connected data analytics is used extensively to identify and recruit the right candidates. Prasad Setty, Google's VP of People Analytics, says that Google applies the same level of analytical rigor to people decisions as it does to product decisions. Interviews are structured, with calibrated rubrics where performance can be analyzed and matched against large data sets that have greater predictive value that one-off individual judgment. It is at the intersection of human resources practices and connected digital technology.[22]

Once again, technology is disrupting another industry. Just as it democratized access to healthcare, education, financial services, and even retail shopping, digital technology is now making it easier than ever for employees and employers to find precisely what they are looking for in terms of work.

If you're an employer and take advantage of the capabilities and opportunities that marketplaces like LinkedIn, Work Market, and others offer externally, or marketplaces like Cisco's Stretch Assignment Marketplace offer internally, you can create a competitive advantage for your company by simply staffing it with the best talent possible. By contrast, you could weaken your company if you don't step up and engage the world of employees who have embraced the new digital economy.

Love it or hate it, this is the new employee-employer relationship dynamic.

That said, finding the right person for the right job is only one piece of the workforce of the future puzzle. Once employers have the right workers in place, they need to provide them with the right tools and workplace environments that enable them to work more effectively. Given the distributed, decentralized nature of so many organizations today, this means equipping workers with the collaborative communications tools that help them overcome time, distance, and other challenges that are commonplace in today's mobile, social, and hyper-connected work environments.

Helping Workers Get More Done: The Collaborative Workplace

If you pour beer along the Texas Gulf Coast in a honky-tonk restaurant or neighborhood bar, you probably know Del Papa Distributing. Founded more than a century ago, the Texas City company distributes 10 million cases of beer annually from 30 different suppliers. In all, Del Papa employs 375 people at its headquarters and in two other distribution centers.

In 2011, the company set out to build a new headquarters on a 27-acre plot of land near the Texas Gulf Coast. But company executives worried that its employees would lose the very intimacy that helped make the family-owned business so productive in the first place. So Del Papa leaders turned to Cisco for help.

Working with a local business partner, Zones, the two organizations showed Del Papa technology that would help the company move into the 21st century without losing the collaborative spirit that it developed in the early 20th. The technology, of course, was advanced video communications. Cisco makes a variety of tools for collaborating across time and distance. For executive communications that require the utmost in video and audio clarity, it offers Cisco TelePresence technology, which facilities life-sized meetings with zero latency and the highest degree of security possible. For virtual get-togethers, it offers videoconferencing software that can run on almost any portable device connected to the Internet, plus a suite of meeting tools that allow people to attend virtual conferences where documents can be shared and face-to-face interactions conducted in high-definition quality at the press of a button.

After seeing Cisco's portfolio of products, executives at Del Papa realized that it could help them in a variety of ways. At a very basic level, they recognized that the technology would increase their communications. But that was just the beginning. They believed the technology would help them better utilize their assets, improve their physical security, and, most notably, sell more beer.

So Del Papa deployed video collaboration technology throughout its entire operations. This included installing video collaboration tools in every office, conference room, break room, warehouse, and more. To prepare for such a complex rollout, Cisco moved to consolidate Del Papa's four separate communications networks that managed voice, data, video, and physical security traffic. Doing so gave the company a single, secure network for physical security, communications, collaboration, and even monitoring inventory temperature, says Steve Holtsclaw, manager of Information Systems at Del Papa.

With the unified network, Del Papa discovered that collaboration improved in several ways throughout the company. The Cisco Tele-Presence units installed by the company allow its workers to connect directly with executives from Anheuser-Busch (one of the brands Del Papa distributes) and fellow employees located in different parts of its massive operation. "Of all the things we can do with our new network, TelePresence is the leadership's favorite," Holtsclaw says. "It's made us more efficient because we can have an in-person experience without the time and costs of driving." This includes time employees formerly spent driving to other offices for departmental meetings, performance reviews, quarterly all-company meetings, or even first-round job interviews. That's big to a company at which every minute of sales time counts toward the bottom line.

"Del Papa isn't selling beer if the salesforce is driving to meetings," Holtsclaw adds. "Meeting with Cisco TelePresence gives reps more time to interact with their customers."

The new network also keeps Del Papa's workforce better informed about the company activities. The latest news and delivery schedules appear on nearly 30 digital signs scattered throughout break rooms, cafeterias, hallways, workout rooms, and delivery entrances. What is more, messages can be tailored on the fly. From 4 a.m. to 6 a.m., for example, the signs in the delivery area display safety messages and weather information. Signs in break rooms, meanwhile, play the latest supplier advertisements and product information.

Connecting previously unconnected people and things has improved safety and security, made business processes more efficient, and even helped improve customer service. Take rush orders. Previously when company sales reps called the warehouse with a rush order, they often got their warehouse colleagues' voicemail. If a warehouse worker didn't check his or her voicemail until the end of the day, that last rush order often didn't make it out the door on time. But with warehouse workers having access to wireless IP phones and instant messaging, by the time reps get back to the Del Papa warehouse after visiting customers, their customers' orders are sitting in the shipping bay, ready for delivery.[23]

The benefits don't stop there.

"These solutions don't just cater to employees within organizations, but are also aimed at expanding their reach across channel partners and customers, thereby expanding their reach across departmental and geographical boundaries," concludes a 2014 report from ReportsnReports, a Dallas-based market research company. According to it, the market for global enterprise social software is expected to top $8 billion in 2019, up from $4.77 billion in 2014.[24]

The growth of the market is being fueled by institutions that believe collaboration technology can unlock employee productivity that is otherwise trapped by barriers and boundaries. When workers can plug into a network of connected peers and tackle meaningful assignments, they often feel a sense of connection and purpose. But when tasked with work that denies them self-determination or a sense of belonging, loyalties can fray and dedication can waiver.

Again, take Cisco's use of collaboration technology. Since deploying video, document sharing, and Web meeting technology almost a decade ago, Cisco calculates that the value created from the effort has returned billions of dollars to the company. The amount of money Cisco has saved from reduced travel alone is estimated to be $210 million annually.

It's not just Cisco, of course, that has seen the benefits of increased employee engagement with collaboration technology. Take a study commissioned by Cisco and published by *Forbes Insights* in 2013. A global survey of more than 500 executives on how cloud-based collaboration technologies could impact their businesses found the following: 64 percent of respondents said cloud-based collaboration tools help businesses execute faster; 58 percent of respondents said cloud-based collaborations have the potential to improve business processes such as purchasing, manufacturing, marketing, sales, and technical support; and 59 percent of executives interviewed agreed that cloud-based collaboration stimulates innovation. When looking at the subset of respondents who have significantly greater experience and familiarity with cloud-based collaboration tools and strategies, the percentages increase to 82, 90, and 93 percent respectively.[25]

This, of course, is just the beginning of Internet-enabled collaboration. Today, a number of companies are developing technologies designed to stimulate what experts call "serendipitous" encounters that lead to unanticipated and impromptu idea sharing. Sociometric Solutions is one such company. Founded by several MIT graduates, the company developed a platform for tracking employee interactions with wearable sensors. With data collected from these sensors, Sociometric then maps employee interactions against performance metrics using sophisticated algorithms. Researchers working with the data look for patterns of interactivity that produce gains in workforce productivity.

If the idea sounds a little bit out there, rest assured the technology is real. Some companies swear by it. Bank of America is one. For three months, Sociometric engineers tracked Bank of America call center employees who were outfitted with sensors that tracked their whereabouts. Everywhere the call center employees went, a computer captured their movements. (To protect their privacy, individuals' names were anonymized by the software.) The experiment, which was chronicled in *MIT News* in 2014 by reporter Rob Matheson, uncovered some surprising findings. Among them: when a specific group of employees would take a lunch break together, organizational productivity increased consistently. Armed with this information, Sociometric data specialists advised the bank to have its call center workers eat together in a communal fashion. "Sure enough, when the bank instituted the changes," Matheson wrote, "Sociometric measured a 15 to 20 percent bump in productivity, a 19 percent drop in stress levels, and decreased turnover, from 40 to 12 percent."[26]

While the above might seem a little extreme, the gains that come from getting people working together more collaboratively—no matter the method—can be extraordinary. In addition to cost savings, increased collaboration helps businesses get work done that otherwise would never happen. When one of my former colleagues wanted to meet with Russia's former minister of economics and trade, German Oskarovich Gref, he was told that an in-person meeting would take several months to set up. But a face-to-face TelePresence meeting? "How about next week?" he was asked.

Video collaboration not only increases the intimacy of business, it accelerates the immediacy of it. This helps employers and employees alike get more done.

This is helping companies around the globe achieve significant gains in productivity—and elevating satisfaction for employees who feel they are far more efficient and effective at getting their jobs done. Taking advantage of this in today's fast-moving world can lead to amazing outcomes; ignoring the digital revolution underway in employee collaboration could lead to serious stagnation.

As beneficial as this technology is, there is still one more tranche of value that digital technology can provide. That's the ability to leverage the creative spark that resides within all of us. In too many instances, this spark is either overlooked or underutilized. But new tools have shown employers how they can put the best thinking of their employees to work—and with good reason. The adage that inspiration can come from anywhere? It's true.

Leveraging the Creative Spark in Us All: The Idea-Sharing Workforce

Scotchgard. Post-It Notes. Super Glue. Saccharin.

Any idea what these popular products have in common? They were all invented by accident.

That's right, the people behind these modern marvels were actually trying to create other inventions when they stumbled across these innovations instead. Thankfully, their creators were not deflated by their failed experiments but inspired to make the most of them.

If you're lucky, one of your employees will step forth one day with a billion-dollar idea born of dumb luck. But don't count on it. Lucky accidents like these don't grow on trees or miraculously appear in laboratory test tubes more than a few times in a generation.

Dumb luck, in other words, isn't a formula for repeatable success. Nor are ivory towers, despite the best efforts of Xerox, AT&T, and others who once isolated their best thinkers in laboratories and research centers located away from their corporate offices. When separated from the company's core workforce, Xerox scientists at the famed Palo Alto Research Center (PARC) created windowing interfaces, scrollable screens, and other inventions.[27] Likewise in Murray Hill, New Jersey, Western Electric and AT&T scientists combined forces to create the famed Bell Laboratories. There, innovators developed radio astronomy, the transistor, and the C computer programming language.[28] As innovative as these centers were, however, they weren't tightly integrated with the heart of the corporations that gave them life. Because of this, the wonderful ideas that sprang from these developments took years to reach market. Many of PARC's ideas, including the computer mouse and graphical user interfaces, for example, languished for years until outsiders—think a shaggy-haired kid named Steve Jobs—recognized their true potential.

To harness the potential of an organization's workforce, organizations need a system and an environment that stimulates creative thinking. Today, a growing number of organizations are applying a variety of ideas for stimulating innovative thinking, not just among product developers, scientists, and engineers but among employees from all walks of life. In companies across the globe, business leaders are finding the answers to some of their most vexing problems can come from anyone within their organizations if they elevate the level of engagement they have with their workers. Take crowdsourcing.

Crowdsourcing, you might already know, is a method of product development and problem solving that leverages the input of a wide spectrum of people. In and of itself, the idea is not new. Recognizing that ideas can come from anywhere—from the factory floor to the corporate boardroom—companies have sought the wisdom of crowds for decades

Today, crowdsourcing is being pursued with digital tools that have taken the idea to an entirely different level. This is especially true of the ways organizations are trying to stimulate "internal" crowdsourcing, the kind that occurs when engaged employees of an organization reach across corporate lines to share ideas with cohorts in other parts of their company. Internal crowdsourcing has proven itself effective for new product development, process refinement, and asset utilization. As a result, it is being received with enthusiasm in a growing number of workplaces. Take Thomson Reuters Corp., the American business information giant.

Like a lot of companies, Thomson Reuters is always looking for new ideas to leverage its core product, which, in its case, is information. The job for creating new ideas at Thomson Reuters typically fell to the 17,000 people who work for the company's engineering and product development departments. But Thomson Reuters employs a total of 55,000 people worldwide. Surely some of them must have some ideas for better running the organization, management thought.

So beginning in 2013, the company launched an internal talent competition, according to the technology news site *TechTarget*.[29] In an article, Mona Vernon, head of Thomson Reuters' innovation data lab, said internal competitions have "been huge" for identifying employee talent that can partner with internal teams and customers to "find data-driven innovations."

In one example, Vernon said Thomson Reuters was desperate to find someone who could help with a tricky problem involving extracting text from digital documents. After its engineers said they couldn't find a solution, Vernon launched an online competition that was open to any company employee. Within the relative blink of an eye, an employee stepped forth with a workable solution to the problem. What surprised Vernon and fellow executives was that the worker who submitted the idea sat just "two or three cubes away from the team," wrote *TechTarget* Senior News Writer Nicole Laskowski. The employee, Vernon said in the article, was, "effectively hiding in plain sight."[30]

The experience taught the company several valuable lessons, not the least of which was that innovation can come from anywhere, including overlooked places. The episode also made Thomson Reuters realize that it needed to specifically ask for employee input and then provide workers with a mechanism or place where they could share their thinking.

In many instances, funding and managing internal Web sites that support these efforts requires the support of an influential executive sponsor, Vernon told *TechTarget*. It also requires some ingenuity and even a little bit of risk-taking. This is what IBM discovered when it launched an innovative internal crowdsourcing project.

In 2012, a team of senior IBM engineers wondered if a crowd-sourcing experiment would generate new ideas from internal research-ers. To prime the pump, the engineers gave 511 IBM researchers $100 each and asked that they spend a month putting various ideas and proposals together. To help them organize their thinking, IBM launched an internal Web site that featured interviews, surveys, and project status updates. Then IBM asked the 511 researchers to evalu-ate the various proposals and vote with their money for the ones they thought were best.

To its surprise, IBM found that the researchers were wildly enthu-siastic about the endeavor. Unlike other internal programs, this one attracted significant participation and attention. Nearly half of the 511 researchers actively participated throughout the project. And though most participants were technologists at heart, the ideas they proposed spanned the gamut from innovation to work culture to morale. The level of employee inter-departmental interaction was almost unprec-edented in company history. The mean number of IBM departments that researchers connected with was seven.

Upon completion, the project's backers, including IBM technol-ogist Michael Muller, chronicled their findings in a research paper published in 2013. Here's some of what they found:

"Major outcomes include: employee proposals that addressed diverse individual and organizational needs; high participation rates; extensive inter-departmental collaboration, including the discov-ery of large numbers of previously unknown collaborators; and the development of goals and motivations based on collective concerns at multiple levels of project groups, communities of practice, and the organization as a whole..."[31]

Cisco has launched similar programs to help solve ongoing chal-lenges and identify new opportunities. Cisco Smartzone was launched in 2010 to capture the best thinking that originated within the Cisco Services organization. "Smartzone" is an open innovation platform that allows any Cisco employee to submit an innovative idea. The best of these are then presented to the company's workforce, which can vote on ideas that it wants to pursue. So far, more than 70 ideas have been identified as worthy of pursuit. In all, the ideas chosen by the company's workforce have produced nearly $40 million in value for the company.

Cisco has also developed an online mechanism called "Street Smart," where sales people can provide their immediate input with their supervisors and managers on customer insights, sales trends, economic conditions, and other factors that influence business. With this tool, executives who oversee Cisco's vast global organization can get immediate insight from the front lines at the click of a button.

Another Cisco program, Connected Recognition, has similarly engaged company employees in an innovative way. The Connected Recognition program replaced a traditional, top-down employee recognition program that identified top performers based on management input.

The problem with the old system was that company managers were often too busy to take time to reward individual contributors for heroic deeds—or too self-absorbed to notice. As a result, employee awards took months to process and even longer to bestow. Recognizing this, Cisco created a new online initiative to reward workers and then left it largely in their control.

Fran Katsoudas, Chief Human Resources Officer at Cisco, points out that the impetus behind Connected Recognition was the realization that the old way wasn't working and that a new way driven by bottom-up employee input and digital innovation would work better.[32]

In addition to changing the way awards are determined, the new system greatly expands who can qualify for recognition. This has dramatically increased the company's ability to shine a light on positive behavior and recognize it with everything from a monetary bonus to a gift card to even a simple "attaboy" distinction.

In the first year since the Connected Recognition program went live, Cisco handed out more than 181,000 awards, 38 percent of which have gone to teams and not any individual, per se. One in six awards have been given to employees who are not based in the country where the honoring team is located.

Organizations that have used internal crowdsourcing programs to increase employee engagement have found that some of the ideas that have come forth are better than the ones produced by teams formally assigned to new product and business development. Employees are not motivated only by monetary rewards; they are motivated to step forward and volunteer their time and energy, and they are doing so for a multitude of reasons. Some are motivated by true altruism and want to help their colleagues. Others are looking for a little recognition. And some just love problem-solving. Writing for the *Harvard Business Review* in 2013, Kevin Boudreau, an assistant professor of strategy and entrepreneurship at London Business School, and Karim Lakhani, associate professor of Business Administration at Harvard Business School, said crowds not only offer organizations scale and diversity, they offer incentives that companies find hard to match, such as the opportunity to polish one's resume.

"Companies operate on traditional incentives—namely, salary and bonuses—and employees are assigned clearly delineated roles and specific responsibilities, which discourages them from seeking challenges outside their purview. But crowds, research shows, are energized by intrinsic motivations—such as the desire to learn—that are more likely to come into play when people decide for themselves what problems to attack," Boudreau and Lakhani wrote.[33]

Better thinking at a lower cost? This greatly enhances the ability of corporations to shape a creative, effective, and rewarding work environment that benefits workers and employers alike.

And digital technology is the catalyst for it.

Conclusion

No matter how you look at it, the workplace is changing in significant ways. It's getting more automated. And more competitive. It's also getting younger and more global.

In this chapter, we've covered the ways digitization is affecting—and will affect—employees' experiences. We've revealed how digitization will lead to greater job mobility and organizational flexibility. We've showcased how it can be applied to improve individual productivity and enrich employee engagement.

Some of the ways technology enhances employee interaction are not new. Contract employment isn't new. Nor is crowdsourcing or simply asking employees to look beyond their own offices or electronic inboxes to the broader challenges facing their employers. What is new are the number of ways digital innovation can be applied to make these and other phenomena *bigger, faster,* and more *accessible.*

The online freelance marketplaces? They are literally connecting workforce supply with workforce demand on a global basis, making connections that never would have been possible previously. Similarly, collaboration technology is helping workers work more efficiently and seamlessly. And broader idea sharing is helping everyone work smarter.

Like any tool, the innovation being developed today can be used for both good and bad. Asking employees to wear sensors to help drive gains in productivity? It's easy to see the pros and cons of this. Likewise, allowing workers to combine their work and personal lives via social media has benefits and consequences. Take the popular professional social media site LinkedIn. If you're connected with your boss, he or she can see how quickly you add new contacts and from where. Without needing your permission—the information is publicly available, after all—your boss can quickly determine if you're looking for new work, what the odds are that you will leave, and if or when you are likely to do so.

On the plus side, it will be almost impossible for "Horrible Bosses" to survive in the new digital economy. In a world where interactions, outcomes, and connections can be easily rated and then shared with everyone, the bad boss of today is likely to be shown the door sooner than later.

As the workplace changes, so will our communities. On any given street in America, you might find people not only working at 10 different employers but also working virtually in 10 different countries, thanks to digitization.

What will it mean for community cohesion, social mobility, and cultural continuity? No one knows for sure. What we do know is that digital, Internet-enabled technologies are creating new employee experiences. For the most part, we believe these are for the better.

So what does this mean for employers? Think of employee effectiveness as a continuum. You can increase organizational flexibility by recruiting the best from anywhere. You can improve individual productivity by providing the tools and freedoms that drive collaboration. And you can increase idea sharing by engaging individuals and teams deeply and leveraging their best thinking.

Though we might marvel at the things machines will one day do in the workplace, the future still belongs to those who achieve the best workforce experience possible.

12

The Digital Revolution
Only the Beginning, Only Just the Start

Change happens fast—or so we are told.

But if you think about the things in your life, including your home, wardrobe, or car, ask yourself, "how many have been thoroughly transformed over the last 20 years?" The answer might surprise you.

Chances are, you have many things in your world that really haven't changed all that much. Take something as basic as your refrigerator. No doubt it is more modern than it was two decades ago. And probably better. The seals are tighter, the shelving more practical. But did the moisture sensor or dual-climate zones make it thoroughly different? Your milk and eggs don't react as though they did.

Likewise, would someone really notice if you wore a suit from 20 years ago to a wedding? Some people with sartorial savvy might, but they would unlikely make it a *thing* if they did. But imagine if you were to pull out a mobile phone from 20 years ago and use it at the reception to call your babysitter. Assuming you could get it to work, there's no way that piece of technology would go unnoticed—or pass without some comment.

Which brings me to my point: While the rest of the world evolves at one pace, technology seems to move at another. It's why the things that technology touches—think communications, entertainment, electronics, and so on—feel so unsettled. In the world of technology, there is no status quo; flux is constant.

For most of us, this takes some getting used to. Traveling, shopping, and even gathering the daily news is so much different than it was just a few years ago. So is working. The rhythm of the office, for example, is so much faster than before, thanks to electronic and digital innovation. Product cycles are shorter, development times compressed. And every business is under more scrutiny (thank you, social media) and under more pressure (thank you, technology-enabled globalization) than before.

So many of us are so busy that we rarely take the time to step back and think about the cumulative effect technological change has on us. Here in America, I rarely do until the world stops for a day or two, such as it does when there's a national holiday such as Thanksgiving. When the world slows in November in the U.S., we collectively take solace that the preparation, enjoyment, and even clean-up of a holiday meal has largely been untrammeled by technology evolution. For a moment, everything seems pretty much the same as it did 20 years ago, save for the kids on the couch with headphones, tapping away at their mobile devices.

But if I've made any point in this book, it should be this: whatever vestige of technology-free life you take for granted is about to change. Personally and professionally. Digital innovation, in other words, is coming to every facet of life as we know it.

Though you may wish to, there's no stopping it. How we live, work, learn, and play is going to radically change, if it hasn't already.

For some, this reality is going to feel more than unsettling; it's going to feel downright wrong. In the next few years, every industry you can think of will undergo a digital revolution. As it does, many existing jobs as we know them will go the way of the movie projectionist, receptionist, travel agent, and stenographer. In a documentary film that debuted at the 2015 Sundance Film Festival, Jeopardy champion Ken Jennings describes the moment that he realized just how widespread this displacement will be.[1] In the film *Most Likely to Succeed*, Jennings recalls the humiliation he felt at the hands of IBM's Watson Cognitive Computer, an earlier version of which beat world chess champion Garry Kasparov in a match in 1997.[2] Chess was one thing, Jennings figured, but subject-matter expertise in a multitude of disciplines? Knowing a little something about artificial intelligence, Jennings thought originally he had the match in the bag.

But quickly into the game against Watson, the Jeopardy champ realized he was about to get unceremoniously dethroned by a machine. Afterward, Jennings realized that for the first time in history, jobs that involved critical thinking, including white-collar jobs in many industries, were in "jeopardy" of technological displacement (if you'll pardon the pun).[3]

If true, this will create significant disruption in the workforce, including where you work. As business practitioners, we have come to expect and even accept that robots will replace task-oriented factory workers in the workplace. But replacing engineers, technicians, and even sales professionals? The very idea sends shivers up the spines of millions.

But it need not.

As I've outlined throughout the chapters of this book, digital innovation is something to be embraced, not resisted. With it, I've shown how everyday business practitioners can increase revenue, reduce expenses, and improve asset utilization. I've also outlined how the technology can be leveraged to engage customers more deeply, delight them more thoroughly, and personalize offers to them more effectively. Finally, I've shown how digital innovation can be used to build a better workforce, one that is more flexible, collaborative, and creative than before.

More than theory, I've also shown how this is being done today in important industries, including healthcare, education, retail, transportation, and more.

Yes, there are significant challenges that this technology revolution will create. In addition to the issue Jennings raises, there are immense concerns that we must address in the areas of privacy, security, and governance.

But imagine that we do. What kind of world will we end up with then?

As I see it, adding intelligence and connectivity to every object you can think of is going to make us smarter and more connected by design. This is a good thing for a multitude of reasons.

If you buy into the adage widely credited to physicist Albert Einstein that says we cannot solve our current problems with the same level of thinking that created them, then digital technology is the higher level of thinking that we have been pining for for decades. Imagine attacking deep-rooted societal problems such as crime, poverty, economic stagnation, environmental degradation, and more with better thinking. Could we make gains against at least a few of these then?

Absolutely.

Today, we have already cataloged the world's information; much of it is already available at our fingertips. And we are amassing new insights from the things we collectively add to the Internet by the minute. As time goes on, we are learning to better apply this knowledge. In practical terms, this means we will surely be able to provide greater access to education, better fight hunger, and increase economic opportunity for all. From there, is it really a stretch to say that we could eradicate most diseases, educate everyone, or reverse environmental degradation?

I believe these are possible—certainly in our children's lifetimes, if not in our own.

Which brings me back to you.

I know the pace of technological change is unsettling. It is to me, even though I've worked inside the epicenter of Silicon Valley for almost 30 years. I think about this during what unfortunately can be a long commute to and from the office. As I poke along the highways of Northern California, I look at the cars and drivers all around me and wonder what many are thinking. Many, I know, are trying to envision the next big thing that will rock our world; it's what we do in the Valley, after all.

More than a few entrepreneurs I know are inspired by what 21st-century innovator Elon Musk has accomplished with the Tesla Model S. When I see one, I remember the quote that is often attributed to 20th-century icon Henry Ford. "If I asked people what they wanted," he said after the introduction of his wildly popular Ford Model T car, "they would have said they wanted a faster horse."

Ford, of course, didn't give them a faster horse but an affordable mode of transportation that literally changed America as we know it.

I don't know whether Ford actually said these words; there's no official record of it. But the sentiment is as true today as it was then. The smart, connected innovations that brilliant thinkers like Musk and others are able to create with digital technology will be as varied and transformative as they are unexpected.

No doubt some will cause upheaval—even pain—as we try to absorb the accelerated pace of change. But as long as these ideas advance the cause of humanity, I say bring 'em on.

From the Ford Model T to the Tesla Model S, innovation is our future.

As it always was.

Endnotes

Introduction

1. http://www.emarketer.com/Article/2-Billion-Consumers-Worldwide-Smartphones-by-2016/1011694

2. http://www.economist.com/news/leaders/21645180-smartphone-ubiquitous-addictive-and-transformative-planet-phones

3. http://wearesocial.net/blog/2015/01/digital-social-mobile-worldwide-2015/

4. http://www.factslides.com/s-Twitter

5. http://www.statista.com/statistics/321215/global-consumer-cloud-computing-users/

6. http://www.cisco.com/web/about/ac79/docs/innov/IoE_Economy.pdf

7. http://blogs.cisco.com/news/cisco-connections-counter

8. http://expandedramblings.com/index.php/new-updated-apple-stats/

9. http://www.cisco.com/c/en/us/solutions/collateral/service-provider/visual-networking-index-vni/white_paper_c11-520862.html

10. http://www-01.ibm.com/software/data/bigdata/what-is-big-data.html

Chapter 1

1. http://www.techinsider.io/tesla-model-s-insane-mode-vs-ludicrous-mode-2015-9

2. http://auto.ferrari.com/en_US/news-events/news/announcing-the-f12berlinetta-the-fastest-ferrari-ever-built/

3. http://www.motortrend.com/oftheyear/car/1301_2013_motor_trend_car_of_the_year_tesla_model_s/viewall.html

4. http://www.consumerreports.org/cro/video-hub/cars/hybrids--alternative-fuel/tesla-model-s-20132014-quick-take/14786539001/2366240882001/

5. http://www.wsj.com/articles/tesla-model-s-the-future-is-here-1428086202

6. http://www.visualcapitalist.com/10-mind-blowing-facts-tesla-motors-tsla/

7. http://www.7x7.com/arts-culture/real-top-10-list-steepest-streets-san-francisco

8. http://www.teslamotors.com/sites/default/files/tesla_model_s_software_6_2.pdf

9. https://newsroom.uber.com/2015/06/5-years-travis-kalanick/

10. http://www.mckinsey.com/insights/business_technology/the_internet_of_things_the_value_of_digitizing_the_physical_world

11. http://blogs.cisco.com/news/at-the-center-of-the-digital-vortex-chaos-disruption-and-opportunity

12. http://blogs.cisco.com/news/at-the-center-of-the-digital-vortex-chaos-disruption-and-opportunity

Chapter 2

1. http://www.oecd.org/health/health-systems/Focus-Health-Spending-2015.pdf

2. http://www.globalissues.org/issue/587/health-issues

3. http://www.uspharmacist.com/content/s/216/c/35249/

4. http://www2.deloitte.com/content/dam/Deloitte/global/Documents/Life-Sciences-Health-Care/dttl-lshc-2014-global-health-care-sector-report.pdf

5. https://www.cms.gov/research-statistics-data-and-systems/statistics-trends-and-reports/nationalhealthexpenddata/nationalhealthaccountshistorical.html

6. http://mercatus.org/publication/us-health-care-spending-more-twice-average-developed-countries

7. https://www.cia.gov/library/publications/the-world-factbook/rankorder/2102rank.html

8. http://www.oecd.org/berlin/47570143.pdf

9. http://www.wcrf.org/int/cancer-facts-figures/data-cancer-frequency-country

10. http://www.worldlifeexpectancy.com/cause-of-death/coronary-heart-disease/by-country/

11. http://healthintelligence.drupalgardens.com/content/prevalence-diabetes-world-2013

12. http://www.oecd.org/els/health-systems/health-at-a-glance.htm#TOC

13. http://khn.org/morning-breakout/health-care-costs-4/

14. http://www.medicarenewsgroup.com/context/understanding-medicare-blog/understanding-medicare-blog/2013/06/03/the-cost-and-quality-conundrum-of-american-end-of-life-care

15. http://www.medicarenewsgroup.com/context/understanding-medicare-blog/understanding-medicare-blog/2013/06/03/end-of-life-care-constitutes-third-rail-of-u.s.-health-care-policy-debate

16. http://www.cbsnews.com/news/the-cost-of-dying/

17. http://khn.org/morning-breakout/iom-report/

18. http://comptroller.defense.gov/Portals/45/Documents/defbudget/fy2015/fy2015_Budget_Request_Overview_Book.pdf

19. https://www.economy.com/dismal/analysis/free/226001

20. http://www.ssa.gov/oact/trsum/

21. http://tricorder.xprize.org/teams/final-frontier-medical-devices

22. http://www.xprize.org/about/our-board

23. http://www.xprize.org/sites/default/files/xprize_backgrounder.pdf

24. http://tricorder.xprize.org/about/overview

25. http://tricorder.xprize.org/about/overview

26. http://tricorder.xprize.org/teams/final-frontier-medical-devices

27. http://www.kgw.com/story/news/health/2014/07/24/12301716/

28. http://www.ohsu.edu/blogs/doernbecher/2012/08/09/saving-babies-40-miles-away/

29. http://www.americantelemed.org/about-telemedicine/what-is-telemedicine#.VfTKlM5d3J4

30. Conversation between Bernard Tyson and Inder Sidhu, June 29, 2015

31. http://www.managedcaremag.com/archives/2015/7/tuning-telemedicine

32. http://usatoday30.usatoday.com/news/science/cold-science/2002-07-17-pole-operation.htm

33. https://www.aamc.org/newsroom/reporter/march2014/374634/telemedicine.html

34. http://www.usnews.com/news/blogs/data-mine/2014/11/18/on-un-world-toilet-day-more-have-access-to-cell-phones-than-toilets

35. http://www.worldometers.info/world-population/

36. http://www.who.int/mediacentre/news/releases/2013/health-workforce-shortage/en/

37. http://data.worldbank.org/indicator/SH.MED.PHYS.ZS

38. http://worldhealthpartners.org/?p=77&utm_content=bufferafadc&utm_medium=social&utm_source=twitter.com&utm_campaign=buffer

39. http://www.ncbi.nlm.nih.gov/pmc/articles/PMC3120773/

40. http://www.ipsnews.net/2014/01/virtual-doctor-will-see-now/

41. http://www.cisco.com/web/strategy/docs/healthcare/stanford_healthpresence.pdf

42. http://www.cio.com/article/2413704/software-as-a-service/how-mayo-clinic-doctors-use-smartphones-to-diagnose-patients.html

43. http://www.azfamily.com/story/28390303/stroke-robot-helps-improve-treatment-for-stroke-patients

44. http://www.azfamily.com/story/28390303/stroke-robot-helps-improve-treatment-for-stroke-patients

45. http://healthjournalism.org/blog/2015/07/indiana-using-telemedicine-consults-to-integrate-mental-health-primary-care/

46. http://www.nytimes.com/2011/09/25/fashion/therapists-are-seeing-patients-online.html?_r=0

47. http://psychcentral.com/news/2014/12/05/for-rural-vets-tele-therapy-an-effective-option-for-ptsd/78229.html

48. http://www.healthcare-informatics.com/article/washington-debrief-cms-proposed-aco-rules-look-boost-telehealth

49. http://www.payersandproviders.com/opinion-detail.php?id=129

50. http://www.chicagotribune.com/business/ct-virtual-doctor-trend-0107-biz-20150106-story.html

51. http://thehealthcareblog.com/blog/2015/01/31/tele-taking-off/

52. http://www.ncbi.nlm.nih.gov/pmc/articles/PMC3670609/

53. http://techcrunch.com/2014/09/22/the-reinvention-of-medicine-dr-algorithm-version-0-7-and-beyond/

54. http://fortune.com/2012/12/04/technology-will-replace-80-of-what-doctors-do/

55. http://www.acog.org/About-ACOG/ACOG-Departments/Deliveries-Before-39-Weeks

56. http://www2.deloitte.com/us/en/pages/about-deloitte/articles/press-releases/deloitte-forge-alliance-around-big-data-and-analytics.html

57. http://www2.deloitte.com/us/en/pages/about-deloitte/articles/press-releases/deloitte-forge-alliance-around-big-data-and-analytics.html

58. https://www.prbuzz.com/health-a-fitness/279499-intermountain-healthcare-led-effort-contributes-to-improved-national-medical-outcomes.html

59. http://www.hhs.gov/news/press/2014pres/12/20141202a.html

60. http://www.modernhealthcare.com/article/20140823/MAGAZINE/308239988

61. Conversation between Dr. Charles Sorenson and Inder Sidhu, July 7, 2015

62. Conversation between Dr. Martin Harris and Inder Sidhu, June 26, 2015

63. http://www.khoslaventures.com/portfolio/kyron

64. http://www.lumiata.com/press/lumiata-raises-4-million-in-series-a-financing-from-khosla-ventures/

65. Conversation between Dr. Charles Sorenson and Inder Sidhu, July 7, 2015.

66. http://espn.go.com/espn/otl/story/_/id/12496480/san-francisco-49ers-linebacker-chris-borland-retires-head-injury-concerns

67. http://espn.go.com/espn/otl/story/_/id/12496480/san-francisco-49ers-linebacker-chris-borland-retires-head-injury-concerns

68. http://www.nytimes.com/2011/05/03/sports/football/03duerson.html?_r=0

69. http://www.fastcodesign.com/3035264/innovation-by-design-2014/reebok-heads-off-injury

70. http://www.mc10inc.com/consumer-products/sports/checklight/

71. http://www.mc10inc.com/company-information/about-us/

72. http://www.fda.gov/scienceresearch/specialtopics/personalizedmedicine/default.htm

73. http://www.fda.gov/scienceresearch/specialtopics/personalizedmedicine/default.htm

74. http://jama.jamanetwork.com/article.aspx?articleid=2108876

75. Email communication between Vance Moore and Inder Sidhu, May 6, 2015

76. http://www.alivecor.com/press/press-releases/alivecor-announces-fda-clearance-for-two-new-automated-detectors-for-normal-recordings-and-noise-interference

77. https://www.scanadu.com/pr/

78. https://gigaom.com/2014/05/13/for-the-truly-health-obsessed-comes-cue-a-spit-kit-that-mimics-five-lab-tests/

79. http://www.dexcom.com/g5-mobile-cgm

80. http://www.dailymail.co.uk/health/article-2997882/Diabetes-epidemic-400-million-sufferers-worldwide-Number-condition-set-soar-55-20-years-unless-humans-change-way-eat-exercise.html

81. https://www.23andme.com

82. http://www.forbes.com/fdc/welcome_mjx.shtml

83. http://blog.23andme.com/news/a-note-to-our-customers-regarding-the-fda/

84. http://www.forbes.com/fdc/welcome_mjx.shtml

85. http://www.forbes.com/sites/davechase/2014/12/29/medical-blockbuster-book-of-the-year-the-patient-will-see-you-now/

86. http://www.wsj.com/articles/the-future-of-medicine-is-in-your-smartphone-1420828632

87. http://www.nytimes.com/2015/01/06/science/the-patient-will-see-you-now-envisions-a-new-era-of-digitally-perfected-care.html

88. http://csdd.tufts.edu/news/complete_story/pr_tufts_csdd_2014_cost_study

89. http://www.riversideonline.com/health_reference/Articles/CA00078.cfm

90. http://www.medicinenet.com/script/main/art.asp?articlekey=55234

Chapter 3

1. http://www.gpo.gov/fdsys/pkg/PPP-1991-book1/html/PPP-1991-book1-doc-pg395-2.htm

2. http://www.webpages.uidaho.edu/engl_258/Lecture%20Notes/jefferson%20on%20education.htm

3. http://www.presidency.ucsb.edu/ws/?pid=24146

4. http://www.gpo.gov/fdsys/pkg/PPP-1991-book1/html/PPP-1991-book1-doc-pg395-2.htm

5. http://blog.usaid.gov/2013/04/education-the-most-powerful-weapon/

6. http://www.un.org/press/en/1997/19970623.sgsm6268.html

7. http://www.oecd.org/pisa/keyfindings/pisa-2012-results-overview.pdf

8. http://www.theprospect.net/inside-a-perfect-score-what-does-it-mean-to-get-a-2400-37827

9. http://www.erikthered.com/tutor/historical-average-SAT-scores.pdf

10. http://www.oecd.org/pisa/keyfindings/pisa-2012-results-overview.pdf

11. http://data.worldbank.org/indicator/SE.XPD.TOTL.GB.ZS/countries

12. http://blogs.edweek.org/edweek/marketplacek12/2013/02/size_of_global_e-learning_market_44_trillion_analysis_says.html

13. http://www.keepeek.com/Digital-Asset-Management/oecd/education/education-at-a-glance-2014_eag-2014-en#page206

14. http://data.worldbank.org/indicator/SH.XPD.PCAP

15. http://www.ers.usda.gov/data-products/food-expenditures.aspx

16. http://documents.worldbank.org/curated/en/2014/05/19556820/student-learning-south-asia-challenges-opportunities-policy-priorities

17. http://www.globaleducationfirst.org/priorities.html

18. http://brokeneducation.tumblr.com

19. http://en.wikipedia.org/wiki/List_of_Nobel_laureates_by_university_affiliation

20. http://www.usnews.com/education/blogs/the-college-solution/2011/09/06/20-surprising-higher-education-facts

21. http://radiowest.kuer.org/post/sundance-2015-most-likely-succeed

22. http://radiowest.kuer.org/post/sundance-2015-most-likely-succeed

23. https://mcluhangalaxy.wordpress.com/2013/11/27/marshall-mcluhan-as-educationist-part-5-the-probe-as-pedagogy-classroom-without-walls/

24. http://www.vlib.us/medieval/lectures/universities.html

25. http://grad-schools.usnews.rankingsandreviews.com/best-graduate-schools/top-business-schools/mba-rankings?int=9dc208

26. https://fnce.wharton.upenn.edu/profile/982/teaching/?teachingFilter=previous

27. http://www.upenn.edu/pennnews/current/2012-01-19/numbers/whartonsan-francisco

28. https://twitter.com/minervaproject/status/556333893738315776

29. Geoff. Garrett in conversation with Inder Sidhu, April 13, 2015

30. http://www.hbxblog.com/hbx-live-the-first-year-infographic

31. http://www.hbxblog.com/dean-nohria-online-education-from-skeptic-to-super-fan

32. http://www.hbxblog.com/dean-nohria-online-education-from-skeptic-to-super-fan

33. http://www.prweb.com/releases/2013/9/prweb11104306.htm

34. http://nearpod.com

35. http://exitticket.org

36. http://exitticket.org

37. http://www.theguardian.com/world/2012/nov/07/greece-austerity-protests-violence

38. http://www.huffingtonpost.co.uk/2012/09/26/spain-riots-protesters-clash-riot-police_n_1915225.html

39. http://world.time.com/2012/07/31/blackout-leaves-600-million-indians-without-power/

40. http://www.foxnews.com/politics/2012/11/06/obama-defeats-romney-to-win-second-term-fox-news-projects/

41. http://www.olympic.org/london-2012-summer-olympics

42. http://www.livescience.com/24380-hurricane-sandy-status-data.html

43. http://www.expomuseum.com/2012/

44. http://mars.nasa.gov/msl/

45. http://poy.time.com/2012/12/19/person-of-the-year-barack-obama/

46. http://www.nytimes.com/2012/11/04/education/edlife/massive-open-online-courses-are-multiplying-at-a-rapid-pace.html

47. https://admission.princeton.edu/applyingforadmission/admission-statistics

48. http://admission.stanford.edu/basics/selection/profile.html

49. https://college.harvard.edu/admissions/admissions-statistics

50. http://www.upenn.edu/about/facts.php

51. http://newsoffice.mit.edu/2014/mit-gives-admissions-decisions-to-the-class-of-2018

52. http://news.berkeley.edu/2015/07/02/berkeley-admits-more-than-13000-prospective-freshmen/

53. Rick Levin conversation with Inder Sidhu, July 23, 2015

54. http://excelined.org/2014/07/09/first-exploration-mooc/

55. http://web.mit.edu/facts/faqs.html

56. http://newsoffice.mit.edu/2012/edx-launched-0502

57. https://www.linkedin.com/pub/daphne-koller/20/3a8/405

58. https://www.linkedin.com/profile/view?id=260012998&authType=OPEN LINK&authToken=p68S&locale=en_US&srchid=174840221428524566 601&srchindex=1&srchtotal=1&trk=vsrp_people_res_name&trkInfo=VS RPsearchId%3A174840221428524566601%2CVSRPtargetId%3A260012 998%2CVSRPcmpt%3Aprimary%2CVSRPnm%3A

59. http://video.cnbc.com/gallery/?video=3000328114

60. http://www.fastcompany.com/3021473/udacity-sebastian-thrun-uphill-climb

61. http://www.fastcompany.com/3021473/udacity-sebastian-thrun-uphill-climbgarr

62. http://news.stanford.edu/thedish/2015/03/16/president-john-hennessy-delivers-aces-atwell-lecture/

63. John Hennessy conversation with Inder Sidhu, June 8, 2015

64. Daphne Koller conversation with Inder Sidhu, April 13, 2015

65. https://www.insidehighered.com/news/2012/06/15/earning-college-credit-moocs-through-prior-learning-assessment

66. http://www.nytimes.com/2012/09/07/education/colorado-state-to-offer-credits-for-online-class.html

67. http://www.nytimes.com/2012/09/07/education/colorado-state-to-offer-credits-for-online-class.html

68. http://blog.coursera.org/post/42486198362/five-courses-receive-college-credit

69. http://www.wsj.com/articles/SB10001424052702304679404579459681722504264

70. Rick Levin conversation with Inder Sidhu, July 23, 2015

71. http://fortune.com/2015/01/21/everybody-hates-pearson/

72. http://www.aspiringminds.in/leadership.html

73. http://www.aspiringminds.com/about-us

74. http://knowledge.wharton.upenn.edu/article/assessing-employability-disrupting-indias-higher-education-model/

75. http://www.aspiringminds.com/press-releases/aspiring-minds-launches-first-standardized-employability-test-in-us-to-bridge

76. http://colleges.usnews.rankingsandreviews.com/best-colleges/georgia-institute-of-technology-139755/overall-rankings

77. http://www.huffingtonpost.com/zvi-galil/proving-grounds-for-a-new_b_5899762.html

78. http://www.huffingtonpost.com/zvi-galil/proving-grounds-for-a-new_b_5899762.html

79. http://www.npr.org/blogs/ed/2015/02/02/382167062/virtual-schools-bring-real-concerns-about-quality

80. http://www.connectionsacademy.com/online-school/technology

81. http://www.npr.org/blogs/ed/2015/02/02/382167062/virtual-schools-bring-real-concerns-about-quality

82. Daphne Koller conversation with Inder Sidhu, April 13, 2015

83. Andrew Jin at Harker Research Symposium, April 11, 2015

84. https://www.youtube.com/watch?v=JC82Il2cjqA

85. https://khanacademy.zendesk.com/hc/en-us/articles/202483630-Press-room

86. https://www.youtube.com/watch?v=kpCJyQ2usJ4

87. https://www.youtube.com/watch?v=mfgCcFXUZRk

88. https://www.youtube.com/watch?v=mfgCcFXUZRk

89. https://khanacademy.zendesk.com/hc/en-us/articles/202260104-How-did-Khan-Academy-get-started-

90. http://www.cbsnews.com/videos/googles-eric-schmidt-on-khan-academy/

91. http://www.forbes.com/sites/michaelnoer/2012/11/02/one-man-one-computer-10-million-students-how-khan-academy-is-reinventing-education/4/

92. https://khanacademy.zendesk.com/hc/en-us/articles/202483630-Press-room

93. http://nypost.com/2014/10/09/khan-academy-founder-has-no-plans-to-turn-passion-into-profits/

94. https://www.khanacademy.org/about/blog/post/105883637645/two-billion-nine-hundred-ninety-nine-million

95. http://www.nobelprize.org/nobel_prizes/physics/laureates/2001/wieman-facts.html

96. https://physics.stanford.edu/people/faculty/carl-wieman

97. https://physics.stanford.edu/people/faculty/carl-wieman

98. https://www.youtube.com/watch?t=39&v=vjFQj7xgB34

99. https://phet.colorado.edu/en/simulations/category/new

100. https://phet.colorado.edu/en/about

101. http://www.colorado.edu/news/content/phet-science-and-math-simulations-take-top-prize-oscars-higher-education

102. https://phet.colorado.edu/en/simulations/translated

103. http://www.colorado.edu/news/content/phet-science-and-math-simulations-take-top-prize-oscars-higher-education

104. https://www.youtube.com/watch?t=45&v=4Hj6GqBRpA0

105. https://khanacademy.zendesk.com/hc/en-us/articles/202260264-What-is-the-impact-of-using-Khan-Academy-

106. http://www.brainrules.net/attention?scene=

107. https://khanacademy.zendesk.com/hc/en-us/articles/202260254-How-is-Khan-Academy-s-site-different-than-other-resources-available-How-is-the-Khan-Academy-model-of-learning-different-

108. http://www.fastcompany.com/3007951/tech-forecast/simple-khan-academy-interface-hack-improved-learning-5

109. http://www.fastcompany.com/3007951/tech-forecast/simple-khan-academy-interface-hack-improved-learning-5

110. http://www.fastcompany.com/3007951/tech-forecast/simple-khan-academy-interface-hack-improved-learning-5

111. https://www.youtube.com/watch?v=Dno9ascsKq8

112. http://ussc.edu.au/news-room/MOOCs-The-iTunes-of-academe

Chapter 4

1. http://autoweek.com/article/car-reviews/2016-audi-tt-and-tts-drive-review

2. http://www.wheelsmag.com.au/reviews/1507/2015-audi-tt-roadster-review/

3. http://www.caranddriver.com/reviews/2016-audi-tt-first-drive-review

4. http://www.audi.co.uk/audi-innovation/audi-city.html

5. http://www.audiusa.com/content/dam/audiusa/myAudi/Magazine/
Audi_magazine_edition_108_rX.pdf

6. http://www.audiusa.com/newsroom/news/press-releases/2015/01/
audi-vr-experience-the-dealership-in-a-briefcase

7. http://global.samsungtomorrow.com/samsung-gear-vr-headset-lets-
audi-customers-take-tt-s-coupe-around-the-track-using-virtual-reality-
technology/

8. https://insights.samsung.com/2015/05/06/the-car-showroom-and-
test-drive-get-a-virtual-reality-check-video/

9. http://www.autonews.com/article/20150427/retail01/304279966/audi-
tests-2-car-sharing-concepts-in-u.s.

10. http://www.cisco.com/c/dam/en/us/solutions/collateral/executive-
perspectives/ioe-retail-whitepaper.pdf

11. http://www.statista.com/statistics/188105/annual-gdp-of-the-united-
states-since-1990/

12. http://www.census.gov/retail/index.html

13. http://www.bls.gov/iag/tgs/iag44-45.htm#about

14. https://nrf.com/who-we-are/retail-means-jobs

15. https://nrf.com/sites/default/files/Documents/Retails-Impact-Printable-
Highlights-REV.pdf

16. http://www.nbcnews.com/id/43797505/ns/business-retail/t/final-chapter-
borders-close-remaining-stores/

17. http://www.dailyfinance.com/2013/01/28/barnes-noble-store-closings-
mitchell-klipper/

18. http://retailindustry.about.com/od/USRetailStoreClosingInfoFAQs/fl/
All-2015-Store-Closings-Stores-Closed-by-US-Retail-Industry-Chains.
htm

19. http://www.nytimes.com/glogin?URI=http%3A%2F%2Fwww.nytimes.
com%2F2015%2F01%2F04%2Fbusiness%2Fthe-economics-and-
nostalgia-of-dead-malls.html%3F_r%3D0

20. http://www.businessinsider.com/shopping-malls-are-going-extinct-2014-1

21. http://www.businessinsider.com/shopping-malls-are-going-extinct-2014-1

22. http://www.cleveland.com/business/index.ssf/2014/12/randall_park_mall_
demo_story.html

23. http://www.bizjournals.com/nashville/stories/2009/09/14/story2.
html?page=all

24. http://www.mckinsey.com/insights/high_tech_telecoms_internet/brand_
success_in_an_era_of_digital_darwinism

25. http://www.cnbc.com/2015/03/30/malls-outperforming-the-shopping-center-industry.html

26. http://fortune.com/2015/05/19/amazon-nyc-pop-up/

27. http://digital.pwc.com/if-stores-had-a-voice/

28. http://www.cisco.com/web/services/portfolio/consulting-services/documents/consulting-services-capturing-ioe-value-aag.pdf

29. http://www.cisco.com/c/dam/en/us/solutions/collateral/executive-perspectives/ioe-retail-whitepaper.pdf

30. http://www.google.com/patents/US8615473

31. http://mashable.com/2014/01/21/amazon-anticipatory-shipping-patent/#eywfVUe6_ZkS

32. http://www.geekwire.com/2014/amazon-adds-30-million-customers-past-year/

33. Conversation between Malachy Moynihan and Inder Sidhu

34. http://www.geekwire.com/2014/amazon-may-50-million-prime-members-according-analyst-estimate/

35. http://www.amazon.com/Samsung-UN55HU8550-55-Inch-Ultra-120Hz/dp/B00ID2HI8O/ref=sr_1_1?ie=UTF8&qid=1441810157&sr=8-1&keywords=85-inch+Samsung+Ultra-HD+LED+television

36. http://www.amazon.com/Schwinn-Protocol-Dual-Suspension-Mountain-26-Inch/dp/B001IANSJ6/ref=sr_1_1?ie=UTF8&qid=1441810273&sr=8-1&keywords=dual-suspension%2C+26-inch+Schwinn+mountain+bike

37. http://www.amazon.com/Sleep-Innovations-SureTemp-Mattress-Warranty/dp/B003CT37L0/ref=sr_1_1?ie=UTF8&qid=1441810355&sr=8-1&keywords=SureTemp+memory+foam+mattress

38. http://www.zdnet.com/article/the-state-of-retail-in-2015/

39. http://www.stagestoresinc.com/about-us/

40. http://www.forbes.com/sites/netapp/2015/02/18/big-data-in-retail/

41. http://www.forbes.com/sites/netapp/2015/02/18/big-data-in-retail/

42. http://www.forbes.com/sites/netapp/2015/02/18/big-data-in-retail/

43. http://www.plattretailinstitute.org/documents/free/download.phx?itemid=499

44. http://www.plattretailinstitute.org/documents/free/download.phx?itemid=499

45. http://www.nytimes.com/2012/02/19/magazine/shopping-habits.html

46. https://hbr.org/2014/10/tescos-downfall-is-a-warning-to-data-driven-retailers/

47. http://www.pwc.com/en_US/us/retail-consumer/publications/assets/pwc-retailing-2020.pdf

48. http://www.theacsi.org/about-acsi/history

49. http://consumerist.com/2014/02/28/survey-says-walmart-is-worst-discount-retailer-worst-supermarket/

50. http://www.businessinsider.com/the-death-of-the-cash-register-2012-11

51. http://www.theatlantic.com/technology/archive/2012/09/the-end-of-the-cash-register-urban-outfitters-will-ring-you-up-with-ipads/262986/

52. http://www.businessinsider.com/the-death-of-the-cash-register-2012-11

53. http://www.dailyfinance.com/2012/07/23/jcpenneys-no-more-cash-registers-cashiers/

54. http://www.bizjournals.com/seattle/morning_call/2015/02/nordstrom-costco-amazon-top-retail-brands-on.html

55. http://www.racked.com/2013/6/17/7664647/nordstrom-rack-to-expand-upgrade-ecommerce

56. http://siliconangle.com/blog/2015/02/25/apple-genius-bar-to-get-iq-bump/

57. http://www.wsj.com/articles/newest-workers-for-lowes-robots-1414468866

58. http://www.hointer.com/main_aboutus.html

59. http://www.hointer.com/main_aboutus.html

60. http://www.cisco.com/c/dam/en/us/solutions/collateral/executive-perspectives/ioe-retail-whitepaper.pdf

61. http://www.gerryweber.com/ag-website/en/ag-website/company/company-profile/rfid

62. http://www.rebeccaminkoff.com/m-a-b-1

63. http://www.rebeccaminkoff.com/m-a-b-1

64. http://www.wsj.com/articles/designer-rebecca-minkoffs-new-stores-have-touch-screens-for-an-online-shopping-experience-1415748733

65. http://www.rebeccaminkoff.com/san-francisco

66. http://www.luxottica.com/en/eyewear-brands

67. http://www.luxottica.com/en/retail-brands

68. http://www.luxottica.com/en/luxottica-announces-agreement-acquire-glassescom-wellpoint-inc

69. https://www.glasses.com/images/misc/GlassesPDRuler.pdf

70. http://www.glasses.com/how-it-works

71. http://www.glasses.com/virtual-try-on

72. http://www.glasses.com/virtual-try-on

73. http://diginomica.com/2015/01/13/nrf-15-eyewear-firm-luxottica-vision-online-customer-experience/

74. http://www.ibmbigdatahub.com/presentation/big-data-analytics-and-retail-industry-luxottica

75. http://www-01.ibm.com/common/ssi/cgi-bin/ssialias?subtype=AB&infotype=PM&htmlfid=IVC03009USEN&attachment=IVC03009USEN.PDF

76. http://www.nytimes.com/2014/04/02/business/billion-dollar-bracelet-is-key-to-magical-kingdom.html

77. http://www.wdwmagic.com/reviews/2014/all.htm

78. http://www.dmeautomotive.com/announcements/1-in-6-car-buyers-skips-test-drive-nearly-half-visit-just-one-or-no-dealership-prior-to-purchase

79. http://www.dmeautomotive.com/announcements/1-in-6-car-buyers-skips-test-drive-nearly-half-visit-just-one-or-no-dealership-prior-to-purchase#.VfIids5d3J5

80. http://www.drivingsales.com/blogs/dealerchat/2013/12/17/new-study-google-says-car-shoppers-online-shoppers

Chapter 5

1. http://www.nytimes.com/2015/03/11/nyregion/the-snow-is-melting-but-what-a-mess-it-left-behind.html?_r=0

2. http://bigbelly.com/spotlight/philadelphia-pa/

3. http://bigbelly.com/places/

4. http://bigbelly.com/timessquare/

5. http://www.enevo.com/solutions/

6. http://siteresources.worldbank.org/INTURBANDEVELOPMENT/Resources/336387-1334852610766/Chap3.pdf

7. http://nypost.com/2014/05/24/new-york-is-top-of-the-heap-in-garbage-hauling-costs/

8. http://siteresources.worldbank.org/INTURBANDEVELOPMENT/Resources/336387-1334852610766/What_a_Waste2012_Final.pdf

9. http://www.trucks.com/Side-Loader-Trucks-For-Sale

10. http://money.usnews.com/careers/best-jobs/garbage-collector/salary

11. http://mirror.unhabitat.org/pmss/listItemDetails.aspx?publicationID=2918&AspxAutoDetectCookieSupport=1

12. https://www.whitehouse.gov/the-press-office/2015/03/09/remarks-president-national-league-cities-conference

13. http://www.cnn.com/2013/07/18/tech/innovation/tvilight-street-lamps-roosegarde/index.html

14. http://www.cnn.com/2013/07/18/tech/innovation/tvilight-street-lamps-roosegarde/index.html

15. http://esa.un.org/unpd/wup/Highlights/WUP2014-Highlights.pdf

16. http://www.un.org/en/development/desa/publications/2014-revision-world-urbanization-prospects.html

17. http://esa.un.org/unpd/wup/Highlights/WUP2014-Highlights.pdf

18. http://esa.un.org/unpd/wup/Highlights/WUP2014-Highlights.pdf

19. http://esa.un.org/unpd/wup/Highlights/WUP2014-Highlights.pdf

20. http://newsroom.cisco.com/press-release-content?type=webcontent&articleId=1492392

21. http://esa.un.org/unpd/wup/Highlights/WUP2014-Highlights.pdf

22. http://esa.un.org/unpd/wup/Highlights/WUP2014-Highlights.pdf

23. http://esa.un.org/unpd/wup/Highlights/WUP2014-Highlights.pdf

24. https://www.osac.gov/pages/ContentReportDetails.aspx?cid=15656

25. http://www.theguardian.com/cities/gallery/2014/jun/24/10-world-cities-highest-murder-rates-homicides-in-pictures

26. http://www.policymap.com/city-crime-rates/los-angeles-crime-statistics/

27. https://www.osac.gov/pages/ContentReportDetails.aspx?cid=15656

28. http://www.mexicogulfreporter.com/2012/01/almost-bankrupt-guatemala-calls-upon-us.html

29. http://www.cnn.com/2012/03/23/world/americas/guatemala-drug-legalization/

30. http://dialogo-americas.com/en_GB/articles/rmisa/features/2014/10/20/feature-01

31. http://dialogo-americas.com/en_GB/articles/rmisa/features/2014/10/20/feature 01

32. http://dialogo-americas.com/en_GB/articles/rmisa/features/2014/10/20/feature-01

33. http://isscctv.com/wp-content/uploads/ISS_Case_Study_Guatemala_City.pdf

34. http://dialogo-americas.com/en_GB/articles/rmisa/features/2014/10/20/feature-01

35. http://www.cisco.com/web/strategy/docs/scc/ioe_citizen_svcs_white_paper_idc_2013.pdf

36. http://www.sunykorea.ac.kr/emergency

37. https://www.umbel.com/blog/big-data/data-driven-cities/

38. http://www.cisco.com/web/strategy/docs/scc/ioe_citizen_svcs_white_paper_idc_2013.pdf

39. http://www.cisco.com/web/strategy/docs/scc/ioe_citizen_svcs_white_paper_idc_2013.pdf

40. http://bigapps.nyc/p/challenges/connected-cities-challenge/

41. http://nationswell.com/mobile-apps-local-governments-citizens-civic-engagement/

42. http://www.cityworks.com/2014/01/elevating-citizen-engagement-cityworks-seeclickfix/

43. http://shoup.bol.ucla.edu/CruisingForParkingAccess.pdf

44. http://shoup.bol.ucla.edu/CruisingForParkingAccess.pdf

45. http://www.fastprk.com/ftp/mailing/brochureFastprk_pro.pdf

46. http://freakonomics.com/2013/03/13/parking-is-hell-a-new-freakonomics-radio-podcast/

47. http://www.nytimes.com/2012/01/08/arts/design/taking-parking-lots-seriously-as-public-spaces.html

48. http://www.statista.com/statistics/183505/number-of-vehicles-in-the-united-states-since-1990/

49. https://mitpress.mit.edu/books/rethinking-lot

50. http://www.cisco.com/c/dam/en/us/products/collateral/wireless/mobility-services-engine/city_of_barcelona.pdf

51. http://www.cisco.com/c/dam/en/us/products/collateral/wireless/mobility-services-engine/city_of_barcelona.pdf

52. http://www.cisco.com/assets/global/ZA/tomorrow-starts-here/pdf/barcelona_jurisdiction_profile_za.pdf

53. http://sfpark.org/wp-content/uploads/2010/11/sfpark_mediakit_FAQ-_v06.pdf

54. http://sfpark.org/how-it-works/pricing/

55. http://www.masstransitmag.com/press_release/10257738/mayor-lee-launches-sfpark-pilot

56. http://direct.sfpark.org/wp-content/uploads/eval/SFpark_Pilot_Project_Evaluation.pdf

57. http://www.sfgate.com/business/networth/article/SpotOn-lets-people-rent-out-unused-space-for-5468453.php

58. http://www.latimes.com/local/lanow/la-me-ln-profit-parking-apps-20150107-story.html

59. http://www.pavegen.com

60. http://www.dubaigolf.com/emirates-golf-club.aspx

61. http://www.thenational.ae/uae/environment/special-report-saving-water-in-the-uae

62. http://www.thenational.ae/uae/environment/special-report-saving-water-in-the-uae

63. http://gulfnews.com/news/uae/society/dubai-population-unbalanced-stats-show-1.1380034

64. http://reports.weforum.org/global-risks-2015/executive-summary/

65. http://www.cbronline.com/news/enterprise-it/server/how-a-3d-printing-technology-sensor-monitors-water-pollution-4341539

66. http://www.cbronline.com/news/enterprise-it/server/how-a-3d-printing-technology-sensor-monitors-water-pollution-4341539

67. http://water.org/water-crisis/water-facts/water/

68. http://qz.com/230689/how-ibm-is-using-big-data-to-fix-beijings-pollution-crisis/

69. http://www.reuters.com/article/2014/03/05/us-china-parliament-pollution-idUSBREA2405W20140305

70. http://www.pv-tech.org/news/china_taps_ibm_for_green_horizon_renewable_energy_program

71. http://qz.com/230689/how-ibm-is-using-big-data-to-fix-beijings-pollution-crisis/

72. http://airqualityegg.com

73. http://airqualityegg.com

74. http://samuelcox.net

75. http://samuelcox.net

76. Communication between Prof. Carlo Ratti and Inder Sidhu, July 20, 2015

77. http://www.cisco.com/web/strategy/docs/scc/ioe_citizen_svcs_white_paper_idc_2013.pdf

78. http://www.cisco.com/web/strategy/docs/scc/ioe_citizen_svcs_white_paper_idc_2013.pdf

79. http://newsroom.cisco.com/video-content?type=webcontent&articleId=1610570

80. http://newsroom.cisco.com/video-content?type=webcontent&articleId=1610570

81. http://www.sensity.com/about-sensity/

82. Communication between Prof. Carlo Ratti and Inder Sidhu, July 20, 2015

Chapter 6

1. http://blog.okcupid.com/index.php/we-experiment-on-human-beings/

2. http://www.npr.org/sections/thetwo-way/2014/06/28/326453204/facebook-scientists-alter-newsfeeds-find-emotions-are-affected-by-it

3. http://www.slate.com/articles/health_and_science/science/2014/06/ facebook_unethical_experiment_it_made_news_feeds_happier_or_ sadder_to_manipulate.html

4. http://techcrunch.com/2014/06/29/facebook-and-the-ethics-of-user-manipulation/

5. http://money.cnn.com/2014/06/30/technology/social/facebook-experiment/

6. http://blogs.wsj.com/digits/2014/07/02/facebooks-sandberg-apologizes-for-news-feed-experiment/

7. http://www.mercurynews.com/business/ci_26064438/facebook-runs-into-uproar-over-experiment-that-tested

8. http://blog.okcupid.com/index.php/we-experiment-on-human-beings/

9. http://www.cbsnews.com/news/the-data-brokers-selling-your-personal-information/

10. https://www.ftc.gov/news-events/press-releases/2014/05/ ftc-recommends-congress-require-data-broker-industry-be-more

11. http://www.wsj.com/articles/richard-clarke-on-the-future-of-privacy-only-the-rich-will-have-it-1404762349

12. http://www.apple.com/legal/internet-services/itunes/us/terms.html

13. http://conversation.which.co.uk/technology/length-of-website-terms-and-conditions/

14. http://southpark.cc.com/clips/382783/i-agreed-by-accident

15. https://www.facebook.com/legal/terms

16. https://www.facebook.com/legal/terms

17. https://www.facebook.com/policy.php

18. https://www.facebook.com/privacy/explanation

19. http://www.theguardian.com/technology/2015/feb/23/ facebooks-privacy-policy-breaches-european-law-report-finds

20. http://www.nytimes.com/2012/06/17/technology/acxiom-the-quiet-giant-of-consumer-database-marketing.html

21. http://www.google.com/about/company/history/#2001

22. http://www.exeter.edu/news_and_events/news_events_5594.aspx

23. http://www.forbes.com/sites/kashmirhill/2012/02/16/how-target-figured-out-a-teen-girl-was-pregnant-before-her-father-did/

24. http://saviance.com/whitepapers/internet-health-industry

25. http://investor.fb.com/releasedetail.cfm?ReleaseID=893395

26. https://materials.proxyvote.com/Approved/30303M/20130409/ AR_166822/

27. http://investor.fb.com/releasedetail.cfm?ReleaseID=893395

28. http://www.marieclaire.com/culture/news/a6294/teen-sex-offender/

29. http://www.pameganslaw.state.pa.us/History.aspx?dt=

30. http://www.marieclaire.com/culture/news/a6294/teen-sex-offender/

31. http://europa.eu/rapid/press-release_CJE-14-70_en.htm

32. http://www.newyorker.com/magazine/2014/09/29/solace-oblivion

33. http://www.newyorker.com/magazine/2014/09/29/solace-oblivion

34. http://www.dailymail.co.uk/sciencetech/article-2629243/Paedophile-misbehaving-politician-GP-unhappy-review-scores-inundating-Google-right-forgotten-requests-EU-ruling.html

35. Michelle Dennedy conversation with Inder Sidhu, October 16, 2015

36. https://blog.wikimedia.org/2014/08/06/european-court-decision-punches-holes-in-free-knowledge/

37. David Hoffman conversation with Inder Sidhu, September 4, 2015

38. http://www.nytimes.com/2015/02/04/opinion/europes-expanding-right-to-be-forgotten.html?_r=0

39. https://www.ftc.gov/system/files/documents/public_statements/581751/140911mentorgroup.pdf

40. http://time.com/3437222/iphone-data-encryption/

41. https://www.youtube.com/watch?v=Bmm5faI_mLo

42. http://fox13now.com/2015/01/23/a-bill-that-shuts-off-the-nsa-data-centers-water-is-back/

43. http://www.americanbar.org/content/dam/aba/events/criminal_justice/2014_USSC_summaries.authcheckdam.pdf

44. http://www.huffingtonpost.com/2014/09/25/james-comey-apple-encryption_n_5882874.html

45. http://www.theguardian.com/world/interactive/2013/nov/01/snowden-nsa-files-surveillance-revelations-decoded#section/1

46. http://www.nytimes.com/2014/06/26/us/supreme-court-cellphones-search-privacy.html

47. http://www.thenation.com/article/supreme-court-says-police-need-warrant-search-your-phone/

48. http://www.thenation.com/article/supreme-court-says-police-need-warrant-search-your-phone/

49. http://www.wsj.com/articles/new-level-of-smartphone-encryption-alarms-law-enforcement-1411420341

50. http://www.wsj.com/articles/new-level-of-smartphone-encryption-alarms-law-enforcement-1411420341

51. http://www.usnews.com/news/articles/2014/11/14/doj-planes-may-be-spying-on-your-phone

52. http://www.wired.com/2012/03/petraeus-tv-remote/

53. http://www.wired.com/2012/03/petraeus-tv-remote/

54. http://www.usatoday.com/story/news/2015/04/07/dea-bulk-telephone-surveillance-operation/70808616/

55. https://www.reformgovernmentsurveillance.com/#111614

56. David Hoffman conversation with Inder Sidhu, September 4, 2015

57. https://www.youtube.com/watch?v=XEVlyP4_11M

58. https://www.law.cornell.edu/supremecourt/text/10-1259

59. https://www.law.cornell.edu/supremecourt/text/10-1259

60. http://www.brookings.edu/~/media/events/2014/06/24-future-technology/20140624_global_tech_privacy_transcript.pdf

61. Doug McNitt conversation with Inder Sidhu, August 28, 2015

62. http://papers.ssrn.com/sol3/papers.cfm?abstract_id=2305882

63. http://gov.ca.gov/news.php?id=18743

64. http://www.brookings.edu/~/media/events/2014/06/24-future-technology/20140624_global_tech_privacy_transcript.pdf

65. http://www.brookings.edu/~/media/events/2014/06/24-future-technology/20140624_global_tech_privacy_transcript.pdf

Chapter 7

1. http://pressroom.target.com/news/a-message-from-ceo-gregg-steinhafel-about-targets-payment-card-issues

2. http://pressroom.target.com/corporate

3. http://pressroom.target.com/corporate

4. http://krebsonsecurity.com/2014/02/email-attack-on-vendor-set-up-breach-at-target/

5. http://www.reuters.com/article/2013/12/25/us-target-databreach-idUSBRE9BN0L220131225

6. http://www.cnsnews.com/news/article/answers-questions-about-target-data-breach

7. http://www.cnbc.com/2014/01/13/target-ceo-still-shaken-by-the-data-breach-vows-to-make-it-right.html

8. http://www.npr.org/templates/transcript/transcript.php?storyId=329838961

9. http://krebsonsecurity.com/2013/12/sources-target-investigating-data-breach/

10. http://pressroom.target.com/news/target-confirms-unauthorized-access-to-payment-card-data-in-u-s-stores

11. http://pressroom.target.com/news/target-confirms-unauthorized-access-to-payment-card-data-in-u-s-stores

12. http://krebsonsecurity.com/2013/12/sources-target-investigating-data-breach/

13. http://money.cnn.com/2015/03/19/technology/security/target-data-hack-settlement/

14. http://www.cnbc.com/2014/01/13/target-ceo-still-shaken-by-the-data-breach-vows-to-make-it-right.html

15. https://corporate.target.com/_media/TargetCorp/global/PDF/Target-SJC-020414.pdf

16. https://corporate.target.com/_media/TargetCorp/global/PDF/Target-SJC-032614.pdf

17. http://www.washingtonpost.com/business/economy/data-breach-hits-targets-profits-but-thats-only-the-tip-of-the-iceberg/2014/02/26/159f6846-9d60-11e3-9ba6-800d1192d08b_story.html

18. http://techcrunch.com/2015/02/25/target-says-credit-card-data-breach-cost-it-162m-in-2013-14/

19. https://nakedsecurity.sophos.com/2014/03/06/target-cio-beth-jacob-resigns-in-breach-aftermath/

20. http://www.startribune.com/target-fired-steinhafel-cut-compensation-proxy-shows/259794771/

21. http://www.commerce.senate.gov/public/?a=Files.Serve&File_id=24d3c229-4f2f-405d-b8db-a3a67f183883

22. https://corporate.target.com/article/2014/01/free-credit-monitoring-and-identity-theft-protecti

23. http://www.theguardian.com/commentisfree/2014/may/06/target-credit-card-data-hackers-retail-industry

24. Conversation with Inder Sidhu, August 14, 2015

25. Conversation between RSA President Amit Yoran and Inder Sidhu, September 14, 2015

26. http://www.starwoodhotels.com/stregis/property/rooms/amenities.html?propertyID=3651&language=en_US

27. http://www.starwoodhotels.com/stregis/property/rooms/amenities.html?propertyID=3651&language=en_US

28. https://twitter.com/verifythentrust

29. https://www.youtube.com/watch?v=RX-O4XuCW1Y

30. https://www.youtube.com/watch?v=RX-O4XuCW1Y

31. https://www.youtube.com/watch?v=RX-O4XuCW1Y

32. https://www.youtube.com/watch?v=RX-O4XuCW1Y

33. https://technet.microsoft.com/en-us/library/dn425036.aspx

34. http://www.networkworld.com/article/2868018/cisco-subnet/
    annual-security-reports-predict-what-we-can-expect-in-2015.html

35. http://www.networkworld.com/article/2868018/cisco-subnet/
    annual-security-reports-predict-what-we-can-expect-in-2015.html

36. http://www.kaspersky.com/about/news/virus/2014/Kaspersky-Lab-is-
    Detecting-325000-New-Malicious-Files-Every-Day

37. http://www.verizonenterprise.com/DBIR/2014/reports/rp_dbir-2014-
    executive-summary_en_xg.pdf

38. Conversation between RSA President Amit Yoran and Inder Sidhu,
    September 14, 2015

39. Conversation between MIT's Prof. Alex "Sandy" Pentland and Inder
    Sidhu, September 16, 2015

40. Conversation with Inder Sidhu, June 26, 2015

41. http://www.ncsl.org/research/telecommunications-and-information-
    technology/security-breach-notification-laws.aspx

42. http://www.wsj.com/articles/morgan-stanley-terminates-employee-for-
    stealing-client-data-1420474557

43. http://www.morganstanley.com/about-us-articles/7f189537-f51c-40b0-
    a963-fc0dc6c65861.html

44. http://www.businessinsider.com/sony-employees-medical-records-leaked-
    in-hack-2014-12

45. http://www.hollywoodreporter.com/news/sony-hack-amy-pascal-scott-
    756438

46. http://www.phillymag.com/ticket/2014/12/12/sony-executive-calls-kevin-
    hart-whore-leaked-emails-hart-responds/

47. http://www.phillymag.com/ticket/2014/12/12/sony-executive-calls-kevin-
    hart-whore-leaked-emails-hart-responds/

48. http://www.cisco.com/c/en/us/solutions/collateral/enterprise/
    cisco-on-cisco/cs-boit-03162015-automate-protection-ip.html

49. http://blogs.cisco.com/security/defensive-security-the-955-approach

50. http://www.ebay.com/gds/Amazing-eBay-Facts-and-Figures-
    /10000000001431688/g.html

51. http://pages.ebay.com/2003annualreport/f96707hme10vk.html

52. http://www.forbes.com/sites/jaymcgregor/2014/07/28/the-top-5-most-brutal-cyber-attacks-of-2014-so-far/

53. http://www.wired.com/2014/05/ebay-demonstrates-how-not-to-respond-to-a-huge-data-breach/

54. https://www.ebayinc.com/stories/news/ebay-inc-ask-ebay-users-change-passwords/

55. https://www.ebayinc.com/stories/news/ebay-inc-ask-ebay-users-change-passwords/

56. http://www.reuters.com/article/2014/05/23/us-ebay-cybercrime-idUSBREA4M0PH20140523

57. http://www.bbc.com/news/technology-29310042

58. http://www.forbes.com/sites/ryanmac/2014/05/23/as-ebay-notifies-users-of-hack-states-launch-investigation/

59. http://www.wired.com/2014/05/ebay-demonstrates-how-not-to-respond-to-a-huge-data-breach/

60. Conversation between RSA President Amit Yoran and Inder Sidhu, September 14, 2015

61. Conversation between Michael Siegel of MIT and Inder Sidhu, September 16, 2015

62. http://www.nist.gov/cyberframework/upload/cybersecurity-framework-021214-final.pdf

Chapter 8

1. http://streeteasy.com/blog/new-york-city-rent-affordability/

2. http://www.gmanetwork.com/news/story/423955/lifestyle/travel/new-york-city-tourism-hit-record-high-in-2014-officials-say

3. http://www.gmanetwork.com/news/story/423955/lifestyle/travel/new-york-city-tourism-hit-record-high-in-2014-officials-say

4. http://www.nycgo.com/articles/nyc-statistics-page

5. http://www.statista.com/statistics/214585/most-expensive-cities-in-the-us-ordered-by-hotel-prices-2010/

6. http://www.nycgo.com/articles/nyc-statistics-page

7. http://blog.airbnb.com/rent-anything-from-a-couchto-a-country/

8. https://www.airbnb.com/about/about-us

9. https://www.airbnb.com/about/about-us

10. http://nypost.com/2014/03/17/airbnb-renter-claims-he-returned-home-to-an-orgy/

11. http://assembly.state.ny.us/mem/Richard-N-Gottfried/story/39019/

12. http://observer.com/2014/05/nys-senator-krueger-says-airbnb-doesnt-give-a-damn-without-sf-info/

13. http://freakonomics.com/2014/09/04/regulate-this-a-new-freakonomics-radio-podcast/comment-page-2/

14. http://www.pewtrusts.org/en/research-and-analysis/blogs/stateline/2015/1/30/a-license-to-braid-hair-critics-say-state-licensing-rules-have-gone-too-far

15. http://www.scrippsmedia.com/ktnv/news/Las-Vegas-cab-drivers-protest-Uber-282526751.html

16. https://www.uber.com/about

17. http://expandedramblings.com/index.php/uber-statistics/

18. https://s3.amazonaws.com/uber-static/comms/PDF/Uber_Driver-Partners_Hall_Kreuger_2015.pdf

19. http://expandedramblings.com/index.php/uber-statistics/

20. http://fivethirtyeight.com/features/uber-isnt-worth-17-billion/

21. http://www.latimes.com/business/autos/la-fi-0628-ford-car-sharing-20150628-story.html#page=1

22. http://www.nytimes.com/2014/11/02/fashion/how-uber-is-changing-night-life-in-los-angeles.html

23. https://media.ford.com/content/fordmedia/fna/us/en/news/2015/01/06/ford-at-ces-announces-smart-mobility-plan.html?adbid=55252792830384 1280&adbpl=tw&adbpr=15676492&scmp=social_20150106_38342167

24. http://www.scrippsmedia.com/ktnv/news/Las-Vegas-cab-drivers-protest-Uber-282526751.html

25. http://www.huffingtonpost.com/2014/12/17/alejandro-done-boston-uber-driver-rapes-passenger_n_6344432.html

26. http://www.theatlantic.com/technology/archive/2015/03/are-taxis-safer-than-uber/386207/

27. http://www.theatlantic.com/technology/archive/2015/03/are-taxis-safer-than-uber/386207/

28. http://news.nationalpost.com/news/uber-criticized-for-charging-minimum-100-fare-to-leave-area-of-sydney-siege-hostage-crisis

29. http://www.huffingtonpost.com/2014/11/28/uber-disciplines-manager-_n_6239050.html

30. http://abc11.com/technology/uber-ceo-offers-lengthy-13-tweet-apology-for-an-executives-controversial-remarks/400914/

31. http://www.wsj.com/articles/uber-valued-at-more-than-50-billion-1438367457?mg=id-wsj

32. http://www.businessinsider.com/heres-everywhere-uber-is-banned-around-the-world-2015-4

33. http://www.washingtonpost.com/world/the_americas/mexico-city-cabbies-are-getting-physical-with-uber/2015/06/07/55b7ba3a-094a-11e5-951e-8e15090d64ae_story.html

34. http://thegazette.com/subject/news/uber-unveils-plans-for-corridor-20141121

35. http://www.nytimes.com/2014/11/02/fashion/how-uber-is-changing-night-life-in-los-angeles.html

36. Conversation between Oleyo Osuru and T.C. Doyle in Salt Lake City, 2015

37. https://www.eff.org/deeplinks/2014/10/octobers-very-bad-no-good-totally-stupid-patent-month-filming-yoga-class

38. http://blog.yogaglo.com/2014/10/yogaglo-update-2/

39. http://blog.yogaglo.com/2014/10/yogaglo-update-2/

40. https://www.eff.org/deeplinks/2014/10/octobers-very-bad-no-good-totally-stupid-patent-month-filming-yoga-class

41. http://cornelllawreview.org/files/2014/01/99CLR387.pdf

42. http://www.cisco.com/web/about/gov/issues/patent_reform.html

43. http://www.eweek.com/networking/cisco-reaches-2.7-million-deal-with-wifi-patent-troll.html

44. https://www.youtube.com/watch?v=lSYpimUE9tk

45. http://www.democracynow.org/2015/2/27/a_historic_decision_tim_wu_father

46. http://www.democracynow.org/2015/2/27/a_historic_decision_tim_wu_father

47. http://www.bloomberg.com/politics/articles/2015-02-26/how-john-oliver-transformed-the-net-neutrality-debate-once-and-for-all

48. http://www.csmonitor.com/USA/Society/2015/0226/Net-neutrality-s-stunning-reversal-of-fortune-Is-it-John-Oliver-s-doing

49. http://www.democracynow.org/2015/2/27/a_historic_decision_tim_wu_father

Chapter 9

1. http://www.seat61.com/UnitedStates.htm#.VfmttHisP5E

2. https://www.aar.org/todays-railroads/what-we-haul

3. https://www.aar.org/Pages/Railroads-and-Coal-A-Unique-Partnership.aspx

4. https://www.aar.org/todays-railroads/what-we-haul

5. http://freightrailworks.org/ever-wonder-what-fits-in-one-rail-car/

6. http://freightrailworks.org/eight-unbelievable-facts-about-americas-freight-railroads-2/

7. http://www.progressiverailroading.com/mechanical/article/Class-Is-employ-fuelsaving-practices-that-promise-stingier-diesel-usage--22736

8. http://www.forbes.com/sites/danalexander/2014/03/27/the-most-efficient-mode-of-transportation-in-america-isnt-a-prius-its-a-train/

9. https://www.aar.org/Fact%20Sheets/Safety/2013-AAR_spending-graphic-fact-sheet.pdf

10. https://www.splunk.com/web_assets/pdfs/secure/Splunk_at_New_York_Air_Brake.pdf

11. http://www.splunk.com/content/dam/splunk2/pdfs/customer-success-stories/splunk-at-new-york-air-brake.pdf

12. http://www.economist.com/news/business/21604598-market-booking-travel-online-rapidly-consolidating-sun-sea-and-surfing

13. http://www.forbes.com/sites/georgeanders/2014/10/15/houzzs-founders-have-become-techs-newest-power-couple/

14. http://graphics.wsj.com/billion-dollar-club/?co=Houzz

15. http://graphics.wsj.com/billion-dollar-club/?co=Houzz

16. http://finance.yahoo.com/q?s=ETH

17. http://www.businessinsider.com/uber-revenue-projection-in-2015-2014-11

18. http://skift.com/2015/03/25/airbnbs-revenues-will-cross-half-billion-mark-in-2015-analysts-estimate/

19. http://www.wsj.com/articles/at-the-weather-channel-gloomy-skies-linger-1428276754

20. https://openforum.hbs.org/challenge/understand-digital-transformation-of-business/data/the-weather-company-using-data-for-more-than-just-reporting-the-weather#comments-section

21. http://www.nytimes.com/2015/10/29/technology/ibm-to-acquire-the-weather-company.html?ribbon-ad-idx=10&rref=technology&module=Ribbon&version=context&region=Header&action=click&contentCollection=Technology&pgtype=article&_r=0

22. http://fortune.com/2015/10/28/ibm-weather-company-acquisition-data/

23. http://www.usatoday.com/videos/money/business/2015/03/31/70733928/

24. https://www.youtube.com/watch?v=tzMkycLRAO8

25. http://www.ispot.tv/ad/73GD/general-electric-software-spot-the-difference-fuel-gauge

26. https://www.youtube.com/watch?v=ss_X7qLomjw

27. http://www.theunitconverter.com/gallon-to-barrel-oil-conversion/
2100-gallon-to-barrel-oil.html

28. https://www.youtube.com/watch?v=ss_X7qLomjw

29. http://www.usatoday.com/story/money/personalfinance/2013/04/03/
bank-of-america-tellers-atm/2025923/

30. http://www.computerweekly.com/news/2240221134/
Bank-of-America-and-Nationwide-use-in-branch-telepresence

31. http://www.usatoday.com/story/money/personalfinance/2013/04/03/
bank-of-america-tellers-atm/2025923/

32. https://www.youtube.com/watch?v=r0iH9r6QJO8

33. http://www.goldcorp.com/English/Unrivalled-Assets/Mines-and-Projects/
Canada-and-US/Operations/Eleonore/Location-and-Geology/default.aspx

34. http://www.goldcorp.com/English/Unrivalled-Assets/Mines-and-Projects/
Canada-and-US/Operations/Eleonore/Overview-and-Development-
Highlights/default.aspx

35. http://www.cisco.com/web/strategy/materials-mining/downloads/
c36-goldcorp-cs.pdf

36. https://www.youtube.com/watch?t=104&v=MkQTMZ1GidE

37. http://www.themiddlemarket.com/news/financial_services/
ge-continues-selling-loan-assets-as-sale-of-ge-capital-256455-1.html

38. http://www.aei.org/publication/fortune-500-firms-in-1955-vs-2014-89-
are-gone-and-were-all-better-off-because-of-that-dynamic-creative-
destruction/

39. http://www.aei.org/publication/fortune-500-firms-in-1955-vs-2014-89-
are-gone-and-were-all-better-off-because-of-that-dynamic-creative-
destruction/

Chapter 10

1. http://newsdesk.si.edu/releases/smithsonian-associates-presents-nation-
s-t-rex-coming-look-out

2. http://www.supplychaindigital.com/logistics/3452/FedEx-successfully-
ships-TRex-across-USA-to-Washington

3. http://fedexcares.com/40th-anniversary

4. http://customcritical.fedex.com/us/services/white-glove/default.shtml

5. http://www.supplychaindigital.com/logistics/3452/FedEx-successfully-
ships-TRex-across-USA-to-Washington

6. http://about.van.fedex.com/blog/behind-the-scenes-access-to-critical-shipments/

7. https://www.youtube.com/watch?v=TaAxEKFlt5s#t=61

8. http://images.fedex.com/ca_english/about/pdf/ca_english_about_decades_innovation.pdf

9. http://about.van.fedex.com/blog/fedex-introduces-fedex-mobile-for-iphone-and-ipod-touch/

10. http://www.informationweek.com/strategic-cio/executive-insights-and-innovation/how-fedex-streamlines-operations-at-freight-docks/d/d-id/1127931

11. http://www.fedex.com/us/fedextracking/#tab1

12. http://about.van.fedex.com/our-story/company-structure/corporate-fact-sheet/

13. http://www.nydailynews.com/news/national/photo-dog-cold-rainy-tarmac-leads-twitter-outrage-article-1.2059940

14. https://twitter.com/keitholbermann/status/549289371770568704

15. https://twitter.com/sia/status/549432122516049921

16. http://www.dailymail.co.uk/news/article-2889799/United-Airlines-faces-angry-backlash-passenger-saw-dog-left-tarmac-pouring-rain-half-hour-despite-alerts-staff.html#ixzz3WCTyuwlA

17. http://www.theacsi.org/news-and-resources/customer-satisfaction-reports/reports-2014/acsi-travel-report-2014/acsi-travel-report-2014-download

18. http://industry.shortyawards.com/nominee/7th_annual/o6g/united-airlines-social-customer-service

19. http://knowledge.wharton.upenn.edu/article/ignored-side-social-media-customer-service/

20. http://industry.shortyawards.com/nominee/6th_annual/2G/united-customer-service-on-twitter-from-black-hole-to-top-shelf

21. http://industry.shortyawards.com/nominee/6th_annual/2G/united-customer-service-on-twitter-from-black-hole-to-top-shelf?category=customer_service

22. http://www.theacsi.org/news-and-resources/customer-satisfaction-reports/reports-2014/acsi-travel-report-2014/acsi-travel-report-2014-download

23. http://www.bostonglobe.com/business/2015/03/30/jetblue-ticketing-outage-delays-some-logan-passengers/9V5Ib6bWggsrYkTnSAkqIN/story.html

24. http://www.bostonglobe.com/business/2015/03/30/jetblue-ticketing-outage-delays-some-logan-passengers/9V5Ib6bWggsrYkTnSAkqIN/story.html

25. http://www.socialmediaexaminer.com/exceptional-customer-service-on-twitter/

26. http://faculty-gsb.stanford.edu/aaker/pages/documents/Jet_Blue.pdf

27. https://twitter.com/search?q=from%3AHyattConcierge%20%40smorrison0%20since%3A2014-01-26%20until%3A2014-02-04&src=typd

28. http://industry.shortyawards.com/nominee/6th_annual/Fu/hyattconcierge-at-your-service

29. http://pogue.blogs.nytimes.com/2011/04/14/the-tragic-death-of-the-flip/?_r=0

30. https://www.youtube.com/watch?v=wPQpdYcZ23k

31. http://investor.gopro.com/releasedetail.cfm?releaseid=895085

32. https://twitter.com/WarbyParker/status/600331823055544320

33. http://www.statista.com/statistics/300087/global-eyewear-market-value/

34. http://www.fastcompany.com/3041334/most-innovative-companies-2015/warby-parker-sees-the-future-of-retail

35. https://www.warbyparker.com/home-try-on

36. http://knowledge.wharton.upenn.edu/article/what-eyewear-startup-warby-parker-sees-that-others-dont/

37. https://www.warbyparker.com/retail

38. http://www.harpersbazaar.com/fashion/trends/a10650/bikyni-is-here-to-solve-your-swimwear-problems/

39. http://blogs.air-watch.com/2014/01/luxottica-airwatch-secure-mobile-enterprise-applications/#.VWZASWCaH5E

40. http://www.luxottica.com/en/luxottica-announces-agreement-acquire-glassescom-wellpoint-inc

41. http://www.ray-ban.com/usa/virtual-mirror

42. http://thesubtimes.com/2014/04/29/55024/

43. http://www.starbucks.com/business/international-stores

44. http://www.huffingtonpost.com/2014/03/04/starbucks_n_4890735.html

45. http://blogs.starbucks.com/blogs/customer/archive/2009/09/15/starbucks-launches-iphone-apps.aspx

46. Rachael Antalek conversation with Inder Sidhu, September 28, 2015

47. http://www.starbucks.com/coffeehouse/mobile-apps

48. https://blogs.starbucks.com/blogs/customer/archive/2014/12/02/portland-we-want-to-hear-from-you.aspx?PageIndex=2

49. Communication between Prof. Fader and Inder Sidhu, April 15, 2015

50. http://www.zdnet.com/article/starbucks-names-tech-execs-after-cio-leaves-for-best-buy/

51. http://bombfell.s3.amazonaws.com/Bombfell_Press_Kit_May2015.pdf

52. http://fortune.com/2015/06/10/spotify-number-users/

53. http://www.digitaltrends.com/music/pandora-spotify-beats-rdio-itunes-radio-algorithm-comparison/

54. http://www.billboard.com/biz/articles/news/global/6029448/ifpis-recording-industry-in-numbers-us-at-44-billion-germany

55. https://www.facebook.com/Burberry?fref=nf

56. http://luxurysociety.com/articles/2014/01/how-burberry-does-digital

57. http://luxurysociety.com/articles/2014/01/how-burberry-does-digital

58. http://www.forbes.com/sites/sarahwu/2014/09/22/how-to-customize-your-own-burberry-billboard/

59. https://twitter.com/hashtag/myburberry

60. http://www.burberryplc.com/documents/results/2005/15-06-05_annual_report_04-05/ar05_report.pdf

Chapter 11

1. http://www.gallup.com/poll/181289/majority-employees-not-engaged-despite-gains-2014.aspx

2. http://allthingsd.com/20130222/physically-together-heres-the-internal-yahoo-no-work-from-home-memo-which-extends-beyond-remote-workers/

3. https://twitter.com/richardbranson/status/306074881433432065

4. http://www.forbes.com/sites/petercohan/2013/02/26/4-reasons-marissa-mayers-no-at-home-work-policy-is-an-epic-fail/

5. http://www.npr.org/2013/03/01/173186526/stay-at-home-workers-defend-choice-after-yahoo-ban

6. https://hbr.org/2015/01/a-working-from-home-experiment-shows-high-performers-like-it-better

7. http://www.sciencedaily.com/releases/2014/09/140918150940.htm

8. http://www.socialsecurity.gov/performance/2012/APP%202012%20508%20PDF.pdf

9. http://www.brookings.edu/~/media/research/files/papers/2014/05/millennials-wall-st/brookings_winogradfinal.pdf

10. http://www.dispatch.com/content/stories/business/2014/03/30/eager-to-work-but-on-their-terms.html

11. http://www.mckinsey.com/insights/organization/making_a_market_in_ talent

12. http://contently.com/strategist/2015/03/27/contently-case-story-inside- marriotts-ambitious-new-travel-mag/

13. https://www.youtube.com/watch?t=489&v=ZOgteFrOKt8

14. http://contently.com/strategist/2015/03/27/contently-case-story-inside- marriotts-ambitious-new-travel-mag/

15. http://www.jeffbullas.com/2014/12/02/25-linkedin-facts-and-statistics- you-need-to-share/

16. https://www.workmarket.com

17. http://info.mbopartners.com/rs/mbo/images/ArdentPartners_ TheStateofCWM.pdf

18. http://www.renitconsulting.com/company.html

19. https://www.accenture.com/t20150827T020600__w__/us-en/_acnmedia/ Accenture/Conversion-Assets/DotCom/Documents/Global/PDF/ Strategy_7/Accenture-Future-of-HR-Rise-Extended-Workforce.pdf

20. http://www.forbes.com/sites/waldleventhal/2014/11/24/5-predictions-for- the-freelance-economy-in-2015/3/

21. Conversation between Cisco HR Vice President Jill Larsen and Inder Sidhu, June 24, 2015

22. Conversation between Google Vice President of HR and People Analyt- ics Prasad Setty and Inder Sidhu, June 30, 2015

23. http://www.cisco.com/web/strategy/docs/del_papa_distributors_cs.pdf

24. http://www.marketwatch.com/story/enterprise-social-software-market- on-premise-on-demand-social-collaboration-enterprise-social-networks- global-advancements-demand-analysis-market-forecasts-2014-2019- research-report-2014-07-29

25. http://www.forbes.com/sites/forbespr/2013/05/20/forbes-insights- survey-reveals-cloud-collaboration-increases-business-productivity-and- advances-global-communication/

26. http://newsoffice.mit.edu/2014/behavioral-analytics-moneyball-for- business-1114

27. https://www.parc.com

28. http://www.alcatel-lucent.com/bell-labs

29. http://searchcio.techtarget.com/opinion/Thomson-Reuters-flushes-out- internal-engineering-talent-with-crowdsourcing

30. http://searchcio.techtarget.com/opinion/Thomson-Reuters-flushes-out- internal-engineering-talent-with-crowdsourcing

31. http://dl.acm.org/citation.cfm?id=2470727

32. Conversation with Fran Katsoudas about IoE implementation in Cisco HR, June 26, 2015

33. https://hbr.org/2013/04/using-the-crowd-as-an-innovation-partner/

Chapter 12

1. http://radiowest.kuer.org/post/sundance-2015-most-likely-succeed

2. http://www.history.com/this-day-in-history/deep-blue-defeats-garry-kasparov-in-chess-match

3. http://www.ted.com/talks/ken_jennings_watson_jeopardy_and_me_the_obsolete_know_it_all/transcript?language=en

Index

V-W-X-Y-Z

About the Authors

Inder Sidhu is a Silicon Valley senior executive with a career spanning three decades in the technology industry.

He has spent twenty years helping build Cisco from $1 billion to $50 billion in annual revenue, most recently as Senior Vice President of Strategy and Planning for Worldwide Operations. Inder has co-led Cisco's highly profitable $16 billion Enterprise business and its fast-growing $7 billion Emerging Countries business. Additionally, he has served as the Vice President and General Manager for Worldwide Professional Services, Vice President and General Manager for Advanced Engineering Services, and Vice President for Strategy and Business Development for Cisco Services.

In his journey, Inder has also been a consultant with McKinsey & Company, an engineer with Intel, and an entrepreneur with a successful Silicon Valley start-up.

In 2010, Inder authored *The New York Times* bestseller *Doing Both: Capturing Today's Profit and Driving Tomorrow's Growth.*

In 2013, Inder was honored to be the commencement speaker at his alma mater, the Wharton School of Business of the University of Pennsylvania.

Inder channels his passion for education by guest lecturing at Harvard Business School, Stanford University, the Wharton School, and the Haas School of Business at the University of California, Berkeley.

He serves on the Graduate Executive Board of the Wharton School and on the Board of Directors of Goodwill of Silicon Valley.

Inder is a graduate of the Advanced Management Program at Harvard Business School and holds an MBA from the Wharton School of Business of the University of Pennsylvania. He also holds a Master's degree in Electrical and Computer Engineering from the University of Massachusetts, Amherst, and a Bachelor's degree in Electrical Engineering from the Indian Institute of Technology, Delhi, India.

T.C. Doyle is a writer, editor, and storyteller who has covered the technology industry for more than two decades. When he's not in Silicon Valley or pursuing a story elsewhere around the globe, he can be found in Park City, Utah, where he resides with his wife and two sons.